DISCARD

The Big Picture

The

BIG PICTURE

The Fight *for the* Future
of Movies

Ben Fritz

An Eamon Dolan Book
Houghton Mifflin Harcourt
BOSTON   NEW YORK   2018

For information about permission to reproduce selections from
this book, write to trade.permissions@hmhco.com or to
Permissions, Houghton Mifflin Harcourt Publishing Company,
3 Park Avenue, 19th Floor, New York, New York 10016.

hmhco.com

Library of Congress Cataloging-in-Publication Data is available.
ISBN 978-0-544-78976-0

Book design by Kelly Dubeau Smydra

Printed in the United States of America
DOC 10 9 8 7 6 5 4 3 2 1

In memory of Riley

Contents

A Note on Sources ix

Introduction: Groundhog Day — How Franchises Killed Originality in Hollywood xiii

PART 1: HOW HOLLYWOOD GOT HERE

1. The Odd Couple: Lynton and Pascal's Glory Days at Sony 3
2. Reality Bites: How Everything Went Wrong for the Movie Business 21
3. Inception: The Secret Origin of the Superhero Movie 37
4. Revenge of the Nerds: The Rise of Marvel Studios 53
5. Spider-Man: Homecoming — Why Sony Gave Up Its Most Valuable Asset 75
6. Star Wars: The Decline of the A-List 83
7. A Star Is Born: Netflix, the New Home for Movie Stars 101
8. Frozen: Why Studios Stopped Making Mid-Budget Dramas 111
9. Trading Places: How TV Stole Movies' Spot atop Hollywood 125

PART 2: WHERE HOLLYWOOD IS HEADED

10. The Terminator: Disney, the Perfect Studio for the
    Franchise Age 143

11. The Producers: Creativity Meets Franchise Management 165

12. The Shop Around the Corner: Amazon Saves the Indie Film
    Business 187

13. Apt Pupil: China's Shifting Relationship with Hollywood 201

14. Field of Dreams: Studio Defectors and the Future of
    Nonfranchise Films 221

15. The Last Picture Show? 231

   Acknowledgments 243

   Notes 247

   Index 265

A Note on Sources

THIS BOOK IS BASED, in part, on stolen material. I won't make any bones about it.

The cyber-breach of Sony Pictures Entertainment in November 2014 resulted in the release of tens of thousands of private e-mails and documents, which became available to the public, whether downloaded from a peer-to-peer network or perused on WikiLeaks.

Sony has called the hack a "malicious criminal act," and that's correct. Executives at the studio have questioned my ethics (and that of many other journalists) in reporting on the contents of the stolen e-mails and documents, and I can hardly blame them. If e-mails revealing the innermost details of my reporting at the *Wall Street Journal* were released to the world, I would be horrified. And if bloggers burrowed through personal e-mails involving my family, my finances, and my online shopping history, I would undoubtedly be embarrassed.

Nevertheless, it's an undeniable fact that much great journalism has used stolen material as its source. While the scale of the theft here was perhaps unprecedented and the import of the material doesn't exactly compare to the Pentagon Papers, the principle remains the same: interesting information worthy of public scrutiny is fair game for journalists.

Now that anyone with an Internet connection can read these e-mails and documents, the question is simply what to do with them. Already, reporters have pored over many, looking for eyebrow-raising scoops, including new details about movies Sony was planning to make and racially offensive jokes about President Obama made by a movie mogul and a power producer.

Of course, I could have just left the hacked materials alone and moved on. That's possibly what some Sony Pictures employees, for whom the hack was a painful incident they'd like to just leave in the past, would prefer I do. But as a longtime reporter on the business of Hollywood, I believed the stolen e-mails and internal documents from Sony Pictures could be the core of a much bigger story — one about the changes in Hollywood and why we get the movies we do. I believed I could put these materials to a productive and enlightening purpose. This book is the result.

Whatever your views, I hope you'll agree that what you're about to read is not exploitative. In researching this book I read or skimmed nearly every e-mail and document released in the hack. I frequently felt uncomfortable, as I think any compassionate human being would, and at times I felt unethical. That happened when I came upon e-mails of a clearly personal nature, particularly when it involved Sony employees' families and doubly so their children. I made it a policy to stop reading e-mails once I realized they were personal. You won't find anything salacious or shocking about anyone's private life in here.

There are, however, extensive details, financial and otherwise, about Sony Pictures, its films, and its senior executives. Much of it comes from e-mails and documents stolen in the hack. Some comes from interviews with more than fifty current and former Sony employees and people who have worked closely with the company. I also utilized internal documents not released in the hack that sources provided to me.

Wherever possible, I have cited the specific e-mails or people I interviewed from which I gleaned quotes or information used in this book. Unless otherwise noted, I have preserved the original spelling and wording of e-mails I quote, including typos.

Some financial data came from internal documents that have no titles, so I can't individually cite them. In addition, I granted anonymity
to some people I interviewed because they feared that being named
would damage their careers in Hollywood.

Introduction

Groundhog Day — How Franchises Killed Originality in Hollywood

IT'S EASY TO BECOME CYNICAL about Hollywood once you've spent much time inside it. No business is as sexy and highly scrutinized from the outside, while managing to feel so small and self-important once you're inside it, as motion pictures.

When everyone around you is constantly assessing the current heat of stars, moguls, and filmmakers and judging movies by their most recent box-office grosses, it's easy to forget that the products created here are profoundly meaningful to millions of people, whether as timeless art or fun pop-culture ephemera.

There's an antidote, however. To remember the grandeur, the tradition, and the cultural significance of an industry that has had a greater impact on imaginations than any in American history, one need only walk onto one of the six studio lots that still take up hundreds of acres in Los Angeles and its suburbs.

None is more inspiring than the forty-four-acre, 102-year-old lot in Culver City, California, that was long home to Metro-Goldwyn-Mayer and is now occupied by Sony Pictures.

The entrance features a giant rainbow that arches ninety-four feet in the air and evokes memories of *The Wizard of Oz,* which was shot here in the late 1930s. Walking down "Main Street," into the heart of the lot, you stroll through a faux downtown lined with buildings named after Cary Grant, Frank Capra, Rita Hayworth, and David Lean, the stars and filmmakers who built the legacy of Columbia Pictures, which Sony acquired in 1989.

Walking farther, past posters for unforgettable Columbia movies like *Lawrence of Arabia* and *Spider-Man,* you come upon the studio store, with T-shirts, mugs, and DVDs of Sony's biggest hits from recent years, including *21 Jump Street, Breaking Bad,* and the James Bond blockbuster *Skyfall.* Visit on the right day and you might see Will Smith drive by on a golf cart or Seth Rogen chowing down in the Harry Cohn commissary building, named after the larger-than-life mogul who co-founded Columbia with his brother and their friend in 1918.

All around you, meanwhile, are nearly thirty soundstages where everything from *Gone with the Wind* to *Rocky* to *Wheel of Fortune* has been shot.

Despite appearances, however, studio lots like Sony's are not what they used to be. Movies are rarely made on soundstages here, as production has fled to places like Georgia and London, in search of big government subsidies. The names of retired actors and directors may appear on the buildings, but the new generation of talent is far less powerful than the world-famous characters they bring to life, like Iron Man and Katniss Everdeen. The moguls who run the studios, meanwhile, have been brought dramatically down to earth and are increasingly indistinguishable from the MBAs who run retail chains and investment banks.

What made the movie business unique in the history of corporate capitalism is captured in the screenwriter William Goldman's maxim, true for many decades: "nobody knows anything." No other industry pumped out so many products so frequently with so little foreknowledge of whether they would be any good. The only feasible business strategy, it appeared, was to sign up the best creative talent, trust your strongest hunches about what looked likely to appeal to millions of people, and hope you ended up with *Back to the Future* instead of *Ishtar.*

Over the past few years, however, something big has happened: finally, people in Hollywood do know something. What they know is
that branded franchises work. People say they want new ideas and
fresh concepts, but in reality they most often go to the multiplex for familiar characters and concepts that remind them of what they already
know they like. Big name brands like Marvel, Harry Potter, Fast & Furious, and Despicable Me consistently gross more than $1 billion at the
global box office, not only raking in huge profits, but justifying studios'
very existence and the jobs of everyone who works on their glamor-
ous lots.

This change has happened slowly over about a decade in Hollywood, making it hard to appreciate its magnitude. But now it is undeniable that the dawn of the franchise film era is the most meaningful revolution in the movie business since the studio system ended, in
the 1950s. That shift ended studios' ability to control creative talent
by essentially owning it with long-term contracts. It also increased the
quality of movies Hollywood made over the next fifty years because
companies had to compete to make the most influential talent happy,
rather than the other way around.

The franchise film era is, in many ways, a return to the studio system. Only now the major entertainment companies don't own the
most important talent — they own the most important cinematic
brands. Instead of fighting for a deal at MGM or Paramount, actors
and filmmakers vie for a chance to make the latest spinoff of *Star Wars*
or *X-Men*. Many of those movies are satisfying crowd pleasers, but nobody is going to compare the 2010s to a standout era of Hollywood
filmmaking like the 1970s.

The studios that adjusted to the implications of the franchise age
with speed and a clear vision have been the most successful in recent
years. Warner Bros. and Disney long ago reshaped their businesses
around big-budget "event" movies that could spawn endless sequels,
spinoffs, and product tie-ins. These studios are now consistently at the
top of box-office and profit rankings, along with Universal, which successfully followed their lead.

A FATEFUL DAY AT SONY

Sony Pictures is a different story. It thrived in the first decade of this century by sticking to a creaky but still workable strategy of focusing on movie stars and original scripts, with the occasional superhero sequel to appeal to teenagers and audiences overseas. The studio's boss, Amy Pascal, is a larger-than-life character who ran her business on the old-fashioned premise that her job was, every year, to make the best slate of movies she could, with the most talented filmmakers and actors, and trust that profits would follow.

It worked until it didn't. Like a newspaper that made a great print product but never invested in its website, Sony succeeded in the early part of the twenty-first century, but its fortunes took a decided turn for the worse in the 2010s. As audience tastes changed, it had little to offer in the way of big-budget "events" that were part of long-popular, well-known franchises.

By 2013, it was clear that Sony could no longer close its eyes to the revolution in the movie business. On a fateful day late that year, the leaders of Hollywood's most talent-friendly studio were finally forced to face the fact that if they were going to have a future, they would have to be more franchise-friendly.

Pascal and her allies would long remember November 21, 2013, as a watershed — the day it became clear that creativity would no longer drive business at Sony Pictures. From now on, it would be the other way around.

On soundstage number eight that morning, no actors or makeup artists or production assistants were preparing to shoot a scene. Instead, dozens of top Sony executives, from Tokyo, New York, and Los Angeles, were preparing to try to impress a gathering audience more important than anyone who bought movie tickets: investors and analysts from Wall Street. The visitors wanted to learn about the studio's plans to cut costs and deliver the kind of consistently growing profits once deemed impossible in the unpredictable roller coaster that is the entertainment business.

Sony Pictures was coming off a disastrous summer in which its two biggest films, the science-fiction vehicle *After Earth,* with Will Smith and his son, and the Channing Tatum action dud *White House Down,* had together lost more than $75 million. Their failure was directly tied to the fact that Sony had almost no popular franchises in its arsenal. To compete with the big summer movies being released by other studios, Sony took a gamble on the type of original, movie-star-driven fare that succeeded in the 2000s but had now fallen out of favor.

For Pascal, who had spent her entire adult life making movies, trying to impress a bunch of Wall Street suits was humiliating. She knew virtually nothing about earnings statements or stock charts and cared even less. As head of Sony's movie business for more than a decade, she schmoozed with stars, gave notes on scripts, and, as the top "picker," decided which films her studio would make each year, at an annual cost of nearly $1 billion.

She relied on others, particularly her longtime business partner Michael Lynton, to handle money issues. And Lynton had for many years done just that, confident that the right business strategy in Hollywood was to insulate creative teams from the day-to-day business pressures. But now, with their performance floundering and pressure from shareholders on Wall Street and corporate bosses in Tokyo ratcheting up, the two were forced to defend their strategy to the financial community.

The pair put on a brave face. Lynton boasted of plans to invest more in television, and Pascal laid out a strategy to do better at the box office.

But in reality, she thought the whole thing was a joke. Once she was done putting on a song-and-dance for the Wall Street analysts, Pascal got busy telling friends in the entertainment industry to ignore everything she and Lynton had just said about financial discipline and focusing on television over film. "Oh please, it's an investor conference," she said. "U know it's bs."

To one close confidant, Pascal admitted what she really thought about the investors, corporate executives, and other suits who didn't have a creative bone in their body but thought they knew better than she did as to what a movie studio needed: "This is my fucking company," she declared. "I have outlasted everyone and always will."

HOLLYWOOD TURNED UPSIDE DOWN

Just a few years earlier, the idea that an uber-mogul like Amy Pascal would have to defend her savvy and relevance to anyone would have been laughable.

Films were the dominant cultural force in America and the dominant economic power in Hollywood. Movie studio bosses were the unquestioned queens and kings of the entertainment industry. That's why Pascal enjoyed the title of co-chairman of Sony Pictures. She was its number two executive, next after Lynton. The head of television, Steve Mosko, was merely a "president" (a title akin to "peon" among showbiz power players) and reported to her, a situation that became increasingly awkward over the years, as his business grew faster than hers.

But that was before Hollywood was turned on its head. It used to be that television, the home of endlessly recycled sitcoms and cop shows, was the medium of the familiar and cinema the medium of originality. Now that axiom has been reversed. We're living in the "golden age of television." Shifting economic and technological factors have fueled an explosion of originality and risk taking that makes the "idiot box" home to arguably the best content Hollywood has ever produced. In 2016, networks and streaming services produced 454 original scripted series, more than double the number created in 2010. Some were good, some were bad, but most were interesting, sophisticated, and made for intelligent adults. It was, to borrow a term from the head of the FX cable network, "peak TV."

Less commented upon was the fact that 2016 was also the year of peak franchise film. Hollywood studios released thirty-seven big-budget sequels, reboots, spinoffs, adaptations, and animated movies. The prior year, it was twenty-four. In 2009, there were eighteen. Some were satisfyingly fun, some were mind-numbingly awful, but it goes without saying that few were substantive and thought-provoking.

The rise of original, risk-taking television is directly tied to the decline of original, risk-taking filmmaking and the dawn of the franchise age of film — one in which studios no longer coddle creative talent, release movies of every type for everyone, or pride themselves for taking risks on quality and new ideas. Instead, movie studios now exist primarily for the purpose of building and supporting branded franchises that continue in sequels, toys, and theme-park attractions.

Of course, "event" movies have been around for more than forty years, since *Jaws* scared a nation and created the idea of a summer tentpole. But they used to just be one element of a studio's strategy. Tentpoles got that name because they were supposed to hold up a structure that also contained dramas, romantic comedies, adult thrillers, and even totally original ideas.

In 1988, *Rain Man* was the number one movie in America. It's worth pausing to consider that fact because today, *Rain Man* would almost certainly never get made. No sane studio executive would bet $50 million (in inflation-adjusted dollars) on an original screenplay and a couple of movie stars because even if it was as good as *Rain Man* — a big "if" before you start production — plummeting home-video sales and the growing importance of international markets mean it would be very difficult to make a profit. Better to spend time and money on the safer bet, sequels to *Batman* and *Mission: Impossible.* Today, anything that's not a big-budget franchise film or a low-cost, ultra-low-risk comedy or horror movie is an endangered species at Hollywood's six major studios.

And as much as some of us may roll our eyes when we walk by a theater marquee filled with superhero spinoffs and sigh when someone has to explain to us what the hell a reboot is, there's no question the studios are acting rationally. Of the top fifty movies at the global box office between 2012 and 2016, forty-three were sequels, spinoffs, or adaptations of popular comic books and young-adult novels (five of the remaining seven were family animation, the sole genre in which originality still consistently works).

Sure, every year a live-action movie without a brand name, like *Gravity* or *La La Land,* becomes a major hit. But those are as rare as a joke in a Christopher Nolan film — no sane company would build a business around them. The studios that made "too many" original films for adults in recent years, like Sony and Paramount Pictures, are not coincidentally the ones that have struggled the most financially.

Any movie can make a profit and every type does, but all the major studios are now owned by huge conglomerates like Sony, AT&T, and Disney, and for them, only mega-profits — the hundreds of millions of dollars created by a global blockbuster like *Jurassic World* or *Deadpool* or *The Hunger Games* — are relevant. These companies also want to tell Wall Street investors that they will deliver profits with the highest possible degree of predictability, another argument for franchise-driven sequels over risky original productions.

Most important, big media conglomerates want movies that generate long-term value. *Despicable Me,* in 2010, wasn't just a hit — it also launched many millions of dollars in merchandise and video-game sales, along with a string of highly profitable sequels and spinoffs for Universal and its corporate parent, Comcast, with more still to come. Compare that to the one-time profits of *La La Land,* and there's no question what type of movies the major studios should invest in.

In reality, even franchises are becoming yesterday's news. Pumping out a new sequel every two or three years is no longer evidence of overly cynical corporate thinking, but rather a lack of imagination. The most important trend in the movie business today is the "cinematic universe."

Pioneered by Disney-owned Marvel Studios, cinematic universes feature overarching narratives that connect two or three movies per year, allowing story lines and characters to weave in and out of them all. Plot points that begin in an Iron Man movie can continue in *Thor* and *Captain America* and be resolved in *The Avengers.* Ant-Man follows up his first solo film with an appearance in Captain America's third, where he also gets his first glimpse of Spider-Man. And fans flock to see them all.

It's quite likely a trend you've noticed and quite possibly one you don't like. Perhaps you've found yourself asking something along the lines of what I'm regularly asked when people find out what I do for a living: Why is there nothing to see at movie theaters for people like me, who are interested in more than sequels and superheroes? What the hell happened to Hollywood?

As a reporter covering the movie business first for *Variety,* then the *Los Angeles Times,* and now the *Wall Street Journal,* I've seen up close what happened to Hollywood. In reporting on the hits and the flops, I've come to know the real people behind those pictures and the forces that motivate them. If you love film, TV, and business as much as I do, it's a fascinating and fantastic job. My task isn't just to see movies, but to understand why we get the movies that we do and then try to explain that to the world.

For years, I've wanted to step back and tell a big story (say, the length of a book) about the new Hollywood — one in which franchises and brands dominate, original ideas and stars are marginalized, and TV and film have swapped places in our culture and our economy. And then I wanted to look forward and explain how new players from Silicon Valley and countries on the other side of the world are reshaping Hollywood and creating a very different future for the movie business. Amazon, Netflix, and would-be media moguls in China are simultaneously a threat to Hollywood as we know it and, perhaps, a savior for the types of films that studios here don't make anymore.

A book made up of my pontifications on those topics would, however, be pretty boring. I really wanted to start by bringing readers into a studio, to give them a close look at how executives develop, produce, and release movies in this new era. But what studio executives in their right mind would invite a reporter to hang out on the lot, with access to every meeting and every memo, for a year or two?

THE WAY INSIDE A STUDIO

Then, in November 2014, came the Sony hack. The cyber-takedown of a Hollywood studio was news worldwide, and like many other reporters in Hollywood, I lived and breathed the twists and turns for two months. Once this died down, though, I began to look through the tens of thousands of e-mails and documents, many of which no journalist had yet examined because there were simply *so many,* and discovered a trove of material that vividly brought to life the trends I wanted to explore and explain. This was, I realized, a way to embed myself inside a studio, a once-in-a-lifetime opportunity to examine the reality of the modern movie business as seen from its central nervous system: a major studio's executive suites.

Fortuitously, Sony Pictures makes for an excellent case study of the franchise age of films. Observing a team led by Pascal, a big personality who thrived in the days of stars and original scripts but struggled to adapt to global audiences and cinematic universes, is an ideal way to see how the industry has changed. The story of Sony Pictures is the story of the movie business over the past few years and an excellent starter course for comprehending the trends that have transformed what we see on the big screen. This book uses material from the Sony hack and dozens of interviews with key Hollywood players to explore what the hell happened to the movie business, where it's going, and what hope there is for cinema to change course in the future.

The first section takes Sony Pictures as a focal point to explain how we got to where we are. We'll get to know Lynton and Pascal and their surprisingly successful relationship, which made the studio successful for nearly a decade, until economic forces sent Sony spiraling down a hole it's still trying to climb out of.

The big-picture business trends that damaged Sony are the reason why certain types of movies are being produced more than ever before. Most significant is the superhero movie, which started with *Spider-Man* at Sony and then revolutionized Hollywood, culminating in the rise and rapidly achieved dominance of the most successful movie studio of this century: Marvel.

As superheroes came into ascendancy, movie stars were suffering. That's particularly true of the Sony favorites Adam Sandler and Will Smith. A close look at them shows how much power A-listers used to have and how they lost it, and why these two actors now make movies for the newest power player in Hollywood: Netflix.

Sony once led the industry in making the smart, mid-budget dramas that are now an endangered species. To see why that happened, we'll closely examine one such film, a biopic of Steve Jobs that would have easily gotten made ten years ago. Sony, however, couldn't find a way to greenlight it in the new Hollywood reality. We'll also take a look at why, desperate to release the film regardless of the odds against it, Pascal turned to a wealthy Silicon Valley heiress who has become a go-to savior for many in Hollywood who are struggling to make sophisticated films for adults.

Sony Pictures also provides a window into the conflicts between motion pictures and television as the latter prospered and the former suffered. You can't fully understand the challenges facing film production and the narrowing of the types of movies studios are willing to make.

The second section of the book leaves Sony behind, along with Hollywood's past, to look at companies, trends, and people that reveal where the movie business is going. It starts with Disney, which, with its obsessive focus on franchises to the exclusion of everything else, has become the studio the rest of Hollywood is striving to emulate. To understand what the American movie business is aiming at, take a look at Disney. And if you hope studios will keep bringing us quirky small movies alongside big-budget franchise blockbusters, prepare to be chilled.

The landscape for filmmakers has changed dramatically in the franchise age, and the filmmakers who thrive now differ from their predecessors in many ways. Directors have become less influential, and producers, including writer-producers, who guide major franchises are now more important. We'll take a look at three of them who are trying, in different ways, to build and guide cinematic universes while still making their own creative imprint.

There is some hope for independent art-house films, but it comes from a surprising source. Amazon is building what could be the biggest and most culturally meaningful independent movie business of this century. We'll discover how this company is working with a set of rules and goals entirely different from those of the Hollywood studios.

No peek at the future of the movie business would be complete without a stop in China. Its consumers increasingly dictate the types of movies that get made, and its money is shaping the way that Hollywood works. Its ultimate effect on filmmaking has yet to be seen, but its impact has already been tremendous.

One other trend could reshape the films Hollywood gives us over the next few years. Studio executives frustrated by corporate mandates that force them to obsess on managing franchises are striking off on their own more and more, using independent money and their decades of experience and connections to try to make the type of interesting mid-budget movies that their former employers have largely abandoned.

At the end, we'll check back with Sony. As I wrote this book the studio continued to linger at the bottom of the box office, took a $1 billion write-down, and changed its leadership team. After its years of struggle, many in Hollywood are asking whether it's even possible for Sony Pictures to make a comeback. If a studio doesn't control great brands, can it find a way to win in the franchise age of filmmaking?

Can it even survive? Rumors have long swirled that Sony might sell its underperforming studio. It seems inevitable that fewer Hollywood studios will exist by the 2020s, since those with big brands that are part of massive conglomerates, like Disney, Comcast-owned Universal, and AT&T-owned Warner Bros., use their power to dominate the franchise film business. Agile digital players like Amazon and Netflix are taking control of the rest.

At the same time, the rise of franchise films and the studios' abandonment of nearly everything else may lead us to the most fundamental questions about movies: What are they? And how much does it matter?

Some still believe that moving images flickering on a giant silver screen deliver a unique cultural experience that must be honored forever. Yet amid the golden age of TV and the ubiquity of streaming media, many now argue that the only difference between a movie and a TV series is how long each one runs. Each Marvel "movie" is, arguably, best understood as a two-hour episode of an ongoing television show, while one season of *Fargo* or *American Crime Story* is, essentially, an eight- or ten-hour film.

Ted Sarandos, the chief content officer of Netflix, has argued that movies are simply stories made of moving images that you consume in one night, whereas TV shows are ones that take several nights. Sure, you can see movies at the multiplex if you so desire, but the size of the screen and the price of the popcorn may no longer be fundamental to the definition of a film.

Ultimately, in the franchise age of filmmaking, perhaps only one thing about movies remains unique: they are home to the biggest, most globally popular brands. If you're a fan of Marvel or DC or Fast & Furious or the Planet of the Apes, you've got to be a fan of the movies. If you're a fan of the most original, moving, and memorable stories that American pop culture has to offer . . . well, the future is very much up for grabs.

PART 1

How Hollywood
Got Here

1

The Odd Couple

Lynton and Pascal's Glory
Days at Sony

IT WAS THE TENSEST TIME in Michael Lynton and Amy Pascal's decade of working together.

After many years of success, Sony's motion picture business was in a slump that just wouldn't end. While big-budget franchise movies were dominating the box office and the studios that focused on them were raking in profits, Sony continued to be known for its mid-budget dramas, genre movies, and star vehicles. There was a lot of talk about the need for more sequels, reboots, and adaptations of well-known intellectual property, but nothing seemed to be clicking.

Lynton was frustrated. He had long stayed out of Pascal's business, figuring he could best help with strategic and financial issues while she was better suited to handle the day-to-day drama of picking and making and releasing movies.

But as the studio struggled, Lynton felt increasing pressure from Wall Street and Sony headquarters in Tokyo. He, in turn, began getting repeatedly frustrated at Pascal for the first time in their eleven-year partnership.

"I did not want to be in this situation, but events have overtaken us and so here we are," he wrote to her in late 2014, not bothering to hide his glumness. "I am only saying this all so you understand the enormous pressure I am under and why I really don't have much patience at the moment."

Pascal would never show to her boss anything but optimism and a can-do attitude. But to others, she admitted she was befuddled.

"Somehow I still can't make sense if what else I have to do to turn the company around," she told Tom Rothman, a confidant who headed Sony's TriStar division. "I can't understand why we are in such a pickle I go over it and over it and all I have is a head ache."

By the middle of the second decade of the twenty-first century, Sony Pictures had lost its way. What at first seemed like an unlucky series of box-office flops had turned into long-term stagnation, revealing a mismatch between the strategy the studio's leadership had adopted and the direction the market was heading in.

The movie business had fundamentally morphed, deriving most of its profits from giving global audiences what they want: branded franchise films, including sequels, reboots, or adaptations based on popular comic books and toys.

But Sony hadn't made that transformation. It was still struggling to shed the strategy that had worked so well for all of Hollywood from the late 1990s through the 2000s: making a diverse slate of films geared first and foremost to domestic audiences, be they fans of comedies, dramas, thrillers, horror, or family fare. In that old-fashioned approach, originality was still considered critical, and branded "event" films were just one part of a successful cinematic recipe.

Because Sony, under Lynton and Pascal, was so good at the old way of doing things and so bad at the new, their story perfectly illustrates what has changed in Hollywood and why the lineup at the multiplex is so full of sequels and reboots and so lacking in fresh ideas.

HOLLYWOOD'S FAVORITE STUDIO CHIEF

When Amy Pascal joined Sony Pictures in 1996, the studio was still reeling from the most disastrous acquisition in the history of the movie industry.

The Japanese electronics giant Sony Corporation had bought seventy-year-old Columbia Pictures in 1989. Sony executives dreamed of leveraging a merger of entertainment and technology, which surely were about to converge, enabling their company to dominate the coming age. Those dreams would ultimately bear little fruit because of bureaucratic ineptitude and Sony's failures in everything from digital music to smartphones to low-cost TVs. But these were not the only issues that made the purchase such a debacle.

Putting up $5 billion to buy Columbia, Sony had grossly overspent and would by 1994 have to write down the asset by $2.7 billion, essentially admitting that the studio behind *Mr. Smith Goes to Washington, Lawrence of Arabia, The Bridge on the River Kwai, Dr. Strangelove, Shampoo, Kramer vs. Kramer, Gandhi,* and *Ghostbusters* was worth less than half of what it had paid.

In addition, the Japanese company spent a total of $1 billion to lock down the management team of Peter Guber and Jon Peters, who proceeded to engage in "the most public screwing in the history of the business," as a book that chronicled their reign put it. They were eye-poppingly extravagant, blowing money on everything from office renovations to talent deals, got the studio caught in a sex scandal involving the prostitute Heidi Fleiss, and oversaw a string of flops still infamous today, including Bruce Willis's *Hudson Hawk,* Arnold Schwarzenegger's *The Last Action Hero,* and the director James L. Brooks's aborted musical *I'll Do Anything.*

When first Peters and then Guber were shown the door, they were replaced by John Calley, an éminence grise if Hollywood ever had one. Urbane, intelligent, and as unconcerned with status as any studio chief could be, Calley had been president of Warner Bros. in the 1970s, when it was a beloved home for filmmakers and turned out classics like *The Exorcist, Dog Day Afternoon, Superman, All the President's Men,* and *Blazing Saddles.*

Then, in 1980, Calley quit. Feeling that he had lost himself and was defined primarily by his phone list, the mogul turned down a seven-year contract worth $21 million and moved to Long Island, then rural Connecticut, where he tuned out business and pop culture almost entirely. He resurfaced as a producer in 1989 and then in 1993 became head of MGM's United Artists division.

Sixty-six years old when he took over Sony, Calley needed a team of young, energetic executives to handle the day-to-day business of developing and making movies. One of his first hires was Amy Pascal.

A rarity in the upper echelons of Hollywood, Pascal is a Los Angeles native who had spent her entire career in entertainment but didn't come from an industry family. The daughter of an economist at a prominent think tank and a librarian who later owned a feminist bookstore, Pascal was born in 1958 and described her upbringing as middle-class Jewish intellectual.

She was interested in human nature as revealed in books, like J. D. Salinger's short stories featuring the Glass family, a septet of precocious children and their parents, who live in New York. Film was the hometown industry, however, and after earning a degree in international relations at UCLA, Pascal answered an ad in the trade paper *Variety* in 1979 and followed a tried-and-true career path: starting at the bottom of the food chain as a producer's assistant, answering phones and fetching coffee. "Movies defined what was possible for a young ambitious girl growing up in Southern California," she would later say.

At the time, motion pictures were a booming business, and anyone with taste and tenacity could rise quickly. Pascal had both, combining an offbeat fashion sense and a rapid-fire speaking style with off-the-charts emotional intelligence and a tireless work ethic. Nobody read more scripts or charmed more creative talent. Her unusual combination of traits — *His Girl Friday* spunk, 1960s flower-child funk, and motherly concern for the filmmakers and actors she adored — gave Pascal the determination to succeed in male-dominated work environments while maintaining her own distinct personality.

It wasn't long until she rose from assistant to "d-girl," a condescending term used in the industry at the time for junior development executives, many of them young women, who scoured piles of script and book submissions in search of the next hit film (today, of course, they'd be scouring Comic-Con and toy shelves). Pascal's first find to make it to the big screen was the comedy *Earth Girls Are Easy*, starring Geena Davis, in 1989. *Earth Girls* garnered attention in the industry as a hot script, though it later flopped at the box office.

Pascal assumed she would one day have the same job as her boss. "Eventually, I want to produce," she said in an interview. "That's where the fun is. That's always been the plan."

It made total sense. Producing was the up-close, get-your-hands-dirty job of making movies, while running a studio was an increasingly bureaucratic job that was more about managing bottom lines and pleasing corporate overlords. With her lack of background in business or in anything, really, besides developing and making films, Pascal seemed ill-suited to such a task.

But in 1985, Scott Rudin, her friend and mentor, and the president of production at Fox, convinced her that she would benefit from some time working at a studio. So Pascal joined him at Fox as a vice president of production. That sent her on a trajectory that would keep her in the studio-executive ranks for more than three decades. By 1989, she had left Fox to take a similar role at Columbia. In 1994, at just thirty-six, she was running her own mini-studio, Turner Pictures, a startup with the backing of CNN and the TBS mogul Ted Turner. There, she oversaw forty people and an annual budget of $100 million.

This remarkable rise put Pascal at the head of the class among her contemporaries. Still, many in Hollywood viewed the bubble-gum-chewing woman who at meetings sat with legs folded under her on a couch, rather than behind an imposing desk, as an odd creature. Her detractors — anyone who reached her level of success in Hollywood was sure to have some — liked to describe her as "crazy."

The moody, insecure, right-brain types who make and star in movies, however, thought she fit right in. "Her self-deprecating thing is charming," said the director James L. Brooks (*Terms of Endearment, As Good As It Gets*). "You tend to trust someone more when they have a degree of self-loathing... they're more like you." Ron Howard described her as "the greatest studio boss out there." George Clooney, who's known for being opinionated but not a brownnose, told her, "I adore you, Amy. You are literally the only person running a studio that loves film." "Amy has the heart and mind of an artist," Jonah Hill once gushed. "I could say I actually love her."

Creative talent didn't fall for just her personality. They also loved Pascal's passion to make the kind of movies they preferred: mid-budget, star-driven, with original ideas. Not necessarily highbrow (though she didn't mind that), but definitely not much "branded entertainment."

She was also widely admired for rising so high and so fast despite rampant sexism in Hollywood and the media that covered it. For example, in a 2002 profile, *Time* magazine reported that "you can gauge her mood by whether her hair is straight (foul) or curly (ebullient)." In interviews, she was constantly asked whether she made too many "chick flicks," like *A League of Their Own* and *Single White Female.* Nobody seemed to ask executives at the studios behind *Die Hard* and *Independence Day* if they made too many movies for dudes.

At Columbia, she had worked on an adaptation of *Little Women* and the still-heralded Bill Murray comedy *Groundhog Day.* The slate she put together at Turner included a Jackie Robinson biopic to star Denzel Washington and to be directed by Spike Lee, an adaptation of Ayn Rand's *The Fountainhead* by Oliver Stone, and original projects about the CIA, women in the space program, and a world in which women disappear.

But in 1995 Time Warner acquired Ted Turner's media empire, and in 1996 it shut down Turner Pictures, deemed redundant at a company that already owned Warner Bros. Only a few movies developed at Turner ever made it into theaters, including the comedy *Michael,* starring John Travolta as an angel, and the Tom Hanks–Meg Ryan hit *You've Got Mail.* "The unfortunate thing about this experience is that it ended before it really had a chance to begin," she said.

Pascal considered becoming a producer or an executive at the startup studio DreamWorks before landing another big job: president of Columbia Pictures under Calley. He paired her with two other top creative executives, vice-chairman Lucy Fisher and co-vice-chairman Gareth Wigan (Sony has a long tradition of lofty, confusing job titles and a multitude of senior production executives, who sometimes butt heads). Nonetheless, the studio's output started to reflect Pascal's taste for midsize interesting movies.

The corporate drama at Sony Pictures ratcheted down considerably in the late 1990s, but the box-office track record was spotty. Some midsize films, such as *Jerry Maguire, Big Daddy,* and *As Good As It Gets,* broke out, but others, like Nicolas Cage's *8 MM,* Robin Williams's *Jakob the Liar,* and the Mike Nichols comedy *What Planet Are You From?,* were major flops. A few were unbelievably expensive, considering the result, including the $100-million-plus biopic *Ali,* a box-office disappointment of 2001 starring Will Smith as the boxer.

And when Sony did swing for the fences, the results didn't impress. Consider the 1998 bomb *Godzilla* and the medieval adventure *A Knight's Tale,* starring Heath Ledger in 2001, another flop.

Other studios were succeeding with original and interesting movies at all budget levels. DreamWorks had *Saving Private Ryan,* Disney *The Sixth Sense,* and Paramount and Fox *Titanic.* Sony's strategy wasn't off; its execution simply wasn't good enough. The studio ranked a disappointing number four at the box office in 1998, and an embarrassing number six or seven every year from 1999 through 2001, until *Spider-Man* not only turned around Sony's fortune but marked a turning point for Hollywood, in 2002.

Amid all this, Pascal remained a survivor, outlasting Fisher, Wigan, and other executives to become Calley's seemingly designated successor. In 1999 she was promoted to chairman of Columbia Pictures ("chairman" being the loftiest title anyone in Hollywood can think of, even though there is never actually a board to chair). And by 2003, when Calley announced he would retire, she seemed poised to take over.

But Sony's U.S. chief, Howard Stringer, and his bosses in Tokyo weren't ready to put her in charge, concerned about her business acumen and her habit of overspending on action movies like *Charlie's Angels 2* (budget: $130 million) and dramas like Brooks's *Spanglish* ($80 million) when they wanted to bring down costs and grow profits, not just box office.

In 2003, Sony had been number two at the box office, with hits like *Bad Boys II, Anger Management,* and *S.W.A.T.* But profits for the motion picture group in the fiscal year that ended March 2004 (the best measure of performance in the prior calendar year) were only $60 million, down 88 percent from the prior year and 75 percent below the company's target, a clear sign that fiscal discipline was needed.

Rumors swirled that Joe Roth, the former Disney film chief who now ran a Sony partner, Revolution Studios, might take over. But instead, Sony shocked Hollywood by turning to an outsider and Pascal's polar opposite.

THE UNLIKELY MOGUL

After he left Hollywood in 1997, nobody thought Michael Lynton would return.

A European-born intellectual who fell into the entertainment industry by happenstance, Lynton could seemingly be deployed to run any company or, thanks to his family wealth, never work at all. People who have known him at all stages of his professional life describe the lanky, lackadaisical Lynton as incredibly smart, extremely decent, and never outwardly excited about what he's doing. Worldly but mild-mannered, he seemed like the type of guy who could say "aw, shucks" in each of the four languages he spoke.

Born in London in 1960 to Jews who fled Germany during the Holocaust, Lynton spent his early youth in the New York suburb of Scarsdale before the family settled in the Netherlands in 1969. There, his father worked as an executive at the window coverings giant Hunter Douglas, which Lynton's maternal grandfather had founded.

Always educated at the best schools, he returned to the United States to attend Phillips Exeter Academy for his last year of high school and then went to Harvard College, where he studied history and literature. After a few years on Wall Street, he decided to return to Harvard to attend business school. Lynton earned his MBA the year that Oliver Stone's *Wall Street* hit theaters, but you could never imagine him standing in front of a room like Michael Douglas's Gordon Gekko, promoting the virtues of greed. He didn't need money, and he had no burning ambition to be a power player or work his way into the 1 percent, since he already belonged to it.

What Lynton wanted was intellectual challenge. The best one to present itself came from Steve Burke, who had graduated from Harvard Business School five years earlier and met Lynton via his former boss at the Wall Street bank Credit Suisse First Boston. Burke, who would later become chief executive of the media conglomerate NBCUniversal, recruited Lynton to work at a company that seemed as un-European and anti-intellectual as they come: Disney.

Under the newly appointed CEO, Michael Eisner, the staid Disney organization had hired a cadre of young MBAs to experiment and expand the company into new businesses. Lynton was assigned to the company's publishing business in New York, and though his first task, licensing coloring books, wasn't too thrilling, he soon launched the magazine *Disney Adventures* and book lines for both children and adults.

Colleagues were certain Lynton would go far — not just because of his acumen and smarts, but because of how easily he seemed to fit in among the elite. "He was in a different world," recalled a Disney coworker. "He always seemed charmed, like he was destined to become a CEO." That prediction seemed well on its way to coming true by 1994, when out of the blue, Lynton was tapped to run Hollywood Pictures, a division of Disney's studio that made films for adults. Calling him a controversial choice would be an understatement. Lynton had no experience making movies and few relationships in a business that ran entirely on them.

Supporters argued that Lynton's background in publishing gave him knowledge of the creative process, along with an outsider's perspective. But in insular Hollywood, he was by his own admission a "stranger in a strange land."

Though he made a goodhearted effort, Lynton never really fit in. He didn't much care for the Hollywood social scene, where connections lead to relationships and then deals. And with a young family, he had other priorities. In an industry full of huge personalities, Lynton was the opposite — an awkward match with the powerful position he inhabited. "It is perhaps true that people like me make the world a less interesting place," he said of himself. Many agents, producers, and other lifelong creatures of the entertainment industry viewed the outsider with mistrust, if not disdain. They considered him an arrogant and unworthy interloper, an opinion that some would hold across his entire career, particularly when he worked alongside the Hollywood native Pascal.

Lynton was the kind of guy who, while CEO of Sony Pictures, could stand awkwardly alone in a corner, dressed in a sweater, hair uncombed, at the Oscars party put on by the super-agent Ari Emanuel. The only reason he even came, he would admit, was because he lived next door and heard the noise.

Pascal herself captured the view of many in the film industry when she described her boss to a management consultant: "he is a very east coast (actually from holland) super brain ... very non California and proud of it ... the kind of guy who wears the same pair of shoes every day but what you wouldn't know is that they were made by the poshest most expensive cobbler in switzerland. he will be the first to tell you he flys coach (yeah sure) but if you check out the pencil holder on his desk its actually a henry miller sculpter."

Though Lynton had a few friends in Hollywood, the people he was closest to were outside the entertainment industry and unsurprisingly, given his background, drawn from the most elite circles. Even in 2013 and 2014, after a decade of running Sony, he only infrequently exchanged e-mails with power players in his own industry.

The people he regularly spoke to were a who's-who of the 1 percent: *The New Yorker* editor David Remnick, the writer Malcolm Gladwell, ABC's anchor Diane Sawyer, CNN's host Fareed Zakaria, Facebook's COO Sheryl Sandberg, and the Obama advisor Valerie Jarrett. When Lynton traveled to Tokyo for work, the pal he tried to catch up with for drinks was the daughter of a president and the ambassador to Japan: Caroline Kennedy. He spent summer vacations with the East

Coast elite on Martha's Vineyard, where he dined with Bill and Hillary Clinton.

"Michael is probably the only media guy you'll meet who reads The New Yorker before he reads Variety (if he reads Variety . . . . . . ?)," said Michael Ryan, a powerful New York attorney and Lynton's brother-in-law.

Lynton's stint running Hollywood Pictures ended ignominiously, though not because of any failure on his part. The division was founded in 1988 to keep the Disney executive who ran it before Lynton from leaving, but it was always duplicative with the studio's other adult live-action label, Touchstone. Joe Roth replaced Jeffrey Katzenberg as chairman of Disney's movie studio just three months after Lynton started, and in 1996 he shut down Hollywood Pictures, ending Lynton's two-year run before the executive had seen a single movie from development to release. If Lynton had any impact, it was his successful bid of $3 million for movie rights to the then-unpublished book *The Horse Whisperer*, which went on to become a bestseller and, in 1998, a hit film for Touchstone, directed by Robert Redford.

"He's a wonderful guy, but I don't think this town embraced him," Jim Wiatt, then head of the agency ICM, said politely about Lynton's departure.

For his part, Lynton seemed glad to be gone.

"For as long as I lived in L.A. I was never entirely comfortable there," he said in 1998. "Imagine living in a town where everything is about movies — where there is no other conversation. That is a horror."

Lynton then headed back to New York for his first job as a CEO, running the book publisher Penguin. The post perfectly combined his European background (Penguin's corporate owner was British), his highbrow education (at Harvard he wrote a dissertation on the author E. M. Forster), and his knowledge of middlebrow tastes and brand marketing from Disney.

Much as he would later do at Sony, Lynton largely left the creative work to subordinates and focused on business strategy. He did get involved in crises, however, including an accounting scandal and Penguin's publication of Salman Rushdie's *Satanic Verses* in 1999. This book provoked the Iranian supreme leader, Ayatollah Khomeini, to issue a fatwa against the author, which led to threats against bookstores and even bombings.

In 2000, Lynton left publishing for America Online, which was then red-hot. He became president of its international businesses just days before the company merged with Time Warner. The ugly corporate politics that followed, along with the dot-com crash of 2001, quickly made AOL a less exciting place to work. And though Lynton succeeded in turning around AOL's European operations, by 2003 he publicly mused about finding a new position in the more traditional entertainment world.

The opportunity came when he was introduced to Sony's Howard Stringer. Once again, Lynton impressed with his stellar résumé and intelligence, and later that year Stringer settled on him to replace Calley as CEO and chairman of Sony Pictures, convinced he could run the business more efficiently and also use his AOL background to bring the studio into the digital age.

There was one problem: Pascal. Convinced that the studio's top job should go to an experienced creative executive and that she had earned it, she expected Stringer to name her as the new boss. When Sony USA's CEO called her at the eleventh hour to inform her that an outsider was about to be hired instead, she threatened to quit rather than report to him.

But Pascal, reluctantly, agreed to fly to New York to meet Lynton. Over dinner in the glass-walled executive dining room atop the Sony Building, she was impressed. The studio's low-key new chief had no intention of horning in on her creative territory. His plan, in fact, was to handle all of the business responsibilities that didn't interest her.

So she agreed to a compromise: Lynton would be named CEO and chairman of Sony Pictures, but she would be given the new title of chairman of the motion picture group and would report directly to Stringer. She and Lynton were partners, in other words, if not quite equal.

It was a "weird, arranged India marriage," Lynton said. The man whose only experience in the movie business had been a brief and sour one and the woman who had never done anything else; the analytical, worldly, and mercurial Harvard MBA and the gut-driven, emotional, and transparent Los Angeles lifer; the man that the corporate suits trusted and the woman Hollywood adored.

"If these two can't work together, I'll eat my hat," declared Stringer.

MAKING IT WORK

The first sign that Stringer was right came in the office assignments for Lynton and Pascal. Rather than exercise the prerogative that came with his title, the new CEO allowed Pascal to have the palatial room that once belonged to the MGM mogul Louis B. Mayer — the literal and metaphorical power center of the Thalberg Building, where the top executives of Sony Pictures worked.

The born-wealthy, double-Harvard-degree-holding CEO didn't need external signs of power as much as his UCLA-graduate partner did, and so was happy to take an office of maybe half the size next door. She got a balcony with a stunning view all the way to the Hollywood Hills. He got a few windows. And even that, he would later say, was more than he needed.

For Pascal, taking the office made famous by Mayer and most recently occupied by Calley was a sign she had arrived. "Everyone knows how I feel about my Louie b Mayer office And what it means," she wrote. To office visitors, she sometimes put things more bluntly: "Don't forget I'm the one who runs this place."

Many couldn't imagine how the man who pulled up to work in a Volkswagen and the woman whose Range Rover was met in the parking lot by assistants could get along. But they did, because Lynton deferred to her on most movie-making issues while handling strategy, administration, relations with Tokyo, and a small but growing television business — all of which she was happy to ignore.

"Amy lives and breathes movies, she works 24/7, and she was really into every detail the way Walt Disney was in the early days of his studio," said Mike De Luca, a producer who worked with Sony frequently and was an executive there from 2013 to 2015. "Michael had opinions, but he was occupied with other stuff and he delegated a lot."

The duo even came to consider each other friends, attending the same synagogue, remembering birthdays, and congratulating each other on successes. "I love you very much And I know you feel the same way about me," Pascal told Lynton. "We are so different I want that to be what's good about us." Conflicts between the two were rare. And in a business where temper tantrums were still considered acceptable behavior by many studio executives, Lynton and Pascal set a different tone.

"For a long time, it was the nicest place to make a movie and the most talent-friendly," said De Luca.

Pascal was a hugger who always lingered too long in conversations and couldn't be more interested in the personal lives of the people she worked with. Lynton was more standoffish, rarely having one-on-one lunches with his executives or inquiring about their families. But he rarely lost his temper and didn't have a mean bone in his body, so though he didn't earn the kind of love and loyalty Pascal did, most of his employees respected him.

Their first year together, 2004, was hugely successful. The fan-pleasing blockbuster *Spider-Man 2*, solid hits like Adam Sandler and Drew Barrymore's *50 First Dates,* and the horror film *The Grudge* brought Sony's motion picture business $550 million in profits — nearly double its internal target and the highest it would reach for at least another decade. The problems of the past seemed to be over and done with.

"Tokyo finally believes this is a business, which, if run in a disciplined way, can be a sound business," boasted Stringer.

The year 2005, however, was a rude awakening. Nearly all of the studio's big bets bombed, including a remake of *Bewitched,* the action movie *Stealth,* and the sequel *XXX: State of the Union.* Motion picture profits plummeted to $31 million. Lynton and Pascal responded in a way that would become a pattern when times got tough at the box office. They replaced their marketing president and promised to take a hard look at costs and their greenlight process. But when things got better, as they did in 2006, with hits like *The Da Vinci Code,* starring Tom Hanks in an adaptation of the best-selling thriller, and Will Ferrell's comedy *Talladega Nights,* all was forgotten and forgiven.

As profits for the motion picture group swung up to $305 million that year, Stringer gave Pascal a five-year contract extension and a new title: "co-chairman" of the studio. (Lynton remained "chairman"; in Hollywood, "co-" does not always indicate equal rank.) In practice, her job of running the movie business stayed the same. But it was the highest title she could be given without usurping Lynton.

Both were well compensated for their work. Pascal made between $6.7 million and $14.2 million annually from 2002 to 2014 ("did I really get this?" she wrote to her lawyer about her peak pay, in 2011). Lynton, who was more circumspect about discussing money in his e-mails, made $13 million in 2013, when Pascal made $12 million.

For most of Pascal's reign, the job wasn't easy, but it was simple: it was just a question of putting together the best slate possible and then hoping that the "movie gods" smiled on her studio.

She wasn't wrong. For a decade starting in the late 1990s, Hollywood experienced one of its flushest moments, thanks to three letters: DVD. Anyone who shopped before 2012 remembers when huge sections of stores like Wal-Mart, Target, and Best Buy were filled with DVDs. The hottest new releases were often priced as low as $13, well below their wholesale cost of $18, in order to lure people into the store. At that price, why not buy a movie and save yourself the trouble of making two trips to Blockbuster Video to rent and return it?

DVD collecting became such an addiction that roughly 15 percent of the DVDs sold in the mid-2000s were never removed from their shrink-wrap, a studio home-entertainment president once admitted to me, with a mix of glee and shame. With studios earning a profit of about $15 on each disc, it became easier than ever to make money in the movie business. All but the biggest flops were profitable.

Hollywood operated like a "welfare state," in the words of one veteran executive, and everyone enjoyed the windfall, from executives to producers to agents to talent. In late 2003, cost control at Sony consisted of a policy to give no more than 25 percent of the revenues of a movie to its stars, director, and producers. A decade later, the concept of "gross points," in which a studio hands out big chunks of revenue to talent before it has even made a profit, would become an embarrassing relic of the past.

In those golden days, it made sense to produce movies for everyone — and a lot of them. The number of movies released annually by the six major studios peaked at 204 in 2006, the same year that home-entertainment revenue hovered near a high of almost $25 billion.

Sony thrived in this environment because Pascal thrived at making all kinds of movies for all types of people. She wasn't much at maximizing the value of a branded franchise, but she knew how to develop a script to perfection, make just the right change in the editing room to take a film from good to great, and how to charm the most talented filmmakers and actors. Stars like Sandler and Smith and Ferrell and Nicole Kidman loved to work at Sony because Pascal loved to have them. She was like a den mother for the industry's A-listers, albeit one who paid her scouts lavishly.

A typical Sony slate at the time could include twenty-five movies in one year, of which two or three were big-budget "event" films like *The Da Vinci Code* and the James Bond sequel *Casino Royale*. The rest were mid-budget movies that crossed genres and audiences, be they dumb comedies like Adam Sandler's *Click*, high-minded dramas like *The Pursuit of Happyness* (which earned Will Smith his second Academy Award nomination), or romantic heart-warmers like *The Holiday*, starring Cameron Diaz, Kate Winslet, Jude Law, and Jack Black.

All around Hollywood, studios were making risky movies. They were not based on well-known intellectual property, and each cost between $30 million and $120 million to make. Alfonso Cuarón's post-apocalyptic *Children of Men*, George Clooney's taut thriller *Michael Clayton*, the psychological crime tale *Zodiac*, Tom Hanks's true-life comedy *Charlie Wilson's War*, the petro-political drama *Syriana*, and the director Michael Mann's *Collateral* and *Public Enemies* are just a small sampling of the films released by major studios in the 2000s that would stand virtually no chance of making their release slates today.

Though she employed a large team of production executives, Sony's film output was ultimately defined by the "Amy factor"— the tastes and sensibilities of Pascal. "If she doesn't get it, we don't make it," said one executive who worked for her. Her tastes weren't narrow— Sony successfully made everything from Adam Sandler comedies to sports stories to *Spider-Man*. But her "comfort zone," as one agent put it, was mid-budget original films for adults rather than global "event" films engineered to spawn sequels.

Sony's motion picture profits did swing up and down in the 2000s, which according to conventional Hollywood thinking was inevitable, since it was tough to tell ahead of time which original films would prove popular and which wouldn't. But with Lynton managing the business and Pascal the moviemaking, financial results were satisfying more often than not. The studio beat its motion-picture-group-profit targets five out of the seven fiscal years from 2002 through 2008, earning an annual average of $329 million.

Over the next seven years, however, the movie division missed its profit targets every year but one, and its average annual profit was nearly unchanged, despite inflation. Sony Corporation expected more from its movie studio as the global economy grew, but Sony Pictures didn't deliver.

It wasn't the recession, during which cinema attendance actually grew, as people cut back on more expensive leisure activities, and it wasn't that Pascal lost her touch. The movie business was turning upside down, and Sony Pictures was painfully slow to react.

2

===

Reality Bites

How Everything Went Wrong
for the Movie Business

IN 2009, TERROR STRUCK at the hearts of Hollywood moguls like
Amy Pascal. The sudden and unexpected drop in DVD sales was like
having a leg yanked out from under a table at which they had feasted
on gourmet food for a decade.

Internet piracy was a major cause. Also, a pair of innovative businesses, Netflix and Redbox, were giving consumers a far more efficient
way to watch movies than buying them at Target or renting them at
Blockbuster. For a dollar per night at Redbox or less than ten dollars
per month from Netflix, consumers could watch as many, or as few,
movies as they wanted and return them in the mail or at the grocery
store. Actual consumption of films went up, but studios' home-entertainment profits tumbled because people were spending far less to
watch them.

Video-on-demand rentals and digital downloads helped a bit as the
years went on, but the movie business never fully recovered. Annual
home-entertainment revenue, and the studio profits that follow from
it, fell by nearly half between 2004 and 2016, from nearly $22 billion to
$12 billion.

At the same time, Americans became much less important to the

American movie business. As the economies of developing nations throughout Latin America and Asia grew, theater construction surged and the rising middle class spent their newfound wealth on what was to them the novel and luxurious experience of a night out to see the latest Hollywood flick. International box office exploded, from $8.6 billion in 2001 to $27.2 billion in 2016. The biggest driver of growth in recent years has been China; its box office grew from $2 billion in 2011 to $6.6 billion in 2016 and is expected to surpass U.S. box office before the end of the decade.

Domestic box office, meanwhile, grew by only 40 percent between 2001 and 2015, to $11.4 billion — reflecting a slight decline in attendance, once you factor in ticket price increases.

Both trends were like a siren's wail to studio executives, urging them to make fewer, bigger, louder movies. DVD sales declines were smallest for movies with budgets of more than $75 million, and as studios tried to cut costs in response to plummeting home-entertainment revenues, risky original scripts and adaptations of highbrow books were the first to go. Annual movie releases by major studios were 139 in 2016, down 32 percent from their peak in 2006, and the decline is explained entirely by the evaporation of interesting, intelligent mid-budget films.

Studios realized their assumption that they had to make every type of movie for everyone was no longer true. So they focused on the types of movies that delivered the biggest and most consistent profits to their publicly traded parent corporations.

Increasingly, that meant movies that appealed to audiences in Russia, Brazil, and China. These consumers weren't likely to understand the cultural subtleties of an American drama or to consider people talking or even running for their lives to be adequate bang for their buck on an expensive night out. They expected spectacle, particularly if they were paying premiums for an IMAX or 3D screen, and they wanted stories that made sense to a villager in China, a resident of Rio de Janeiro, or a teenager in Kansas City.

Transformers, in other words. And *The Avengers.* And *Jurassic World* and *Fast and Furious* and *Star Wars.* With the exception of 1997's *Titanic,* which made a spectacle out of the sinking of a cruise ship and

Leonardo DiCaprio's eyes, the forty-eight highest-grossing Hollywood films overseas are all visual-effects-heavy action-adventure films or family animation.

The transformation of Hollywood into a foreign-first business has also made sequels, spinoffs, and cinematic universes the smartest bet in the movie business. Newly minted middle-class customers in developing nations like China love prestige Western brands like Apple, Louis Vuitton, and Gucci. The same logic applies in cinemas. American cineastes may reach for the Advil when offered the choice between the latest superhero, dinosaur, or talking robot spinoff, but to many foreign moviegoers, that response is somewhere between condescending and confounding — the equivalent of complaining that there aren't enough modern art installations at Disneyland.

One more trend fundamentally changed the movie business this decade: the golden age of television. As TV has gotten better, the pressure on major movie studios is not to keep up with *Breaking Bad, Orange Is the New Black,* and *Fargo* (a property that was perfect for the movie business of the 1990s and for the TV business of today), but rather to stand out by offering something different. Most people, particularly middle-aged adults, simply don't go to the movies for sophisticated character dramas anymore. Why would they, when there are so many on their DVR and Netflix and Amazon queues at home?

Why go to the movie theater at all, audiences have asked over the past few years, when movie tickets, snacks, and a babysitter can easily cost a hundred bucks and there is so much good TV to watch and so many apps on their tablets to interact with?

Moviegoing is no longer a habit the way it used to be, particularly for people ages eighteen through forty-nine. They saw two fewer films per year on average in 2016 than they did in 2012. When they do go to the cinema, modern consumers increasingly prefer to know what they're in for, which means a brand-name franchise. Even big-budget, star-driven action movies with stellar reviews, like Tom Cruise's excellent *Edge of Tomorrow,* have struggled. And in the same year, *Star Wars: The Force Awakens* destroyed box-office records by essentially re-creating a movie from forty years ago.

SONY'S STRUGGLES

Some in Hollywood adapted well to this new reality. Disney, as we'll explore in depth later, reoriented its studio with brands like Marvel and Star Wars and movies based on fairy tales. Warner Bros., which pioneered the global tentpole in the early 2000s with *Harry Potter* and owned DC superheroes such as Batman and Superman, as well as Lego and the Hobbit, was consistently at or near the front of the pack.

Sony was not. Between 2003 and 2009 it was ranked in the top three of the six major studios in domestic box office every year but two. Between 2010 and 2016, it was in the bottom half of the pack every year but two.

More troubling, as international box office became more important, the weakness of Sony's overseas operations hurt it more and more. It was ranked fifth or sixth among the major Hollywood studios in foreign grosses every year between 2010 and 2016 except one. While other studios hired people with overseas expertise for top positions, Pascal and her team remained far too U.S.-oriented for far too long.

The biggest reason for Sony's box-office struggles, however, was that it hadn't acquired or built many cinematic series that qualified as global franchises. Sony's focus on mid-budget star vehicles had kept the studio lights on when that type of film was consistently profitable. But as the industry shifted, Sony's cupboards were almost bare.

Still stung by the big write-down it took on its initial purchase of Columbia, the Japanese parent company was reluctant to make the kinds of investments that drove the success of competitors like Disney, which bought Pixar, Marvel, and Lucasfilm, or Warner Bros., which signed a costly partnership with J. K. Rowling, the creator of the Harry Potter stories. Discussions about big investments for Sony's movie business rarely translated into action.

The studio's slate still largely reflected the singular version of the mogul who oversaw it. But as the economics of the film business and the tastes of global audiences evolved, Amy Pascal's vision grew increasingly misaligned with what the job required.

"The truth [is] that we do not have as many frnachises aas other companies," she wrote to her friend Doug Belgrad, president of Sony's motion picture group, in a candid admission of failure. "The cornerstones of our slates were Adam Sandler, Will S[mith] and Will F[errell]. For a long period of time these relationships provided a steady stream of reliable, profitable films. This was an advantage we had vs. other studios, but it was about talent rather than properties ... Over time, like any franchise, the freshness wore off. And unlike a property or brand, you can't reboot a movie star ... We stayed too long at the party and got behind, as our competitors built their businesses for the future."

Sony essentially had three major franchises: James Bond, Men in Black, and Spider-Man, all of which came with baggage from bad decisions in the past. That was illustrated dramatically in 2012, the only year in the 2010s when Sony ranked number one at the box office. Unbeknownst to many, though, the profits from its trio of blockbusters that year were shockingly small.

Sony's highest-grossing movie, and the fourth highest in the industry, was the Bond sequel *Skyfall,* which collected a phenomenal $305 million domestically and $1.1 billion worldwide, a record for 007. Typically, studios make several hundred million dollars in profit on such movies. Sony made only $57 million (measured as an "ultimate," or the expected profit over the next decade, which is standard in the industry).

The reason? Sony didn't actually own the Bond franchise. Another studio, MGM, did. Executives at Sony Pictures had advocated buying MGM, but the company never pulled the trigger. Instead, MGM emerged from a bankruptcy in 2010 as a small independent entity that needed a partner to co-finance and distribute its movies. Sony bent over backward to add one of the industry's highest-profile franchises to its otherwise lackluster slate. It agreed to pay 50 percent of the Bond movies' costs, but keep only 25 percent of the profit. "Who else is gonna make such a one sided deal with mgm?" Pascal asked, rhetorically but tellingly.

Men in Black 3, Sony's third-biggest movie of the year, was even uglier. It grossed $624 million worldwide. But after dishing out $90 million in gross points to talent like Will Smith and Steven Spielberg under deals set in place with the first two MIB movies in 1997 and 2002, the studio earned no profits at all. It broke even.

The Amazing Spider-Man, a reboot of Sony's most successful franchise, earned about $110 million on $758 million of worldwide ticket sales, a respectable amount. Still, that was less than half the profits of 2007's *Spider-Man 3* and one-quarter of the profits of 2002's original movie about the web-slinger. "Even though we were #1 at box office in 2012," Pascal would later admit, "it was a shitty year."

There were still solid hits in the 2010s that fell right in with the Pascal wheelhouse of high-quality, mid-budget dramas and comedies, like the hilariously subversive *21 Jump Street* and the Oscar-nominated *Moneyball, The Social Network,* and *Captain Phillips.* Each could throw off profits of around $40 million to $60 million — real money, but nothing compared to a global blockbuster.

Yet some movies made under the "old" Sony model were outright debacles. One of the most damaging to the studio's bottom line and its claims of financial discipline was 2010's *How Do You Know?* from Pascal's old friend James L. Brooks. It cost a staggering $120 million to make and grossed less than $50 million. It was both a major money loser and an embarrassment, given that its budget was three or four times higher than that of most romantic comedies.

A new low came in 2013. With no franchise properties for the summer, Pascal and her team were forced to take big swings on movies they weren't totally confident in. These included *After Earth,* a Will Smith passion project whose main star was actually his son, Jaden, and whose director, hand-picked by Smith, was the ice-cold M. Night Shyamalan; another was *White House Down,* a Jamie Foxx–Channing Tatum action movie whose script Sony bought for $3 million in 2012 and then rushed into production. It wasn't fast enough, however, to beat the very similar *Olympus Has Fallen,* which came out in March 2013 and left June's more expensive *White House Down* looking like a shiny but unappealing leftover. *After Earth,* meanwhile, simply lacked an audience for its moralistic science-fiction tale about a boy lost on a post-apocalyptic planet.

Perhaps most important, both films felt like relics — star-driven movies in a summer when big brands surrounded it, from *Fast and Furious 6* to the Superman reboot *Man of Steel* to the animated sequels *Monsters University* and *Despicable Me 2*. *After Earth* and *White House Down* each cost about $150 million to make and both bombed, and *White House Down*'s foreign grosses were particularly dismal. It lost more than $50 million, while *After Earth* lost about $25 million.

And these films appeared right in the midst of the activist investor Dan Loeb's assault on the studio. He gleefully compared them to infamous industry bombs such as *Ishtar* and *Waterworld*. Sony rejected Loeb's criticisms (though it did agree to host that entertainment investors' day in November to try and placate him), but the stink of that summer's bombs never washed off.

"It was two fucking movies . . . . . . how long does this go on," Pascal complained to Lynton.

It would go on for several years. And get much worse.

Along with the Loeb settlement, Sony also agreed to find $350 million in annual savings, resulting in more than two hundred layoffs. The studio's headcount was in the midst of a dramatic shrinkage — from nearly eight thousand in 2009 to six thousand by 2014.

The number of movies released shrank too, from twenty-two in 2011 to just thirteen in 2015. And annual development spending, the R&D of the movie industry, fell dramatically, from $127 million in fiscal 2010 to $71 million in 2015. Pascal even had to let go of her longtime assistant, Mark Seed. He made her life run so magically that she nicknamed him "Mark Poppins," but he made more than $250,000 per year.

Pascal had less to work with and at the same time, Sony Corporation demanded more from her, as it responded to pressure from Loeb and the struggles of its electronics business. One result was growing tension between Pascal and Lynton, who in 2012 had been promoted to CEO of Sony Entertainment, putting him in charge of the company's music businesses and officially making him Pascal's boss, not her partner.

Their relationship grew less familiar, and he privately admonished her about the company's faltering financial situation. "Why is everyone freaking out[?]" she asked, when the *Hollywood Reporter* revealed her assistant's eye-popping salary. "Because we said no cost is too small," responded Lynton. "An assistant paid that amount suggests a lack of controls. We claim to have those controls."

Despite her frustrations, Pascal was determined to turn things around. "I'm trying to put this company back together," she told Scott Rudin, now long gone from Fox and one of the industry's most powerful producers. "It's not so easy."

But she believed she couldn't do it with just her current senior team, which included Doug Belgrad and Columbia's president of production, Hannah Minghella, a young and fast-rising favorite of the mogul, whom she referred to as "My Hannah." So Pascal brought in two more senior executives (a decision that played poorly among the studio's rank and file, given that the executives were paid multi-million-dollar salaries while so many were being laid off): De Luca became a second head of production for Columbia, alongside Minghella, while Tom Rothman, recently fired as chairman of 20th Century Fox, was given a largely dormant Sony label, TriStar, to run.

To Rothman, who quickly became a trusted friend, Pascal admitted what many around her had been noticing: that her confidence in herself, in her ability to pick the movies that audiences wanted to see and whose profits Sony would be happy to take home, was shaken. Rothman responded with tough advice. "What is happening to you is that the financial pressures, and your desire to please your bosses, are causing you to doubt your instincts," he told Pascal. "In our jobs, we must be able to hear our inner voices clearly and yours are getting undermined and hence confused."

Lengthy, sometimes barely comprehensible late-night e-mails from the boss, panicking about the latest crisis and the state of Sony's business, had long been a fact of life for Pascal's subordinates. But as stress at the office grew, these communications became even more common. "The un marvel marvel world that is rooted in humanity but instead of it being like a trilogy or a story this is the opening of a world that will be unleashed," Pascal wrote one night at 10:48 in an attempt to figure out what to do with Spider-Man. "A little too late for me to decipher your poetry," responded Belgrad.

The Hollywood trade press, meanwhile, was speculating about whether Pascal was about to lose her job. "I've been miserable for two years," she confided to CAA partner Bryan Lourd, one of her best friends, in 2014. She even had to reassure her parents she wasn't about to be fired.

She wasn't the only top executive at Sony who seemed to have lost all joie de vivre. "Work is drudgery," Michael Lynton told a friend just a month after Pascal complained that she was miserable. Facing his toughest times yet after more than a decade on the job and unsure about his relationship with the new CEO of Sony, Kaz Hirai, Lynton was considering escaping Hollywood entirely. Working with a recruiter, he lobbied aggressively to be considered for jobs in academia and the nonprofit world, such as president of New York University, or Tulane, or the Smithsonian Institution.

As he traveled for interviews and meetings with academic acquaintances who could help his cause, Lynton had a good sense of what his current colleagues in Hollywood would think. "We have to keep this very confidential," he told Walter Isaacson, another friend and a superstar writer. "With all that is going on at Sony if word got out about this it could be v harmful to the company."

His time was also taken up by one of the nation's hottest tech startups: Snapchat, the app on which messages disappear after a set time. Lynton had gotten to know the founder of Snapchat, Evan Spiegel, after the Sony CEO's wife noticed their daughters were using it. Lynton e-mailed the young Stanford dropout, who had attended the elite private school where the Lynton girls were students. Within an hour, Spiegel was at their house, and the couple agreed to invest in the startup, among the earliest to make that commitment. Not long after, Michael Lynton joined Snapchat's board, eventually becoming its chairman.

As Snapchat grew rapidly and eventually had a $24 billion IPO, the Lyntons' personal stake reached more than $500 million.

DESPERATELY SEEKING FRANCHISES

Among the rest of the studio's movie executives, meanwhile, it was a time of heightened urgency. Almost every weekend as De Luca left work with a pile of scripts to read, Pascal would ask him, "Where's our tentpole?! Where's our tentpole?!"

By the mid-2010s, it was clear that the most consistently successful studios had the most franchises in their quiver, which they used to cycle sequels and spinoffs while enjoying the freedom to develop the next hits. Disney and Warner held that status for most of the decade, while the rest struggled, with varying degrees of success, to reach that elite level. None had a harder time than Sony Pictures.

De Luca, Minghella, and other Sony staffers eagerly picked up anything that smelled like a potential franchise. They bought the rights to make movies based on Barbie, the Fifth Wave series of young adult books, and Stephen King's Dark Tower novels. Looking to expand the successful but relatively small Jump Street franchise and reinvigorate Men in Black, Sony cooked up a plan to combine the two in a single film ("jump street merging with mib i think that's clean and rad and powerful," commented the star Jonah Hill). They tried to get movies that had been languishing in development for years into production: a remake of *Cleopatra,* a third Ghostbusters, another Bad Boys, and adaptations of the toy-based animated TV series *He-Man and the Masters of the Universe* and of Sony's Indiana Jones–esque video game *Uncharted.*

And instead of putting out a new sequel to *Spider-Man* every few years, Pascal and her team started developing spinoffs they could release annually, like those based on the Sinister Six team of villains, in order to create their own superhero universe to rival Marvel's.

But few of these development projects turned into actual movies. By 2013 and '14, the trend in Hollywood was to announce a prime release date for major franchise films years in advance, before a script was even in place, and then marshal resources to reach that goal. Sometimes it worked brilliantly to focus attention, and sometimes it resulted in creative disaster when the date proved unrealistic — but at least it got movies out the door.

The new model called for a studio chairman to set a big goal and then direct his or her deputies to make it happen, come hell or high water. That wasn't how Pascal typically worked, though. She loved to get her hands dirty, working personally with writers, directors, and producers to get a project just right. And no matter how important the big movies were, the lure of small, prestigious, and potentially Oscar-winning films, like a biopic of Steve Jobs, kept stealing Pascal's attention.

Lynton, in his typical manner, which some considered respectful and others passive-aggressive, expressed his concerns to her: "I worry that we are signing up a lot of smaller movies and that the big ones, 5th wave, Masters of the universe, ghostbusters, unchartered are not crossing the line. If columbia is spending all this time on the smaller ones, how are they getting the big ones done."

Pascal, writing to Belgrad, vented in her typical way: "barbie is in freeefall and we paid a fucking fortune for it . . . when are scripts cpoming in on things that can be movies uncharted monkeys we don't have a writer on barbie we don't have a writer on the chris hemsworth movie sinister 6 is a scary problem because of marvel and warners when do you think we are getting the gb script can we make jump street real what is happening with winters knight and hood and eden and dishonorables and narnia and bad boys . . . .michael bay isn't doing it i don't know what to do with my frustration so I'm writing you."

Only two of the big ideas in the works in 2013 and 2014 would make it to the big screen by 2016: the female-led *Ghostbusters* reboot and *The 5th Wave,* and both disappointed at the box office. In the meantime, Sony faced a conundrum: how to produce the big results that Tokyo wanted ASAP, given the lack of vibrant franchises they had to work with. One answer, which often blew up in their faces, was to overpromise.

When Hollywood studios greenlight movies, they typically make a box-office projection that will create an acceptably big profit, after considering all the revenue expected to follow from DVD, digital, and television sales. Such projections are based on comparisons to similar movies with similar budgets released at similar times of the year, and they always include some level of subjectivity. (Is the remake of *Ghostbusters* most similar to other Melissa McCarthy comedies? To buddy comedies? To generic summer action films? To the first two Ghostbusters films in the 1980s?) But because executives are judged on whether their movies hit the projections made at greenlight, not whether the movies are simply profitable or not, the projections are supposed to be made as objectively as possible.

That was always challenging at Sony, because when Pascal really wanted to make a movie, she sometimes rejected projections she deemed too low. She certainly wasn't the only studio chief who bent others to his or her will, but it was telling that some executives referred to greenlight meetings at Sony as "enablement sessions" for Pascal. That's how 2004's dour James L. Brooks dramedy *Spanglish,* for instance, was greenlit, with a projection that it would make more than $100 million domestically (it ended up with $43 million).

Pascal's willingness to go with her gut could pay dividends, though. *Superbad,* in 2007, seemed like a risky bet: an R-rated comedy about high school (meaning most of its target audience would be too young to buy tickets), featuring Jonah Hill and Michael Cera, totally unknown then. But she believed it would succeed and so the film was greenlit, with a target domestic box office of $30 million, which seemed like a stretch to some inside Sony. It ended up grossing $121 million.

By 2013, Sony Pictures was regularly projecting very high grosses on its films, both in order to make it seem like they could achieve the big profits its parent company wanted and to justify budgets that, while shrinking, still weren't exactly the tightest in Hollywood. So 2014's *The Amazing Spider-Man 2,* which cost $260 million and grossed $709 million worldwide, was a major disappointment because it was projected to make $865 million.

A rash of other movies that year and the next were greenlit with optimistic expectations and failed to deliver: the R-rated comedy *Sex Tape* (projection: $180 million; result: $126 million); the robot film *Chappie* (projection: $200 million; result: $102 million); 2015's only summer tentpole, *Pixels,* featuring video-game characters alongside the fading stars Adam Sandler and Kevin James (projection: $282 million; result: $245 million); the drama *Ricki and the Flash,* starring Meryl Streep, from Rothman's TriStar label (projection: $100 million; result: $41 million); the drama *Concussion,* starring Will Smith (projection: $135 million; result: $49 million); the comedy *Aloha,* directed by Cameron Crowe (projection: $90 million; result: $20 million); and the comedy *The Brothers Grimsby,* starring Sacha Baron Cohen (projection: $200 million; result: $25 million).

Some movies overperformed, most notably 22 *Jump Street* (projection: $215 million; result: $331 million) and the animated *Hotel Transylvania* 2 (projection: $325 million; result: $473 million), but Sony was too frequently stretching, and many inside the studio knew it. "The projections were insane," admitted De Luca.

Another movie with a big number on it was Sony's R-rated 2014 comedy *The Interview,* starring Seth Rogen, which cost $41 million to make and was projected to gross $100 million at the worldwide box office after its debut on Christmas Day. Instead, it grossed $11 million, but not because of miscalculations by Sony's production executives. Its release was aborted because of the worst corporate hack in American history.

THE HACK AND THE AFTERMATH

Tens of thousands of e-mails and documents were posted online by the hackers and then covered breathlessly by press around the world. Among the most embarrassing were offensive jokes Pascal and Scott Rudin made about which movies with African American casts President Obama would like best, criticisms of A-list stars like Angelina Jolie, and a copy of the script for 2015's James Bond movie *Spectre.* There were even internal discussions at Sony as to whether North Korea would seek to retaliate over *The Interview,* which mocked the country's dictator, Kim Jong-un — discussions that unwittingly presaged the hack itself. The U.S. government and most experts eventually concluded that hackers backed by North Korea broke into Sony's computer system, most likely in retaliation for *The Interview*. The issue was never fully resolved, though, and some still believe that disgruntled ex-employees are to blame.

For Pascal, the end of 2014 was a never-ending nightmare, as she told anybody who would listen. Not only were bloggers' deep dives into her e-mails humiliating, but the harm done to Sony Pictures was painful for a woman whose identity and self-worth were inextricably tied to it. I'll never forget talking to her on the phone as I drove down Santa Monica Boulevard and explained why I'd be using a few of her stolen e-mails in a business story.

"I'm not using anything personal," I said, thinking I could separate myself from the bloggers who wrote about her orders on Amazon.

"You don't get it!" she retorted. "It's all personal!"

Lynton, meanwhile, got personally involved in a way he never had before. He dined in the cafeteria and invited employees to approach him with questions about what FBI agents were doing on the lot, how payroll would be processed, and when security guards would be able to stop hand-writing passes for visitors (that would end up taking more than a year).

He took charge when people claiming to be the hackers threatened violence against any theaters that played *The Interview*. Major cinema chains quickly caved, with the backing of other studios fearful that audiences would avoid multiplexes entirely and harm their holiday releases too. Though Sony had the contractual right to force theaters to play the film, executives decided not to do so. "No movie is worth a human life," Belgrad declared at a meeting in Pascal's conference room, earning nods from the rest of the studio's leadership team.

Sony executives expected they would be credited for not forcing anyone to play their film, but instead they were perceived to be bowing to a terrorist threat and were widely criticized. Even President Obama said the studio "made a mistake."

Lynton was furious that Hollywood wasn't uniting to defend Sony against terrorists who threatened the industry's freedom of expression, as book publishers had rallied around Penguin when, under his leadership, it released Salmon Rushdie's *Satanic Verses*. The heads of other studios, meanwhile, grumbled that the aloof Lynton had long lacked interest in getting to know them and working together until this moment of crisis, when he needed them.

He did find friends, however, in Silicon Valley. Right after theater chains passed on playing *The Interview*, Lynton began secretly calling the heads of major cable and Internet companies, from Comcast to Amazon to Apple, seeking a partner to release it online. Most said no, but Google's chairman, Eric Schmidt, agreed that his company would offer *The Interview* online by Christmas. Microsoft joined too, as did 331 independent theaters, and the comedy got a release, of sorts, on Christmas Day.

By the new year, coverage of the hack seemed to die down as the regular release of stolen e-mails and documents throughout November and December ended, and the public turned its attention elsewhere. Inside Sony, however, the drama continued.

Lynton still faced a key question: whether to keep Pascal. Her contract would expire in March, and before the hack, extensive negotiations had been underway to continue her employment. But the fact that she hadn't been renewed by November indicated Sony's uncertainty and became yet another source of anxiety for Pascal, who one evening e-mailed, texted, and called Sony's head of human resources multiple times on his cell phone to demand an update.

Instead of continuing to base her annual bonuses on the performance of the entire studio — giving her the benefit of the success of a television business she technically oversaw but had almost no involvement with — Sony had before the hack proposed basing 70 percent of Pascal's bonus on the business that she spent 99 percent of her time on: motion pictures. And they wanted to reduce her maximum annual pay from $21 million to $16 million. "In all cases the new offer has me earning substantially less money," she complained to her lawyer. "That sounds like an insane thing to ask me to agree to."

The most insulting part for Pascal, though, was that after her tenure of nearly twenty years at the company, Lynton wasn't enthusiastically urging her to stay. "You know ml will be as rude as possible and try and make me feel AKWARD instead of loved," she told Lourd.

Still, Pascal seemed confident that she would return, one way or another. And she didn't even mind that Lynton wanted to shorten the length of her contract from that of the previous renewal: five years. She just wanted enough time to make Sony a winner again and then bid adieu. "3 years I'm done for good," she said.

On Saturday, January 31, 2015, Lynton visited Pascal's house to inform her that she wouldn't get the chance. He was letting her go. The poor performance of the movie business over the past several years was the ostensible reason. But there was no denying that, fairly or not, the hack had done severe damage to her reputation in Hollywood and around the world, and thus it had hurt her ability to perform her job.

The hack had also heightened Pascal's unhappiness in the job, so she didn't put up too big a fight. She agreed to stay on the Sony lot with a multi-million-dollar deal to become a producer, the job she had envisioned twenty years earlier.

Her eleven-year partnership with Lynton, once hailed as among the most successful in Hollywood history, was now at an end. The two would remain on cordial terms, but Sony's reputation as the most talent-friendly studio in Hollywood — one that had prospered under an unlikely partnership that defied expectations — was officially over. It was the end of an era.

Lynton's choice to replace her was Tom Rothman, whose bottom-line orientation and knowledge of the global market also delivered a signal that Sony was finally bowing to the realities of the worldwide franchise-driven movie business, even if it meant killing the studio's talent-friendly reputation.

But as they announced Pascal's departure (laughably spinning that it was entirely her choice), the now former partners had a secret: just a few days earlier, Lynton had traveled with Pascal to Palm Beach, Florida, where they agreed to relinquish control of one of their most valuable assets in a deal that demonstrated how power in Hollywood was slipping out of the hands of major studios like Sony.

3

Inception

The Secret Origin of the
Superhero Movie

IT WAS A WARM TUESDAY NIGHT in November when Amy Pascal reached out to one of Hollywood's top directors with a desperate plea.

"I really need your help with you know who I've made a mess of it," she told Sam Raimi. "I don't want to blah blah blah about how badly Peter needs to be rescued [but] I don't know where to turn . . . i realize i sound like i am talking about a person . . . probably anyone beside you would think ive lost my marbles."

The "Peter" in question was Peter Parker — not a real person, but the alter ego of Spider-Man, one of the world's most famous superheroes. He was the basis of one of Hollywood's most successful franchises and the single biggest source of profits for Sony's movie business. For Pascal, working with Raimi on 2002's *Spider-Man* and its 2004 and 2007 sequels was a career highlight — her skills in working with creative talent and finding the emotional heart of stories were paired perfectly with a marquee property that could achieve box-office success and earn acclaim from audiences.

Many still believe *Spider-Man 2* is the best superhero film Hollywood has made. And the four most profitable fiscal years for Sony's motion picture business this century were, not coincidentally, those in which it released the first four movies starring the red-and-blue web-slinger.

But, along with the rest of Sony's movie business, Spider-Man suffered in the 2010s.

In 2014 *The Amazing Spider-Man 2* grossed $709 million. That sounds like a big number, but it's the lowest box-office take of any movie in the series and of any superhero movie that year. Sony spent $260 million to make the picture, in hopes that it would be a blockbuster. The studio internally targeted $865 million in ticket sales, but Pascal was privately urging her colleagues to aim higher and get Peter Parker "in the billion dollar club."

Its underperformance blew a hole in Sony's financials for the year. Instead of earning $138 million in profits as expected, it made less than $20 million. Just as disappointing, the film was a creative dud — something Pascal had privately known for months but had hoped wouldn't impact the box office.

"Uneven skitzo tone . . . Repetitive Long doesn't ever hit the center bullseye for a long enough time weird disjointed not one single great set piece because action is just big and not story telling not funny at all," she wrote to Belgrad two months before *The Amazing Spider-Man 2* was released, insightfully listing many of the flaws upon which critics and fans would later pounce. "Prob if I'm really honest," she added, "wring director and wrong casting."

Still, she believed, "We will almost get away with it."

In fact, *The Amazing Spider-Man* opened to a respectable $91.6 million domestically. But then, as word of mouth spread, ticket sales fell off a cliff. The next weekend, Sony and most of Hollywood was shocked when the superhero sequel was beat at the box office by the low-budget Seth Rogen comedy *Neighbors*. "They just kicked our ass on Spider-man and look like geniuses for betting against our most important franchise," Belgrad lamented to Pascal.

One of the main reasons audiences rejected *The Amazing Spider-Man 2* is that four weeks earlier, the company that actually owned Spider-Man had released a far better movie and raised quality expectations for superheroes beyond what Sony seemed able to satisfy. *Cap-*

tain America: The Winter Soldier was the latest in a nearly nonstop string of hits from Marvel Studios, which included *Iron Man, Thor,* and *The Avengers.*

The rise of Marvel Studios over the past decade has been one of the most extraordinary stories in Hollywood history. Utilizing a crew of second-rate superheroes and run by a team of unproven executives, Marvel upended the industry's conventional wisdom. Previously, almost everyone in Hollywood believed that the general public was interested only in marquee superheroes like Batman and Spider-Man, and nobody would see a movie about Ant-Man or the Guardians of the Galaxy; that the resources and experience of major studios gave them an unbeatable advantage over upstarts; that tightly managing budgets on would-be global "event" movies was penny-wise but pound-foolish; that tying together the plots of disparate films was too risky because if one failed, they all would; and that the only Hollywood brand name that meant anything to consumers was Disney.

The massive success of 2008's *Iron Man* and almost every Marvel Studios release that followed proved each of those precepts wrong, throwing the entire movie industry on its heels. Studios nearly a hundred years old struggled to understand what had happened and how to compete with a new, unstoppable cinematic universe of superheroes. More than any other company, Marvel Studios is responsible for the dominance of branded movies at the box office and the rush by every studio to create their own cinematic universes, in the process tossing most original films for adults aside like foul-smelling trash.

Marvel's rise particularly stung Sony, which until 2008 could justifiably brag that with its first three Spider-Man movies, it was king of the superheroes. At that point, *Spider-Man* and its two sequels were the most successful superhero pictures of all time. By 2016, though, the original *Spider-Man* had been knocked down to number seven, and four of the top six spots were taken by films from Marvel Studios (the other two were held by the Dark Knight Batman films produced by Warner Bros.).

Pascal had to admit Sony was "being eaten by Marvel." Resurrecting Spider-Man was absolutely critical to the survival of her studio and her career. By late 2014 she concluded that she needed help and cast a wide net in search of answers, including her ultimately fruitless flirtation with bringing back Raimi to direct or produce another installment. Nothing seemed likely to succeed, however, except one option that would mark a humiliating creative defeat: admitting her team no longer had the chops to make a blockbuster superhero movie in the current environment and allowing Marvel, which first licensed Spider-Man to Sony in the late 1990s, to take back control.

That such a partnership was even on the table was ironic, and not just because twelve years earlier, Sony had shown Marvel how it's done by producing the first global blockbuster based on one of its comic books.

The two companies' stories had actually been intertwined for more than a quarter-century. During that time, Sony had missed the opportunity to own the entire Marvel cinematic universe but had made so much money off Spider-Man that it inspired the comic book company to enter and ultimately dominate the movie business.

SPIDEY'S SORDID HISTORY

In 1990, a young lawyer named Peter Schlessel working for Columbia Pictures' home-video operation in New York was asked to help unwind a deal with a B-movie schlock-meister named Menahem Golan. Columbia had previously agreed to release twenty of Golan's movies on videotape, and Schlessel, who would later hold a number of top posts for the studio, including president of production, had no problem letting go of most of the low-budget movies on Golan's slate except for one that caught his eye: *Spider-Man*.

Created in 1962 by Stan Lee and Steve Ditko, Spider-Man was the first superhero whose story combined fantastic adventures with the problems of a geeky teenager, including trouble with girls and bullies and an initial reluctance to use his powers to help others (thus the famous motto "With great power comes great responsibility"). Kids who read comic books could relate more to Peter Parker than they could to the square and stolid Superman and Batman. A sales sensation, the web-slinger with super-strength and "spidey sense" quickly became Marvel's most popular character, both in comic books and toys. Nearly five decades later, in the late 2000s, Spider-Man would account for an astounding 62 percent of Marvel's total profits.

Golan, whose filmography includes the second Texas Chainsaw Massacre film, the embarrassingly bad *Superman IV: The Quest for Peace,* and an adaptation of Marvel's Fantastic Four so awful it was never released, bought the movie rights to Spider-Man from the perennially cash-strapped Marvel in 1985 for just $225,000.

Companies run by Golan spent $2 million developing a Spider-Man film, and in 1989 he held a press conference at the Cannes Film Festival to announce that the picture would soon begin production. But Golan was never able to get the financing together to start the cameras rolling. He did, however, manage to make a mess of the rights, selling the television rights to the media company Viacom, which would later buy Paramount Pictures, and the theatrical rights to Carolco Pictures.

Schlessel didn't know when, or whether, a Spider-Man movie would actually be made, but he knew he had heard of the character and that name recognition was fast becoming a valuable asset in the movie business. It took him a year to reach a settlement with Golan that would keep the Spider-Man home-video rights at Columbia. And it would take another decade for that bet to pay off.

In the early 1990s, Carolco agreed to pay James Cameron, arguably Hollywood's hottest writer-director (just coming off 1991's *Terminator 2: Judgment Day*), $3 million to adapt Spider-Man. He wrote a forty-seven-page "scriptment," a mixture of narrative and screenplay-style dialogue, and it was set to become a $50 million blockbuster production (big money at the time).

But Spider-Man's path to the big screen would continue to prove as tortured as his personal life in the comics. Golan sued Carolco for allegedly trying to shove him out of the picture. A financially struggling Carolco sued Viacom and Sony in an effort to reunite the movie rights, and they both countersued Carolco, as well as Marvel and Golan. Another studio, MGM, also got involved, claiming it actually owned the

Spider-Man rights through a deal it had made with one of Golan's many companies.

As if that wasn't enough, Marvel in late 1996 filed for bankruptcy, weighed down by $700 million in debt, as well as bonds with a face value of $1 billion. It was one of the most contentious and protracted bankruptcies in American history. The Wall Street titans Ron Perelman and Carl Icahn turned a small, struggling comic book publisher into the vehicle for a titanic battle of egos. During the process, deal-making essentially froze, including any effort to make movies out of Marvel characters. Most people involved in the company recognized that films could be a growth driver due to the success of the 1989 hit *Batman,* produced by Warner Bros. and directed by Tim Burton.

During the bankruptcy, a court-appointed trustee tried to sell Marvel, and numerous entertainment companies kicked the tires, including MGM and Warner Bros., the owner of Marvel's competitor DC Comics, which publishes Superman and Wonder Woman comics. But the Hollywood company that came closest to buying Marvel, unbeknownst to many, was Sony Pictures.

John Calley, the former MGM and Warner executive who took over Sony in 1996, recognized the value of Spider-Man on the big screen and encouraged executives to try to expand their home-video rights to take full control of the character. The key player for Sony was Yair Landau, a young, aggressive Stanford MBA looking to make his mark. Working with the toy manufacturer Hasbro, Landau put together a $500 million offer. Each company would put up half the money to buy Marvel. This represented a rare willingness on the part of the Japanese parent company to take a gamble on a long-term investment. Hasbro, one of the world's most successful toy manufacturers, would handle consumer products under the plan, while Sony would make movies. The films would spur toy sales, of course, while toys would spur more people to see the movies.

Spider-Man was the crown jewel, but Landau believed that a legal loophole would allow him to take back Marvel's most popular superteam, the X-Men, whose film rights had previously been sold to Sony's competitor 20th Century Fox for just a few hundred thousand dollars.

This would have enabled Sony to make movies featuring any and every one of Marvel's characters (except for the Hulk, controlled by Universal), which numbered more than five thousand.

The Sony-Hasbro team hired bankruptcy counsel, visited a "data room" at a law firm's conference room in New Jersey where Marvel's financial records were available, and met with debt holders. But amid a series of almost-not-quite agreements to save Marvel between Icahn, Perelman, and a dizzying roster of banks and bondholders, the Sony-Hasbro offer never gained traction.

Instead, Marvel ended up in the hands of a man whose initial interest in comic books was as minimal as Michael Lynton's in entertainment: Ike Perlmutter. An Israeli veteran of the Six-Day War who immigrated to the United States in 1967 at age twenty-four, with $250 in his pocket, Perlmutter had an uncanny ability to smell value where others held their nose. The thin businessman who spoke with a heavy accent initially made his fortune in super-discount stores like Odd Lot, where he would buy seemingly worthless products, like last year's toys that nobody else wanted, and sell them to value-conscious consumers for as little as one dollar.

He was always on the lookout for nearly dead companies he thought he could turn around, including Coleco, the manufacturer of Cabbage Patch dolls, and Remington, the razor company. Surplus goods could catch his eye too. In the 1980s, when Gimbels, the department store, went out of business, Perlmutter agreed to buy all of its fixtures, from mirrors to clothing racks — basically everything but the retail inventory itself. He started looking on a Wednesday, closed the deal the next Monday for about $10 million, and within a week sold it all for close to $50 million. The deal went through so fast that he had no time to conduct due diligence, title searches, or the other risk-protecting moves that businesses usually undertake.

Perlmutter had a reputation for extreme stinginess. He scrutinized every single cost at the businesses he bought, from the thermostat temperature to the thickness of the paper, and had no shame about personally calling employees to ask why they arrived at the office fifteen minutes late (as evidenced by the electronic time clocks he installed). But people who worked closely with him said that when Perlmutter saw a much bigger upside than downside, he was willing to take gambles.

That was what led him to Toy Biz, a struggling toy company. Perlmutter acquired it in 1990, with plans to revive it. One of his first moves was to strike a deal with Ron Perelman, then the owner of Marvel, to stop paying a licensing fee to manufacture toys based on the comic book company's superheroes. In exchange, Marvel got 46 percent of Toy Biz's equity. It saved Toy Biz millions, but also embroiled it in corporate chaos when Marvel filed for bankruptcy.

Most plans to revive Marvel called for using the bankruptcy court to cancel Marvel's royalty-free license with Toy Biz, enabling a new owner to generate much-needed cash. Perlmutter's investment in Toy Biz would have been ruined in the process, and he was prepared to go to any lengths to avoid that. His solution was to pitch a plan to merge Toy Biz and Marvel and for *him* to take over.

It was an audacious proposal, given the power of Icahn and Perelman, but Perlmutter had a unique asset: Avi Arad. A toy designer and fellow Israeli veteran of the Six-Day War who, like his business partner, could converse in Hebrew or accented English, Arad met Perlmutter at Toy Biz and the two became unlikely friends. He was in many ways the Pascal to Perlmutter's Lynton — he had no interest in the business side of entertainment, but he was creative, he understood the value of story and characters, and he could charm almost anyone.

And he had an idea that initially seemed outlandish, but made more sense the longer you thought about it: Marvel, a bankrupt comic book and toy company, was perfectly positioned to become a major player in Hollywood.

The bearded, gray-haired Arad, who rode Harleys and liked to wear leather jackets, skull caps, and oversized rings featuring the logos of Marvel characters, could charm even a room full of conservative bankers with that vision. "I feel certain that Spider-Man alone is worth a billion dollars," he declared in just such a setting, at a critical moment in the bankruptcy process. "But now at this crazy hour, at this juncture, you're going to take 380 million — whatever it is from Carl Icahn — for the whole thing? *One* thing is worth a *billion!* We have the X-Men. We have the Fantastic Four. They all can be movies. Not to mention television and all the products and the other rights."

That speech helped sell Marvel's lenders, who wanted a solvent company that could pay back as much of its debt as possible, on the plan to put Arad and Perlmutter in charge of Marvel. And when the duo finally took the reins, at the end of 1998, job number one was to start selling film rights, especially those of the highly valuable Spider-Man.

Perlmutter, now Marvel's biggest shareholder and its de facto chief, understood that hit movies would sell a lot of toys. Arad believed that films could transform Marvel from a publisher of comic books for kids into a media powerhouse. And both knew the fresh-out-of-bankruptcy company desperately needed the cash that a movie-rights deal would bring.

Landau had gotten to know Arad and Perlmutter when putting together Sony's bid for Marvel with Hasbro, and he reapproached them in an effort to finally secure the rights necessary to make a Spider-Man movie. Another Israeli American who loved the art of the deal, Landau was able to forge a connection with the Marvel duo and recognize that, for Perlmutter, the exclamation "Go fuck yourself!" was the beginning of a negotiation, not the end.

He had an ace in the hole: the home-video rights that Schlessel had secured nearly a decade earlier. Without those, it would be very difficult for another studio to profit from a Spider-Man film, particularly as the era of huge DVD sales was dawning.

But when he approached Arad and Perlmutter, Landau found that the two had something bigger in mind. Looking to get as many movies going and as much cash in their account as quickly as possible, they offered him the rights to every single Marvel character (save for the X-Men, the Fantastic Four, and the Hulk, who were at other studios) for $25 million.

That included Spider-Man, who would go on to gross $4 billion over five movies, plus virtually every character that now makes up the

Marvel Studios cinematic universe — Iron Man and Captain America and Thor and Black Widow and Ant-Man and others, who through 2016 would gross $10 billion in one dozen films.

Landau brought the offer back to Calley and the heads of Sony's motion picture business, a small group of executives that included Amy Pascal. It didn't take long for them to quickly and decisively respond: no way. "Nobody gives a shit about any of the other Marvel characters, we don't want to do that deal," they told Landau, as if he were Jack coming home with a handful of magic beans. Their instructions to Landau, they thought, were quite simple: "Go back and do a deal for only Spider-Man."

It was the mistake of a lifetime, a deal that could have made Sony billions of dollars and potentially turned it into the juggernaut that Marvel's current owner, Disney, is today.

But that's with the benefit of hindsight. At the time, it was a deal nobody wanted. Who, besides the obviously biased Arad, could have possibly foreseen that as a result of economic forces not yet on the horizon, cinematic universes would take over the movie business and superheroes, no matter how obscure and seemingly absurd, would be the most valuable currency in Hollywood? In 1998, the number three movie was the gross-out comedy *There's Something About Mary,* and in 1999 it was *Toy Story 2.* Nobody at the time — not even anyone working at Marvel, if they were honest — imagined that in 2014 it would be *Guardians of the Galaxy,* based on a poorly selling Marvel comic featuring a foul-mouthed raccoon and a grunting tree-man.

Indeed, Arad and Perlmutter couldn't find any other takers for the deal, which is why six months later they ended up back in talks with Landau, offering him Spider-Man alone for $20 million. Even Marvel's most valuable character, the Sony executive figured, wasn't worth 80 percent of the cost of the entire library, and so he balked. But eventually, the two sides reached an agreement: Sony would pay $10 million up front for each Spider-Man movie, plus an additional 5 percent of the revenue once it exceeded that initial payment.

The deal also specified that the two companies would evenly split revenue from Spider-Man merchandise, with a hitch that would prove important later: Sony would take the lead on selling products related to the movie, while Marvel would handle "classic" Spider-Man products and would have to split only the money above the baseline that existed before any films were produced.

One issue remained: Sony still needed to settle all of Peter Parker's courtroom headaches. MGM was the most viable legal rival, and Calley, who had previously worked there, figured out an ingenious way to resolve the matter. In 1997, he had announced that Sony would produce a James Bond sequel, even though rights to the super-spy had for decades rested with MGM and its corporate sibling United Artists. Due to a complex dispute over the rights to 1965's *Thunderball* and its 1983 remake, *Never Say Never Again,* Calley claimed his studio had acquired the rights to make its own series of Bond movies. MGM was, of course, outraged. Its CEO called Sony's claim "delusional" and filed a lawsuit.

In March 1999, the two sides settled. To the outside world, they disclosed only the financial terms, which called for MGM to pay Sony $5 million. Behind the scenes, though, Calley had agreed to give MGM the disputed Bond rights in exchange for MGM giving up its claim to Spider-Man.

It was a huge victory for Sony. This was not yet the era of franchises, but nonetheless studios needed a few "event" movies every year to drive outsized box office and to prop up their diverse and riskier release slates. And Sony, as would always be true, was short on "event" films.

"The idea is to do it now, as fast as we can," Pascal said after the Spider-Man deal closed. "It's a big, tentpole movie."

SWINGING TO SUCCESS

Arad hoped Cameron would still be interested in making his nearly decade-old scriptment and took the director, who was now working on *Titanic,* to lunch, only to find he had moved on. "It was like a girl you chased in high school, now she's in college and she's finally ready for you, but you don't feel the same," said Arad. "Jim was spent. He was done."

Sony Pictures under Pascal was never known for developing its movies quickly, and it took the studio more than three years to get Spider-Man to the big screen. But they did it just right. After considering directors such as David Fincher, who was hot coming off *Fight Club,* Pascal chose Sam Raimi. Since launching his career with the campy, cult classic Evil Dead horror trilogy, Raimi had become a respected but only modestly successful studio director. His Hollywood movies like *The Quick and the Dead, For Love of the Game,* and *The Gift* were more mainstream, but none were major hits.

Raimi's choice for his main character, with the studio's backing, was the even-further-from-the-A-list Tobey Maguire, who had played sensitive teenagers in movies like *Pleasantville* and *The Ice Storm.*

The more recent template for hit superhero movies had been the last two Batman movies, packed with stars like George Clooney, Arnold Schwarzenegger, and Jim Carrey, along with the A-list director Joel Schumacher. Fox's *X-Men,* the first Marvel movie released since the bankruptcy ended, boasted the well-known Patrick Stewart and Ian McKellan in lead roles, along with the red-hot indie director Bryan Singer.

The *Spider-Man* roster, meanwhile, reflected the fact that Amy Pascal, though hardly a comic book nerd, had come to love Peter Parker. She correctly intuited that while a Spider-Man movie needed jaw-dropping visual effects that showed its title character swinging through the streets of Manhattan, its success would really come from the heart-wrenching story of an insecure teenage loser, inspired by the tragic death of his uncle to become a hero.

Raimi, a long-time nerd himself, knew how to tell that story. And Maguire was perfectly suited to play the sad-sack teenager pining for the girl he can't have until he covers his face with a superhero mask. As for Spider-Man himself? Visual effects, produced by Sony's internal Imageworks unit, took care of that.

"I remember seeing a cut of the first 'Spider-Man' before most of our effects were in and the film worked just as a story," said Landau. "That's when I knew it was going to be unbelievably successful."

In the United States and Canada, *Spider-Man* grossed $404 million. It remains the highest-grossing Sony release ever domestically, despite a nearly 50 percent rise in ticket prices since then. Overseas it grossed $418 million, an astounding figure at the time, when China wasn't even a factor in the global box office. Most important, with stars and a director who weren't yet able to command massive salaries and cuts of ticket sales, the $140 million production was hugely profitable. Once DVD, television, merchandise, and all other revenue sources were counted, that one movie alone generated $442 million in profits. *Spider-Man* is still Sony Pictures' most profitable film of all time.

Everyone at the studio was elated. The year 2002 broke records for Sony at the box office and on the bottom line. Executives fanned out around the lot to give every employee a hundred-dollar bill in celebration.

Hollywood is an industry of followers, and in the wake of the success of *Spider-Man*, everyone jumped on the Marvel superhero train. Arad had been in Los Angeles full-time since soon after the bankruptcy, making a slew of deals to license as many characters as possible. After the moderate success of 2000's original *X-Men* and the blockbuster returns from *Spider-Man*, studios rushed to get those projects on the screen.

Between 2003 and 2007, twelve movies featuring Marvel superheroes were released, quadruple the number that had ever been in theaters before. Five different studios were in on the action, and their results were decidedly mixed. *Spider-Man* sequels reigned supreme, with Fox's *X-Men* sequels ranking a strong second. *Fantastic Four* and *Daredevil*, also from Fox, did decent business, while Universal's *Hulk* was a disappointment and Fox's *Elektra* and Lionsgate's *The Punisher* were major flops.

Plenty more were in development, still trying to find their way to the big screen, including Iron Man at New Line, Black Widow at Lionsgate, Deathlok at Sony, Namor at Universal, and Dr. Strange at Miramax.

From the outside, it seemed like a golden age for Marvel. Arad's vision had come true: the comic book company was now a major player in Hollywood, and its characters had become valuable brands. Marvel stock rose from less than $1 in 2001 to $20 by 2003. But in the dingy offices of Marvel Comics back in New York, Ike Perlmutter wasn't smiling. *X-Men* had been a disaster for his company in 2000, when Fox unexpectedly moved up its release from the Christmas season to the summer. That ruined Marvel's plans to sell toys in conjunction with the big-screen release, which meant it made little money off the movie. The pre-bankruptcy deal Arad had made gave the company no piece of the box office.

Spider-Man was a different story. Sony paid Marvel $11 million in royalties in 2002, on top of the initial $10 million. Marvel's toy sales rose 69 percent that year, to $155 million.

But paradoxically, the healthier Marvel became, the more bitter Perlmutter felt about the deal his company had struck with Sony. Marvel had been at its weakest point then, just out of bankruptcy. Not only were most of the profits staying with the Hollywood studio, but to the general public, Spider-Man was associated with Sony, not Marvel. A *Newsweek* article about the Japanese company listed among its iconic assets the Trinitron, the Walkman, and Spider-Man.

"When we started to understand the business, we realized the 5 percent was pitiful and the deal on DVDs was even more insulting," said Arad. "And Sony carried the banner for Spider-Man. It's our brand, but they're getting all the benefit."

So in 2003, Marvel sued, claiming Sony was unjustly withholding merchandising revenue and attempting to disassociate Spider-Man from the comic book company that owned him. Marvel wanted $50 million and, most significant, a termination of its licensing deal with Sony. That would leave it free to negotiate a far more lucrative agreement with any competitor that wanted to make sequels.

Sony executives first discussed the lawsuit during a meeting in Tokyo, attended by, among others, Landau, Calley, and the CEO of Sony Corporation, Nobuyuki Idei. "What's the meaning of this?" a surprised Idei asked.

"Our Israeli is tougher than their Israeli. We won. They're upset," responded Calley.

And so Sony fought back, filing a countersuit of its own, alleging that Marvel was trying to force a renegotiation of a contract it signed with eyes wide open.

The dueling complaints didn't stop Sony from rushing to get *Spider-Man* 2 into theaters in 2004. The only major obstacle was Maguire, who wanted more money for the sequel and complained of a bad back from riding horses while filming *Seabiscuit*. Sony expected to pay more, but not as much as the actor was demanding, and so Pascal made a contingent offer to Jake Gyllenhaal, essentially positioning him to take over the role if Maguire didn't come around. The ploy worked, and by March 2003, Maguire went to a "come to Jesus" meeting at Pascal's house, where he apologized to Raimi, and the two "hugged it out, literally," one witness recalled.

Spider-Man 2 grossed $783 million at the box office, slightly less than its predecessor, on a production budget that rose to $200 million, due to bigger visual effects and higher pay for Maguire, Raimi, and the other talent. The result: Sony's profits on the sequel plummeted 45 percent from those of the original, to a still substantial $244 million.

This was also Michael Lynton's first year as CEO of the studio. Always more likely to search for an amicable solution than battle to the bitter end, Lynton quickly settled the litigation with Marvel. Without disclosing any details to the public, the two companies agreed that Marvel would now handle all of the licensing work for Spider-Man, whether related to the movies or not. There would be less fighting over what qualified as "classic" versus "film" merchandise and whether one was being promoted at the expense of the other. In return, Marvel would keep 75 percent of all merchandise revenue and Sony would get 25 percent.

Some at Sony felt it was a mistake to settle because the merchandise rights were too valuable to give up. Certainly, if Lynton thought the agreement would bring peace between the two sides, he was wrong. Perlmutter continued to be a thorn in Sony's side, constantly searching for any foot faults on their agreement. Calling from his $3.2 million condo in Palm Beach, where he spent much of his time and worked the phones starting early in the morning, Perlmutter would scream about the smallest details, from the costs of DVD displays at Best Buy to marketing restrictions in Thailand to free drinks at press junkets. The fact that Perlmutter was known to be a licensed gun owner only added to his ability to intimidate.

The two companies also clashed over creative control. Marvel wanted guarantees, for instance, that Peter Parker would be a heterosexual male who didn't lose his virginity before age sixteen and never slept with anyone under sixteen (which Sony agreed to) and that he would be a Caucasian of average height who doesn't smoke, drink, use drugs, or curse (which Sony would not accept). Both sides were regularly auditing each other, and Sony eventually formed a committee that met weekly just to deal with the nonstop barrage of Marvel-related issues.

Bottom line: the more successful Marvel movies were, the more pissed off Perlmutter became. In his view, studios were making too much of the money and getting too much of the credit for his characters. And the movie-based toy sales and royalties that now made up the bulk of Marvel's profits depended on the whims of studio executives, who had their own agendas. Instead of becoming a master of Hollywood, Marvel was subservient to it.

Perlmutter was a constant pain in Sony's ass because, like any schoolyard bully, he was trying to compensate for the fact that deep down he felt powerless. What Marvel really needed was to become the master of its own destiny.

4

Revenge of the Nerds

The Rise of Marvel Studios

AS THE RELEASE OF *SPIDER-MAN* in 2002 approached, Avi Arad made what he thought was a simple request: he wanted to spend $80,000 to produce an animated Marvel logo that would run in front of that movie, and all future films based on Marvel comics, to remind audiences where the characters came from.

But Ike Perlmutter didn't see the point. If Arad really wanted it, the art department could make one, he said, though designing a movie logo for a movie screen was very different from creating the cover of a comic book. Arad eventually won that battle, and the result was an eleven-second animation of comic book panels flipping, until the name Marvel emerges from them. It still plays, in an updated form, on the company's movies today.

This tiny battle illustrated Perlmutter's attitude toward Hollywood. He hated it: the egos, the grandiosity, and most of all the wasteful spending on luxurious offices and talent. One of his first moves upon taking over Marvel had been to try to slash the salary of the company's only in-house star, Stan Lee, by half, down to $500,000. Arad and others prevailed on him to be less severe, and so he trimmed it to only $800,000.

Perlmutter's unwillingness to spend money on anything associated with Hollywood, while at the same time griping that Marvel wasn't making enough money off Hollywood, was a difficult position to defend. If he wanted studios to put up all the money and take all of the risk, he could hardly ask them for a bigger reward.

It took an outsider to come up with a possible solution. Amir Malin, a veteran independent film executive, had been part of the Sundance scene since its infancy, in the 1980s. He went on to lead a company called Artisan Entertainment that's best remembered for the horror hit *The Blair Witch Project.* In 2000, he signed a deal for Artisan to make movies, some of which would be direct-to-DVD, with a cadre of mostly unknown Marvel superheroes that nobody else wanted, such as Ant-Man, Deadpool, and Black Panther (the first two would go on to become hit movies, and a Black Panther film appears poised to be a hit in 2018). Most of those projects never went anywhere, in part because Artisan was bought by a competitor, Lionsgate, in 2003, and the character rights returned to Marvel.

But Malin, another Israeli American, became close to Arad in the process, and by 2003, as he prepared to leave Artisan as part of the Lionsgate sale, the businessman had an idea. In the wake of the mega-success of *Spider-Man,* he thought Marvel should take a new approach to moviemaking. "Why don't you finance your own pictures?" he told his pal Arad. "Why don't you collect the lion's share of the benefits from this wonderful brand you have? If you're successful, you have a multi-billion-dollar enterprise."

Arad, who wanted nothing more than to become a movie mogul himself, thought it was a great idea. But the toy designer turned producer hated spreadsheets and financial projections, so he asked Malin to put together a business plan. Over the next few months, Malin and associates wrote a seventy-five-page document titled "Marvel World." An independent entity that would be 80 percent owned by Marvel and 20 percent owned by Malin and his business partners, Marvel World would raise its own capital to produce movies based on any superheroes the comic book company hadn't already licensed out, a list that at the time included Thor, Captain America, and the characters originally licensed to Artisan.

It was risky, for sure, but Malin thought it was a calculated risk, one whose high potential returns would appeal to Perlmutter, whom Malin had met when Marvel once considered acquiring Artisan. But Perlmutter, officially Marvel's vice-chairman but as the largest shareholder also its key decision-maker, still thought investing in movies was too risky. A business in which a few major hits were supposed to cover the losses of a bunch of flops and in which even experienced studios regularly went on multi-year cold streaks was not appealing to him. Nor was giving up even 20 percent of the equity in anything to do with his company's characters.

So when Arad took Malin's plan to the board in late 2003, "they looked at me like I was going to lose my mind," he recalled.

"Ike's scared of the film business," Arad reported back to Malin. And so Marvel World died.

Perlmutter would consider making movies only if he didn't have to give up any equity and couldn't possibly lose money. To anyone who knew anything about Hollywood, it sounded like refusing to sit down at a blackjack table without a guarantee you'll be dealt twenty-one every time.

A MAN WITH A PLAN FOR MARVEL

Most people would take that attitude as an invitation to get lost and not forget to close the door on the way out. David Maisel took it as a challenge.

A Harvard MBA and a former McKinsey consultant, Maisel spent the early part of his Hollywood career working alongside the mogul Michael Ovitz, first at the Creative Artists Agency, then at Disney, then with the theatrical producer Livent. After a stint at the Endeavor Talent Agency with another agent turned mogul, Ari Emanuel, Maisel was introduced to Ike Perlmutter.

Brimming with confidence but socially awkward — people who worked with him semi-seriously questioned whether he had Asperger's syndrome — Maisel first met Perlmutter at Donald Trump's ex-

clusive Mar-a-Lago Club in Palm Beach in late 2003. Seated at the luxury beachfront restaurant, the boyish, floppy-haired young executive
convinced his skeptical breakfast partner that he could do the only
thing Perlmutter cared about when it came to movies: make more
money from them.

So he was hired in the new position of president and chief operating
officer of Marvel Studios, under Arad, the division's CEO. Marvel Studios wasn't actually a studio then — it was an office above a Mercedes
dealership in Beverly Hills. There, a small team that included a young
red-haired executive named Kevin Feige, who read scripts and carried
Arad's bags to and from meetings, consulted on the movies that other
studios made with their characters.

Maisel told Perlmutter he could get more than 5 percent of the gross
in new deals for Marvel movies, which he did for properties like Deathlok (set up at Paramount but never made). But negotiating higher licensing fees was just a Trojan horse by which Maisel hoped to earn
Perlmutter's trust, in order to make a big pitch.

His plan was similar to Malin's Marvel World concept, which Perlmutter had rejected: raising the money for Marvel to make its own
films. Except, in Maisel's scenario, the company wouldn't give up any
equity. Maisel would do all the work and Marvel would own 100 percent of the movies it made.

Maisel was a lifelong fan of comic books, and he was ambitious.
Well known as a business executive, he wanted to also be a producer
respected for his creativity. Marvel, he believed, could be the launching
pad he needed. He knew how deep the lore of seemingly second-tier
characters like Thor and Iron Man actually was and how compelling
they could be on the big screen.

And a basic financial analysis told him that if Marvel could produce
movies that performed at just the average level of the ones partner studios had made for the company — *Spider-Man* and *Hulk* and *Daredevil*
and the two X-Men films — the potential profits were massive.

"This is an opportunity worth billions!" he told the board, in a pitch
similar to the one Arad had made to lenders during Marvel's bankruptcy five years earlier. Not only could Marvel keep all the movie prof-

its, he argued, but it wouldn't have to share a penny from sales of consumer products. And instead of having to tell Wall Street that it really hoped Tom Rothman at Fox or Amy Pascal at Sony would release its next movie by the upcoming holiday season, Marvel alone would determine when its films hit theaters, on dates that were most ideal for its toy sales.

The *X-Men* debacle of 2000 would never be repeated.

Maisel's argument went even further: he also contended that Marvel could make *better* films than the studios. "The movies should be made by people who love the characters, love the stories, and really care about these movies being the best they can," he argued. "People who don't just make million-dollar salaries regardless, while they're making lots of other movies." It was a ballsy claim, given Sony's success with *Spider-Man*. But Maisel believed it would prove true as films came to be based on less-well-known characters. Most people knew the basics about Spider-Man, after all, but how many would know how to make a good movie about Ant-Man?

It was certainly undeniable that Marvel employees, who knew more about their characters than anyone, were struggling to be treated with respect in Hollywood. Even for hits like *X-Men*, Marvel executives had to fight over minor details such as the hairstyle of Hugh Jackman's Wolverine, which has an iconic pointy-but-not-devil-horns look in the comic books. And the fact that Arad and Feige were only consultants, not producers who had to be listened to, was evident in duds such as 2003's *Daredevil*, which was more of a second-rate star vehicle for Ben Affleck than an exciting superhero adaptation.

But the board's response was similar to what they said about Malin's plan: "David, stop talking so much. Your last name's not Spielberg and we're not going to risk the whole company on this. Don't talk about this anymore unless you find a way to do it with little or no risk.'"

They weren't necessarily saying no, but by demanding that he come back with a specific plan that met their outrageous demands, many board members thought they would never hear from Maisel again. Still, he wanted time to try, and he asked the board for one concession: that they put a freeze on new licensing deals, particularly ones that were already in the works to sell Captain America to Warner Bros. and Thor to Sony. "If you license them out," he said, "I'll never be able to do it, even if I get the capital we need."

Perlmutter was intrigued, particularly by the potential for Marvel to control the movie release dates that drove toy sales, and the board agreed to put a pause on licensing and give Maisel the breathing room he wanted. If he could raise half a billion dollars of risk-free money, they'd be happy to hear back from him.

At any other time, this would have been an impossible task. But as Maisel, working with consultants, put together his business plan and began meeting with banks throughout 2004 and into early 2005, he realized that what Perlmutter and the board wanted really was doable. The financial bubble that would crash the global economy four years later was growing, and major financial institutions were looking for new vehicles in which to invest their money, with little regard for risk.

Hollywood was fast becoming an attractive home. One studio after another was setting up "slate deals," in which hedge funds and banks pledged hundreds of millions of dollars to fund half or a quarter of the costs of most movies that would come out over the next several years. It seemed safe enough, since a few movies could easily lose a lot of money, but several dozen meant an investor was certain to participate in hits as well as flops.

What Wall Street didn't count on, however, was that DVD sales would soon start plummeting and that the "distribution fees" studios charged — typically 8 to 12 percent off the top in order to cover their costs — would subsume the profits on all but the biggest hits. Most slate deals ended up as losers.

Then again, nobody invested in Hollywood purely for the money. Even the savviest investor was prone to be a little more flexible in judgment when given the opportunity to read scripts, hang out with stars on a red carpet, and get an "executive producer" credit onscreen.

Maisel, a bachelor who can't resist showing off texts on his phone from Sean Penn or mentioning that he and Leonardo DiCaprio took their moms out together for Mother's Day, played that card to the hilt.

After more than a year of negotiations, he found partners who were willing to give him everything he wanted, a deal that even Ike Perlmutter might find impossible to resist.

Working with the Wall Street bank Merrill Lynch, Maisel secured a commitment of $525 million in debt. Marvel could use the money to make any movie it wanted over the next seven years, so long as it was rated PG-13 and cost less than $165 million. Marvel kept all of the consumer product rights and didn't have to share a penny if toy sales shot up because of a film.

Marvel could even cover the costs of the extra staff it would have to hire to oversee and make the movies with the Merrill debt. The comic book company wouldn't have to spend an extra dollar on payroll.

In addition, for its work producing the movies, Marvel got a 5 percent cut of all revenues. That's what it got from other studios when they made movies with Marvel characters. But in this case, Marvel got to pay *itself* 5 percent, ahead of the investors who actually put up the money.

And that was from all the revenue the films made, including on DVD. Typically, so-called "participations" for actors or licensors like Marvel apply to only one-fifth of the revenue from DVDs, a protection that studios built in to ensure profits for themselves. Maisel kept waiting for the bankers to request just such a provision, to which he would have replied, "OK, you're right." But, inexperienced in the ways of Hollywood, they never did.

That 5 percent would apply regardless of whether the movie was actually profitable. Combining it with a lowball estimate of consumer products sales tied to a movie, Maisel figured the worst-case scenario was that Marvel would make between $25 million and $50 million per film and get at least four swings before it was forced to give up, unable to pay interest on the debt.

"We're guaranteed to make $100 million to $200 million just by signing. That's our downside," he told the board of directors in the spring of 2014. "Our upside, if it works, is billions."

That was all great, but it didn't address Perlmutter's biggest concern: the collateral. No matter how low an interest rate you get on your mortgage, after all, if you can't afford the payments, the bank takes your house. That's why the board wanted the Merrill Lynch deal for the movies to be "non-recourse" to Marvel, meaning that the company wouldn't have to give up any assets if the films flopped and they couldn't pay back the money.

Amazingly, Maisel achieved it. The collateral for the movies was . . . the rights to make the movies themselves. Ten characters or groups of characters were included in the deal, and Marvel was guaranteed the right to make films based on at least four. After that, if it couldn't afford the debt payments anymore, Merrill would take the rights. Marvel would still be able to make comic books and toys based on those superheroes, just not movies.

But if Marvel made four consecutive flops, Perlmutter would almost certainly flee the production business anyway. And, indeed, the entire genre of films based on Marvel properties would likely be dealt a serious blow. So, if Marvel couldn't pay, the rights Marvel gave up would be virtually worthless to it.

"There's little risk, there's no risk, and there's guaranteed-to-make-money," Maisel explained. That was an approach to the movie business that even Ike Perlmutter could get behind. And so, after more than a year of saying no first to Malin and then to Maisel, Marvel's board of directors agreed to get into the film business.

"The idea was that hopefully the movies break even, we'd get our 5 percent fees, and then we'd make most of our money on products, because we'd control the timing and we'd make sure the movies were toyetic," said a person close to Perlmutter, using industry jargon for a film that naturally lends itself to products on the shelves of Toys "R" Us.

Paramount Pictures agreed to distribute and market the movies — a cost-intensive process Marvel couldn't afford to replicate — for 10 percent of the revenue, which is standard in such deals (later on, following the success of *Iron Man,* Marvel would get that number down to 8 percent).

WINNING WITH THE B-TEAM

Now the question wasn't whether Marvel could make movies, or if it would make movies, but how exactly it would do so. And there was one big problem: the ten characters included in the Merrill deal weren't exactly A-listers. With the exception of Captain America, in fact, calling them second-tier would be generous.

Hawkeye, a guy who's really good with a bow and arrow? Power Pack, a quartet of young siblings given superpowers by an alien who looks like a horse? Ant-Man, a guy who can shrink and mind-control ants? Nick Fury, a spy who's . . . well, he's basically just a spy?

Their prospects for turning into hit movies looked dubious. Certainly, they didn't seem like a lineup that a new company starting from scratch could use to compete with the likes of Warner Bros., Disney, and Sony. No matter how savvy the financial structure, it was easy to dismiss Marvel Studios' new aspirations as hubristic folly.

"If you needed to launch a Hollywood franchise — are those the superheroes you would really turn to?" asked a skeptical *Los Angeles Times.*

But luck was on Marvel's side.

A project based on Iron Man had been stuck in development hell for years. Initially optioned by Fox in the 1990s, it was picked up in 2000 by New Line Cinema's president of production, Mike De Luca (the future production chief for Sony). New Line went through several different writers and spent nearly a year trying to sign the director Nick Cassavetes, who was hot after 2004's weepy romance hit *The Notebook,* but couldn't seal the deal. At the same time, Tom Cruise became interested in playing Iron Man. But "interested" and "committed" are two very different things for Tom Cruise. And when a star of his magnitude is flirting with a project, all other plans grind to a halt as everyone waits to see what the capricious A-lister will do.

Even under the best of circumstances, adapting Iron Man for the big screen would be no easy feat. The character was goofy on the outside but troubled on the inside. Created in 1963 by Stan Lee and the writer Larry Lieber, with artists Jack Kirby and Don Heck, Iron Man was not technically a superhero but rather a super suit, made of metal, which allows its wearer to fly and shoot lasers and missiles. The man under the armor was Tony Stark, a weapons designer with a devil-may-care attitude and a Howard Hughes–esque lifestyle, who secretly battles self-hatred and alcoholism.

New Line's co-CEO Bob Shaye was not a true believer. Though his executives had convinced him the character was valuable and he could see Sony's grosses for Spider-Man films, he maintained that nobody would buy a character in a bulky metal suit soaring through the air. "I'll never make a movie in which Iron Man flies!" he told Arad during one of several arguments the duo had. "It just doesn't make any sense! Steel cannot fly."

It was a typical attitude for a Hollywood producer who thought movies had to be relatable to the average non-geek and understandable for anyone not immersed in the world of comic books. But it also illustrated Maisel's point — nobody understood Marvel characters better than the people who worked at Marvel.

So when New Line's option on Iron Man expired in late 2005 and it tried to renew the deal, as it had done before, Marvel pounced. Arad and Maisel refused to extend the agreement, which was within their rights but certainly not standard decorum in Hollywood, where contract renewals are usually little more than a formality. New Line executives were shocked, and mad, but they had no choice.

"It was a great gift," said Maisel.

It wasn't the only gift to come Marvel's way that year. After hemming and hawing about making a sequel to 2003's *Hulk*, which grossed a mediocre $245 million at the box office and was panned for director Ang Lee's overly psychoanalytical approach to the character, Universal agreed to give Marvel back the movie rights to the giant green monster, so long as it could release the film instead of Paramount.

In addition, Maisel and Feige finally prevailed upon Arad to include Thor, a Norse god who becomes a human superhero, in the Marvel Studios slate. Arad had initially been hesitant because he didn't believe a proper film about the character, who spends much of his time in the mythological and expensive-to-produce world of Asgard, could be made within the $165 million maximum budget of the debt facility. But as Marvel's plans accelerated and the group started discussing an idea that would leave the character stranded on Earth for most of the movie, Arad relented.

Now, instead of starting the slate with Captain America, as had been Arad's initial plan, Marvel had options. Sure, none of them were on par with Spider-Man and the X-Men. But between Iron Man, the Hulk, Thor, and Captain America, the company at least had multiple characters with a little name recognition outside comic book shops.

To decide which film to make first, Marvel convened focus groups. But they weren't convened in order to ask a random cross-section of people which story lines and characters they would most like to see onscreen. Instead, Marvel brought together groups of children, showed them pictures of its superheroes, and described their abilities and weapons. Then they asked the kids which ones they would most like to play with as a toy. The overwhelming answer, to the surprise of many at Marvel, was Iron Man.

"That's what brought Iron Man to the front of the line," said a person who helped to decide which movie Marvel would self-produce first.

Marvel executives in New York went ahead with plans for a slew of new Iron Man toys set to come out in 2008, while Arad, Maisel, and their team, including the fast-rising Feige, got to work on a movie intended to sell those toys.

Though they were technically using the bank's money, every dollar they spent was an extra dollar they'd have to pay back, which meant Marvel Studios still had to play by Ike Perlmutter's rules. The same scrutiny that kept employees sweltering in the summer, freezing in the winter, and retrieving paper clips from the trash meant Marvel couldn't spend anything close to the $200 million-plus that Sony had put into 2004's *Spider-Man 2* and Fox into 2006's *X-Men: The Last Stand. Iron Man* cost only $109 million — $30 million less than Sony had spent on the first *Spider-Man* six years earlier.

That meant no A-listers who could demand big salaries or, even more abhorrent to Perlmutter, gross points — revenue off the top before Marvel made its profits. In other words, there was no longer a chance that Tom Cruise would be Iron Man.

Jon Favreau, who had only three directing credits, none particularly big budget, and whose latest release, *Zathura*, had been a flop, was everyone's first choice to direct. He impressed Arad with his knowledge of the character and his plan to balance the story's political elements with comedy. Because Marvel wouldn't be spending a lot on big action scenes, it was critical that the director bring energy to characters standing around talking. Favreau, who wrote *Swingers* and directed the comedy *Elf,* had proven skills in that arena.

Maisel and the Marvel executives in New York, meanwhile, liked that Favreau wasn't particularly powerful in Hollywood, meaning that if battles over costs or creative choices arose, and they needed to push him around, they could. "We would never have a final cut director," said Maisel. "Our movies were not the director's fiefdom."

Terrence Howard, who had recently been nominated for an Oscar for *Hustle & Flow,* was the first actor cast, as Tony Stark's best friend, and paid the most of anyone in the film: $3.5 million. The company figured it needed one somewhat prestigious actor to attract other talent, and by putting him in a supporting role, they could spend the least amount possible doing it.

According to Marvel's philosophy, the characters, not the actors, were the stars, and pretty much everyone was expendable. Indeed, when Howard later demanded $5 million to return for *Iron Man 2,* he was replaced by the more affordable Don Cheadle.

Casting Iron Man was tricky. Marvel considered Colin Farrell and Patrick Dempsey, but Feige really wanted Robert Downey Jr., whose own public struggles with addiction matched Tony Stark's demons. Marvel certainly liked the fact that his career, hot in the 1980s, had cooled considerably and he would be a bargain. The question was whether he was worth the headache, particularly when it came to getting insurance for the film. But Downey was so eager that he agreed to audition for the role, showing up in a tuxedo and wowing everyone in the room. Marvel relented, agreeing to pay him $2.5 million (he and the rest of the cast would earn more from bonuses based on the movie's box-office performance).

After considering making the Mandarin, a mustache-twirling Asian villain from the comics, Iron Man's first foe, the new studio instead decided on Obadiah Stain, played by Jeff Bridges. He was less fantastical, had a more personal connection to Downey's character, "and saved us $10 to $20 million we would have had to spend going to China," noted Maisel.

The first twenty minutes of the movie take place in a cave, and there are surprisingly few scenes of Iron Man flying or doing battle in his combat armor, which kept the budget down. Nonetheless, Perlmutter kept as close an eye on the script as he did on office supplies. When a convoy attack at the beginning of the movie was supposed to include ten Humvees, the frugal executive said, "No, too many, too expensive, we can do it with three." Another scene, in which Iron Man saves villagers from a group of terrorists, was going to cost $1 million, and Perlmutter wouldn't authorize the money until the last minute, figuring it could be trashed if costs rose elsewhere.

All of this backseat driving by Perlmutter, who became Marvel's CEO in 2005, drove Arad insane. Arad was now head of a Hollywood movie studio. So what if he wanted to have nice offices, fly first class, and make his own decisions without constant oversight? Nobody was looking over Amy Pascal's shoulder every moment, questioning every penny she spent. He thought the leadership team in New York didn't understand Hollywood, and he particularly hated it when they tried to get involved in creative matters, such as the time a board member gave him notes on a script that was "boring." Board members and other executives at Marvel, meanwhile, privately called Arad a greedy "pig" who cared more about his own ego than the company's bottom line.

Even within Hollywood, Arad was a divisive figure. Some admired his bravado and his undeniably successful track record, while laughing at his personal eccentricities. Others thought he was a blowhard who didn't truly appreciate Marvel superheroes and relied on subordinates like Kevin Feige to do the real work. Maisel and Arad, meanwhile, clashed with increasing frequency over creative issues, financial control, and who deserved the most credit for Marvel's burgeoning movie business.

When push came to shove, it wasn't a contest. New York favored Maisel, the Harvard MBA, who spoke the board's language and, though he privately harbored an ego more akin to Arad's than Perlmutter's, wasn't nearly as flamboyant and obnoxious as his rival for power.

So in May 2006, Arad quit, selling Marvel stock worth nearly $60 million and setting himself up as an independent producer who would work on, among other projects, *Spider-Man* sequels. He remained close to Perlmutter, his friend since the mogul took over Toy Biz in 1990, but few at Marvel were sorry to see him go. Marvel Studios was now officially the purview of Maisel, who was named its chairman in 2007.

Increasingly, though, the power was shifting to Feige, who had risen from being Arad's bag boy to the president of production. As personally geeky as Maisel and as socially adept as Arad, but without the outwardly apparent ego of either, he made the perfect ambassador for the brand both within Hollywood and to the outside world. With Maisel and others, he plotted out what would become the Marvel cinematic universe, in which superheroes all exist in the same fictional reality. After each was established in his own film, the plan was for them to join together in a blowout Avengers-style team-up. It was Feige who came up with the scene at the end of *Iron Man* in which Samuel L. Jackson, as Nick Fury, first tells Tony Stark that there's a wider world of superheroes out there.

Nobody at Marvel was yet using the term "cinematic universe," but they knew the movies would interconnect, for creative and business reasons. Loyalty to the source material was paramount, after all, and in Marvel comic books, most of its superheroes soar, swing, or drive flying cars in New York City, where they regularly team up or throw punches at each other over misunderstandings. Marvel Studios also had the business insight, completely new at the time, that by linking movies with different characters, it could get the benefit of sequels without having to wait two or three years to reunite the same actors.

"One of the best businesses in movies is sequels because you can better predict the revenue and the costs," said Maisel. "I knew by interspersing our characters, I was making every movie a quasi-sequel."

At most studios, the "president of production" oversaw ten to twenty movies in a given year, with dozens more in development. He or she relied on producers like Jerry Bruckheimer or Joel Silver or Brian Grazer to handle the grunt work of spending every day on set and ensuring the films were done on time and on budget, with the original creative vision intact. Maisel, who had been around Hollywood for nearly two decades but had never before worked at a studio, thought the traditional divide between production executives and producers was wasteful and illogical. "Forget how things have been done," he said of his approach. "How should they be done?"

And so Kevin Feige became Marvel's sole producer. This change in the typical way of doing things appealed both to Perlmutter's cost-consciousness (producers could easily earn millions of dollars per picture) and to Maisel and Feige's belief that the best people to make Marvel movies were the people who worked at Marvel. The unusual arrangement was doable because Marvel had just two movies scheduled for 2008: *Iron Man* and *The Incredible Hulk.* The fledgling studio prioritized the latter project because Marvel's deal with Universal meant it had to move ahead ASAP or lose the rights, even though Ang Lee's *Hulk* had been a bust just five years earlier.

The pre-production offices for both films were located at Marvel's Beverly Hills office, in rooms that required a key card to enter, so the company could precisely allocate costs.

Production on *Iron Man* went well. Shockingly so, in fact; under Favreau's direction, Downey was improvising and adding more comedy and joie de vivre than anyone expected in a superhero movie. The recent *Spider-Man* and 2005's Batman reboot, *Batman Begins,* were known for their darker undercurrents, but *Iron Man* would set a tone of almost sitcom-esque playfulness, more similar to Stan Lee's comics in the 1960s. This differentiation would become a trademark of Marvel Studios movies, which fans loved. Sometimes, as it turned out, it was OK if superheroes had fun.

Still, Marvel executives in New York were worried. *Iron Man* was a big gamble in a business they knew little about. And toy manufacturers and retailers were not jumping on the bandwagon as they had hoped. Marvel Studios was an upstart with no track record, after all, and Iron Man was a seemingly goofy and not particularly popular character. Marvel tried to force companies that wanted toys tied to 2007's *Spider-Man 3* to make and stock Iron Man toys for 2008 as well, but few agreed. "We couldn't give Iron Man away, nobody wanted it," said one Marvel executive. "So there was not very much merchandise on the shelves for the first movie."

Marvel's business plan to break even on the movies and make big profits from toys was not looking promising. *Iron Man* would actually have to be a hit at the box office. But initial projections called for it to gross only $100 million in the United States, which meant it would make barely any money.

But as *Iron Man*'s May 2, 2008, release approached, expectations grew. A trailer at Comic-Con in 2007 convinced fanboys that *Iron Man* would be a pitch-perfect adaptation of a character they loved. Later, more mainstream advertising began to draw in a broader audience interested in a big action movie with robots, tanks, and visual effects. To others, *Iron Man* looked like a fun romantic comedy with two actors who had great chemistry: Downey and Gwyneth Paltrow, who surprised many at Marvel when she agreed to play the love interest, Pepper Potts, at an affordable salary.

The movie was such a huge deal for Marvel that the obsessively private Perlmutter, who never gave interviews to the press or allowed himself to be photographed, showed up at the premiere at Hollywood's Chinese Theatre. He wore glasses and a fake mustache so no one would recognize him.

The opening weekend ended up blowing away everyone at Marvel and throughout Hollywood. Its $99 million domestic debut was the second highest ever for a non-sequel, behind only *Spider-Man*. Its $97 million launch overseas was spectacular as well.

Not coincidentally, Marvel scheduled its quarterly earnings call for the Monday after *Iron Man* opened. The company raised its profit and revenue projections for the year and announced it would release *Iron Man 2* in 2010. Its stock jumped 9 percent in a single day. The movie would ultimately gross $585 million globally and generate more than $100 million in profits, not to mention spurring toy companies to finally jump on the bandwagon and make Iron Man a popular action figure.

Perlmutter was so thrilled, he allowed Maisel to buy Downey a Bentley and Favreau a Mercedes as thank-you gifts.

Iron Man's success more than made up for that July's *Incredible Hulk*. The result of Marvel's most difficult production right up to the present, the second Hulk film starred Ed Norton, who proved a terrible fit for Maisel and Feige's philosophy that studio executives should be the ultimate creative authority. Undeniably one of the best actors of his generation, Norton is also famous in Hollywood for being "difficult" and highly opinionated, refusing to allow artistic choices he disagrees with and seeking to rewrite scripts he doesn't like, which is what he did on *The Incredible Hulk*.

The clashes intensified in post-production, and the director, Louis Letterier, sided with Norton over the studio. They both learned who has the ultimate power at Marvel, though, when Feige took control of editing. He excised many of the darkest scenes, including a suicide attempt meant to portray how much the scientist Bruce Banner wants to rid himself of the curse of transforming into the Hulk when he's mad.

The resulting movie was still darker and more dramatic than any other Marvel Studios production and not different enough from the Hulk movie of 2003. It grossed only $263 million at the box office and barely broke even, the worst performance for any Marvel Studios film to date.

The Incredible Hulk never got a sequel, but the character has returned in Avengers films, played by the easygoing Mark Ruffalo. The usually cheerful Feige stated that the decision to recast the role was "rooted in the need for an actor who embodies the creativity and collaborative spirit of our other talented cast members."

THE HAPPIEST COMIC BOOK
COMPANY ON EARTH

Marvel set an earnings record in 2008, with profits up almost 50 percent. By the end of the year, its stock was trading at more than $30 per share, up from less than $1 in the dark days of 2001.

But still, Perlmutter was nervous. He was no expert on Hollywood, but he knew a smash success out of the gate, which Marvel had with *Iron Man,* was a rarity. Maybe, he thought, they had just gotten lucky, and their experience with *The Incredible Hulk* would be the norm. Perhaps, with the stock at an all-time high, they should consider getting out while the getting was good.

After years of concentrating on building the company, Perlmutter was open to discussions about a sale or a merger. Maisel pitched the idea of a combination with DreamWorks, the company behind *Shrek* and *Madagascar,* arguing that their animation assets could pair nicely with Marvel's live-action business. But it never went beyond the idea stage.

Following the success of *Iron Man,* many at Marvel expected offers to flood in, particularly from Paramount's owner, Viacom, which would seemingly want to double down on the success it was enjoying through releasing Marvel films. Or perhaps Sony would make another offer, this time without Hasbro, as some within that studio were eager to do. But Sony didn't.

Maisel figured that Marvel would be the best fit for, and thus get the best price from, his former employer, Disney. Under Bob Iger, who became CEO in 2005, Disney was focusing on brands and franchises above all else, and Marvel was fast becoming one of the most distinct in the entertainment business. Disney had paid a huge premium to acquire the biggest brand in animation, Pixar, in 2006, and now Iger and his team were considering Marvel as their next target.

Maisel and Iger finally met in February 2009. For Iger, it was a chance to find out what Marvel had to offer and whom he should be talking to. The ultra-secretive Perlmutter never even spoke to the investment community, and Iger was unsure who at Marvel actually had the authority to make a deal.

It took another four months for the pair to meet again, but that June, Iger told Maisel he might be interested in a deal. Maisel left behind a copy of *The Marvel Encyclopedia,* with information on every one of the company's characters, numbering more than five thousand. In the parking lot outside the Team Disney building, where executives run the world's largest media company behind a façade featuring seven twenty-foot-tall dwarves, Maisel called Perlmutter to let him know they officially had a suitor. Maisel knew that if his boss didn't like the idea of a combination with Disney, he could fire his subordinate for approaching Iger without permission. Instead, an intrigued Perlmutter told Maisel to come to New York and discuss the possibility further.

Perlmutter wanted the money that would come from a sale, as well as the security of not having to worry how far back a few box-office flops would set his company. But although he was sixty-seven, he was definitely not ready to retire. Ike still wanted to keep leading the company that he had resurrected from the grave over the past decade. Once again, he wanted all of the upside possible in a deal, with none of the downside.

A few weeks later, Iger began a charm offensive to prove that was possible. He flew to New York and met with Perlmutter at his office. "I like this man, I really like this man," the Marvel CEO told an associate afterward. That night, Perlmutter and his wife, Laurie, had dinner with Iger and his wife, the journalist Willow Bay. The next morning, Perlmutter was feeling even better. "I trust this man," he told the colleague.

There was no way of guaranteeing in a sale document that Iger would leave Perlmutter in charge and allow him to preserve the unique, and uniquely cheap, Marvel corporate culture. So Perlmutter began talking to people who had worked closely with Iger, including Steve Jobs, who sold Pixar to Disney in 2005 and was now the company's biggest independent shareholder. "He's great. Everything he said he was going to do, he's done," Jobs told Perlmutter.

With Iger's encouragement, Feige and other Marvel Studios executives flew to Pixar headquarters outside San Francisco to confirm for themselves that a distinct creative culture was possible within the Walt Disney Company behemoth. On August 31, Disney announced it would buy Marvel for $4 billion. Perlmutter personally made about $1.5 billion. Maisel, who left following the sale, made more than $20 million.

For years, the deal worked out exactly as both sides had hoped. Perlmutter was allowed to run the company his way, continuing to split his time between New York and Palm Beach. Working out of a dingy office in the L.A. suburb of Manhattan Beach, with none of the trappings of a Hollywood lot, Marvel Studios continued to be famously cheap.

Stars were signed to multi-movie contracts and paid tiny salaries, by Hollywood standards, with rewards in the form of bonuses for box-office performance, not gross points. The virtual newcomer Chris Hemsworth was paid $150,000 to star in the first Thor movie, and Chris Evans received $1 million for *Captain America: The First Avenger.*The only star to make huge money was Downey, because his contract ended after three films and he was able to renegotiate with leverage on his side. He earned more than $50 million for 2012's *Avengers* alone.

As pugnacious and controlling as ever, Perlmutter threw his weight around at his new company. He even successfully pressured Iger to replace the chairman of Disney's consumer products business. Executives became used to screaming phone calls from Palm Beach while the sun was still rising in California.

Disney, meanwhile, got the most consistently successful live-action movie brand in Hollywood history. Post–*Incredible Hulk,* everything worked. *Iron Man 2* grossed $624 million, and *Iron Man 3* grossed $1.2 billion. *Avengers,* teaming all of Marvel's superheroes together, grossed $1.5 billion. *Guardians of the Galaxy* grossed $773 million. Even the widely mocked *Ant-Man* sold $519 million in tickets. Maisel and Feige's bet proved exactly correct: for fans, movies set in the same "cinematic universe" would feel like sequels, and they would show up for all of them if the films had the same lighthearted, fun tone.

By 2015, Feige was chafing under Perlmutter's scrutiny. He was now one of the most powerful moguls in Hollywood and, like Arad a decade earlier, he hated having to justify his every decision to an obsessively cheap executive on the other side of the country. Their clashes became increasingly intense as the movies got bigger, more expensive, and more complex, with characters regularly showing up in each other's sequels and budgets exceeding $200 million.

Feige demanded his freedom and Iger granted it, allowing the Marvel chief to report to Disney's more laid-back movie studio chairman, Alan Horn. Marvel Studios moved to a new home on the Disney lot that was nothing like the dumpy, no-frills offices, with old carpets and bare walls, that Marvel Studios used to operate out of in Manhattan Beach. The new digs were decorated with superhero wallpapers, statues, and props. Feige bragged about the track lighting Disney installed in Feige's conference rooms, to spotlight marketing concept art that hung on the walls. Perlmutter, who jammed three comic book editors into each office at Marvel's office in New York, would have never sprung for such an unnecessary feature. Perlmutter remained with Disney, overseeing Marvel television, toys, and comic books, but this change was an undeniable insult.

It was other studios, however, that were most damaged by Feige's success. Why, their corporate bosses wanted to know, couldn't they be as successful as Marvel? Of course other studios had hits, but nobody was pumping out two surefire blockbusters per year (soon to be three) like Marvel, with nary a flop in the bunch. Even the movies that clearly weren't as good as the rest, like the second Avengers film, seemed to get a pass from audiences and critics, engendering no small amount of bitterness throughout the rest of Hollywood. "Marvel could have made a movie about someone picking his nose and it would have been 98 on Rotten Tomatoes," complained Arad, who as a producer of Sony's Spider-Man films now competed with his former employer.

It wasn't as easy as Marvel made it look. Though its films weren't all perfect, they shared a consistent tone that balanced old-fashioned adventure, *The Office*–style workplace comedy, and a perfectly sized dollop of contemporary characterization and political concerns — enough to engage adults but never so much as to turn off a ten-year-old anywhere in the world.

Warner Bros. had arguably better-known superheroes in its DC

Comics library, but 2013's *Man of Steel* and 2016's *Batman v Superman* were widely disliked by fans and not as successful at the box office, in large part because they were too serious and somber. *Suicide Squad* was a hit in 2016, but a barely competent piece of filmmaking despised by critics, fanboys, and even executives within Warner. It wasn't until 2017, with the fresher and more optimistic *Wonder Woman,* that Warner finally found its footing with DC.

Everyone now had cinematic universes on the agenda. Paramount was turning Transformers into one, Universal did so with its monsters Frankenstein and the Wolfman, and Warner with King Kong and Godzilla. Nobody, however, was as much affected by Marvel's ascendancy as Sony Pictures.

5

Spider-Man: Homecoming

Why Sony Gave Up
Its Most Valuable Asset

"I AM SURE YOU ARE GETTING THIS," Michael Lynton wrote to Amy Pascal in July 2014, his sigh almost audible within an e-mail. "[I've] gotten these for the past 12 years," Pascal wrote back.

"This" was an Internet petition, forwarded to the Sony Pictures CEO, urging him to give the movie rights to Spider-Man back to Marvel. There were, in fact, a number of them circulating online. "With The Amazing Spider-Man 1 and 2 not being 'Amazing' and you (Sony) not having a plan for the franchise, the character Spider-Man is dying," read one. "Because Sony can't make a good spider man movie," read another. "Sony has had their chance with the property and failed, we the people want spiderman back with marvel," pleaded a third.

What the fans didn't know was that in the wake of the failure of *The Amazing Spider-Man 2*, Sony was considering just that.

It was a long time coming. Sony had been struggling with Spidey since 2007's *Spider-Man 3*. Though it grossed more than any other film with the character, thanks to growth in international markets and residual goodwill from *Spider-Man 2,* the threequel was a mess. Raimi appeared to have lost his touch, turning Peter Parker at one point into an emo buffoon who literally dances in the street. And Maguire, now in his thirties, was getting too old to play the character as a teenager or even a young adult.

Worst for the studio, because the costs of talent and visual effects were getting so high, the profits from *Spider-Man 3* were $159 million — nothing to sneeze at, but down 35 percent from *Spider-Man 2* and 64 percent from the original.

As Sony executives started planning the fourth Spider-Man movie, they realized that they had financial problems along with creative problems. In order to bring back Maguire and Raimi and spend the more than $200 million now necessary for a large-scale "event" film, they'd be giving away all their profits. Projections showed that the best Sony could do with a *Spider-Man 4* was break even. And after multiple rewrites from big-name screenwriters, Raimi had lost his passion. One night he called Pascal at home to inform her that he was done with the web-slinger.

So in 2010, Sony decided to "reboot," a term that originated in the computer industry. Decades ago, comic book creators adopted the word to refer to their occasional practice of pretending prior stories had never happened and retelling a character's origins from scratch. As she had for the first Spider-Man movie, Pascal identified a promising young director (Marc Webb, coming off the indie romantic comedy *500 Days of Summer*) and a sensitive, talented young star, the little-known British actor Andrew Garfield. They would once again tell the tale of a teenage Peter Parker, granted amazing powers when he's bitten by a radioactive spider.

But as Marvel had discovered with *The Incredible Hulk,* audiences don't get excited about retellings of stories that they've recently seen. In 2012, *The Amazing Spider-Man* was shockingly similar to the original *Spider-Man* of 2002. With $758 million, it grossed less than any of the first three Spider-Man films — a bad sign, particularly in the same year that Marvel's *Avengers* made twice as much.

IF AT FIRST YOU DON'T SUCCEED . . .

With no other hit global franchises and with pressure mounting from the staggering success of Marvel Studios, Sony had to up the ante for the next go-round in 2014. Not only did it spend a hefty $260 million to make *The Amazing Spider-Man 2* as big an event as possible, but it also announced plans to give Spidey his own cinematic universe. In addition to sequels featuring the superhero every other year going forward, the studio was developing spinoffs featuring the Sinister Six team of villains and the web-slinger's most vicious foe, Venom.

Publicly, Sony executives boasted that they had a "rich universe" that could stand up to the competition. Privately, they knew it was a stretch to build a cinematic universe off a single superhero and his supporting players. "I only have the spider universe not the marvel universe," Pascal complained. "And in it are only his villains and relatives and girlfriend. No superhero team up here."

Among *The Amazing Spider-Man 2*'s flaws were the too-obvious attempts to build out a cinematic universe, introducing superfluous characters and story elements clearly meant as seeds for spinoffs. Marvel was able to accomplish this with a light touch in its movies, but Sony couldn't seem to do so without using neon-red arrows.

Marvel had helped promote *The Amazing Spider-Man 2,* as was its responsibility and in its interest, if the company wanted to sell more toys. Perlmutter, in fact, had been laying off Sony for years, since a deal in 2011, by which Sony gave up its participations in Spider-Man merchandise and Marvel, in return, gave up its 5 percent share of the movie revenue. It also paid cash-strapped Sony $175 million, plus $35 million for each future film released.

Lynton thought it was a smart way to end the acrimony, but as with his prior Marvel settlement, a number of senior executives were opposed to it. The studio had made a total of $245 million from its share of Spider-Man merchandise through 2010, and the detractors thought Sony should be fighting to grow that business, rather than give it up.

But the deal, not publicly disclosed except in the broadest of terms, went ahead. Whether smart or not, it stopped Perlmutter's incessant complaints from Palm Beach. Combined with the success of Marvel Studios, now part of the Disney empire, and the struggles of Sony's motion picture business, it also flipped the power dynamic in their relationship. Though they were ostensibly partners, Pascal now feared that executives at Disney and Marvel didn't think her Spider-Man movies were that good anymore.

"It s weird im geting great reaction to film from everyone except the disney folk," she wrote to a colleague as Sony was screening *The Amazing Spider-Man 2* before its release.

Soon after the movie opened, the Sony executive Rachel O'Connor, who oversaw the Spidey movies most closely, e-mailed Feige, asking for his help on the next sequels and spinoffs. Ten days later, he hadn't replied.

The affable Feige would never admit it to Pascal's face, but he and his team at Marvel had for years disliked what Sony had been doing with the character. He thought that restarting with *The Amazing Spider-Man,* rather than moving on from Raimi's mistakes in *Spider-Man 3,* had been a big mistake.

"In a million years I would never advocate rebooting . . . Iron Man," Feige wrote to Marvel Entertainment's president, Alan Fine, and its vice president of production, Tom Cohen. "To me it's James Bond and we can keep telling new stories for decades even with different actors."

Fine concurred: "I think that it is a mistake to deny the original trilogy its place in the canon of the Spider-Man cinematic universe. What are you telling the audience? That the original trilogy is a mistake, a total false-hood?"

He had even harsher words for the script of *The Amazing Spider-Man 2* that the Marvel trio had recently read: "I found this draft tedious, boring, and had to force myself to read it through . . . This story is way too dark, way too depressing. I wanted to burn the draft after I read it never mind thinking about buying the DVD."

THE HUNT BEGINS

It hurt the hearts of Feige and many on his team that Sony was doing such a poor job with Marvel's most beloved character. Perlmutter,
meanwhile, was hurt where he felt it most: in the wallet. Sales of Spider-Man toys were slowing, and he attributed that in part to audiences'
dissatisfaction with the movies.

Marvel Studios, he and his team felt, could do a better job with the
character. But he had no way to make that happen. Under the 1998
deal, as long as Sony released a Spider-Man movie every five years and
nine months, it could retain rights to the character forever.

Perlmutter needed to convince Sony that it would benefit from giving the character back. He targeted Lynton, an old acquaintance who
had briefly served on Marvel's board of directors in the late 1990s, in a
series of e-mails and phone calls in the months after *The Amazing Spider-Man 2* opened.

Feige, meanwhile, targeted Pascal. At lunch on a patio outside her
office, in the summer after *The Amazing Spider-Man 2,* he pitched his
fellow creative executive on the benefits of having Marvel Studios produce the next film, so that Peter Parker could join the same cinematic
universe as Iron Man, Captain America, and Thor. "I love Spider-Man
and I want to help," he told her.

Pascal was so offended, she threw her sandwich at Feige and told
him, playfully but truthfully, to "get the fuck out of here." Turning the
character over would be an insult, she felt, not just to her but to the entire studio.

But Marvel didn't relent. At the Sun Valley conference for media
moguls in 2014, Perlmutter's boss, the Disney CEO Bob Iger, brought
up the issue to Lynton's boss, Kaz Hirai, Sony's CEO. He approached
Hirai at the luxury Idaho resort and urged him to consider that the recent run of bad Spider-Man movies was hurting both their companies
and that Marvel could do a better job. But Hirai was cool to the idea,
in part because he was surprised to hear that fans hadn't been pleased

with the Amazing Spider-Man reboots. Apparently this was news to him.

Perlmutter and Feige's plan was for Marvel to reintroduce Spider-Man in 2016's *Captain America: Civil War,* paving the way for a fresh new take on the web-slinger in his next solo movie, in 2017. Global audiences had eagerly devoured the stories that bounce from one Marvel Studios film to the next, and the Marvel executives were confident that Spider-Man would enjoy the same benefit once he was part of the same cinematic universe as Captain America, Iron Man, and Thor.

Spider-Man, in other words, would be saved by the very characters that Sony had refused to spend an extra $15 million to buy back in 1998.

Many Sony executives saw the undeniable wisdom of Perlmutter's pitch. "It's still your baby," the production president De Luca reassured Pascal. "Feige is just maybe the right babysitter for this moment." The problem was the economics. Sony certainly wasn't going to give away its valuable rights, and Disney wasn't going to write a check for the potential billions of dollars Spider-Man movies would make into the indefinite future. So the two companies discussed plans to invest in each other's movies as part of an arrangement to share the characters. Perlmutter, unsurprisingly, thought any such deal should heavily favor Marvel. He proposed that his company take a 50 percent stake in the next Spider-Man film, while Sony would get a 5 percent stake in the third Captain America movie.

After taking time to reflect, following her lunch with Feige, Pascal ran hot and cold on the idea. At times she saw it as a potential coup and at others as an unthinkable insult. "Unless I partner with marvel And have spiderman join their world I'm running out of options," she complained to Jeff Robinov, a former Warner Bros. movie chief whose new company had a deal with Sony.

"U got to figure out spidey," he urged her. "Can't go back to marvel."

Lynton thought a deal with Marvel was a no-brainer. "Michael had no ego about who creatively oversees Spider-Man," said De Luca. "He felt this is a giant asset for the studio, so let's get the best movie made. I think Amy felt personally guilty the fans didn't love the last Andrew

Garfield movie and felt she owed Peter Parker a better outing. She wanted to deliver that outing."

For a while, Pascal's hopes to do that lay with *The Sinister Six*.

In July, Sony had announced a change to its prior plans to release *The Amazing Spider-Man 3* in 2016, with the fourth in the series following in 2018. Now the studio would release *Amazing Spider-Man 3* in 2018, it said in a press release, and deliver *The Sinister Six* in 2016. In reality, though, Sony had already given up on the Amazing Spider-Man series. The announcement about *The Sinister Six* was intended to distract fans from that fact. Pascal was done with "the Marc Webb experience," particularly since after paying him $6 million to direct *The Amazing Spider-Man 2*, which she admitted was "crazy," she was obligated to pay him $10 million if she brought him back for a third installment.

She now was prepared to bet on Drew Goddard, a rising star who wrote and directed the cult horror hit *The Cabin in the Woods* and was writing and directing *The Sinister Six*. Envisioned as *The Dirty Dozen* for Spider-Man villains, Pascal dreamed of casting major stars like Matt Damon, Daniel Craig, and Leonardo DiCaprio. Initially, Andrew Garfield was going to have a role in it, but that plan fell apart in the wake of *The Amazing Spider-Man 2*.

In fact, by November 2014, when the talks with Marvel appeared dead due to conflicts over financial terms, Sony began planning to use *The Sinister Six* to reboot the web-slinger for a second time. Goddard was turning the movie into a more lighthearted adventure, which used a story line from the comics involving the Savage Land, where Spidey and a team of villains would do battle in a world filled with dinosaurs. Spider-Man, who would be recast and aged down to sixteen, was going to ride a tyrannosaurus rex.

But just as Goddard delivered his draft, the hackers hit Sony. Work ceased while fans gleefully dissected the revelation from leaked e-mails that Sony and Marvel had been in talks to partner on Spider-Man. The pressure was higher than it had ever been, and Sony couldn't afford to spend months or years on the risky goal of fixing Spider-Man on its own. The safe choice was to reapproach Marvel.

Feige and Pascal met again, this time for dinner at her house, and things went quite differently. It was a creative meeting of minds, and they excitedly shared ideas for a new Spider-Man movie with a decidedly John Hughes tone.

In a matter of weeks the two companies reached a deal: a new, high-school-age Spider-Man would debut in May 2016, in *Captain America: Civil War,* to be released by Disney. Next, he would appear in his own film in 2017, which would be creatively supervised by Marvel but released by Sony. It was titled *Spider-Man: Homecoming,* a none-too-subtle allusion to his return to the Marvel universe. Rather than haggle over co-financing arrangements, Marvel and Sony agreed they would each fully finance and keep the profits from their respective releases. Marvel, however, would pay less than the standard $35 million to Sony for *Homecoming* if the movie grossed more than $750 million.

Just a few days before she was fired, in January 2015, Pascal flew with Lynton to Palm Beach, where they hammered out the terms with Perlmutter and Feige at the Marvel chief's condominium. A few days later, their handshakes turned into a nine-page document that the two sides signed. In a surprising twist, Marvel agreed to let Pascal, in her new post-mogul life, serve as a producer on the next Spider-Man film. She would be the first person besides Feige with a producer credit on a Marvel Studios film since 2008 and the first outsider ever to actually be on set every day and oversee one of its films. It was a sign that despite their companies' conflicts over the years, Feige and Pascal saw each other as kindred spirits — studio executives who believed the job was still about the hands-on details of making movies they loved.

It also meant that by giving up Peter Parker, Amy Pascal would finally get the chance to do what she had long desired: redeem him.

6

Star Wars

The Decline of
the A-List

MICHAEL LYNTON HAS LONG been known as one of the most easygoing, even-tempered men in Hollywood. But when he returned from his annual vacation to Martha's Vineyard in August 2014, he was pissed off. The object of his anger: movie stars.

"Michael seems to have gotten annoyed with the movie star drama business in a big way since he's been away," Doug Belgrad reported to his boss, Amy Pascal.

Why, Sony Pictures' CEO wanted to know, was his studio considering making both a Brad Pitt World War II movie and casting Leonardo DiCaprio in a biopic of Steve Jobs? Why were they considering casting Will Smith in a drama about NFL concussions — a subject Lynton felt strongly about but believed should be dramatized at a very low cost — when the star wanted $15 million for what was supposed to be a passion project?

"Why," he demanded, "do we have so many of these movies that take so much time and energy, are risky, and can never make us very much money?"

The movies Lynton was talking about, mid-budget vehicles for major stars, were not that long ago among the easiest to make, most consistent, and most profitable movies in Hollywood.

Sony's CEO was not griping about them because he was in a bad end-of-vacation mood. His attitude reflected a painful reality that was upending decades of accumulated wisdom in Hollywood and the status of the closest thing America has to royalty: our movie stars.

A-listers like Tom Hanks and Julia Roberts once commanded $20 million salaries or 20 percent of the first dollar gross — box-office and certain other revenues — and were able to get nearly any project made that they fancied because their names on the marquee and faces on a poster practically guaranteed box-office success, as well as huge DVD sales. They were the beating hearts of the movie business, and everything else revolved around them. Their productions were called "star vehicles" because everything — the script, the setting, the direction, the supporting actors — was in service of the celebrity who was the reason the film existed and would likely make money.

Audiences deciding what to see at the multiplex or buy at Wal-Mart often made their decisions based on the face on the poster or the box cover because they knew what they were going to get. No matter the role, Tom Cruise was likely to be sexy and masculine. Jim Carrey would be wacky and hilarious. Sandra Bullock would be goofy but goodhearted, and relatable.

In the first decade of this century, even as "event" movies and superheroes were starting to make their box-office power known, about ten of the twenty highest-grossing films annually were star vehicles. Among the most successful were star vehicles like Tom Hanks's *Cast Away* (number two in 2000), Jim Carrey's *Bruce Almighty* (number five in 2003), Brad Pitt and Angelina Jolie's *Mr. and Mrs. Smith* (number ten in 2005), Will Smith's *Hancock* (number four in 2008), and Sandra Bullock's *The Blind Side* (number nine in 2009).

But by the 2010s, as few as three movies of the top twenty each year was, generously defined, a "star vehicle." DiCaprio in *The Revenant,* Bullock and Melissa McCarthy in *The Heat,* and Kevin Hart and Dwayne Johnson in *Central Intelligence* were becoming the exception, rather than the rule.

Movie stars didn't become irrelevant, but they became very inconsistent in attracting an audience. People used to go to almost any movie with Tom Cruise in it. Between 1992 and 2006, Cruise starred in twelve films that each grossed more than $100 million domestically. He was on an unparalleled streak, with virtually no flops. But in the decade since then, five of Cruise's nine movies — *Knight and Day, Rock of Ages, Oblivion, Edge of Tomorrow,* and *The Mummy* — were box-office disappointments. This was an increasingly common occurrence for A-listers. Will Ferrell and Ben Stiller couldn't convince anyone to see *Zoolander 2*. Brad Pitt didn't attract audiences to *Allied*. Virtually nobody wanted to see Sandra Bullock in *Our Brand Is Crisis*.

It's not that they were being replaced by a new generation of stars. Certainly Jennifer Lawrence and Chris Pratt and Kevin Hart and Melissa McCarthy have risen in popularity in recent years, but outside of major franchises like The Hunger Games and Jurassic World, their box-office records are inconsistent as well.

What happened? Audiences' loyalties shifted. Not to other stars, but to franchises. Today, no person has the box-office track record that Cruise once did, and it's hard to imagine that anyone will again. But Marvel Studios does. Harry Potter does. Fast & Furious does.

Moviegoers looking for the consistent, predictable satisfaction they used to get from their favorite stars now turn to cinematic universes. Any movie with "Jurassic" in the title is sure to feature family-friendly adventures on an island full of dinosaurs, no matter who plays the human roles.

Star vehicles are less predictable because stars themselves get older, they make idiosyncratic choices, and thanks to the tabloid media, our knowledge of their personal failings often colors how we view them onscreen (one reason for Cruise's box-office woes has been that many women turned on him following his failed marriage to Katie Holmes).

In a franchise-dominated business, stars matter only in the right roles. Tom Hanks in *Sully*? Yes. Matt Damon in *The Martian*? Absolutely. Jennifer Lawrence in *The Hunger Games*? Nobody else could do it. But put them in *A Hologram for the King* or *Monuments Men* or *Passengers,* and fans are just as happy to skip it.

It's no wonder that their salaries have fallen too. While A-listers still occasionally get $20 million for the right role, nearly all have seen their paychecks drop significantly. Now $15 million, $10 million, or $5 million are more likely when it's a mid-budget movie the star really wants to make, or a franchise in which the role could go to any number of actors. Gross points, meanwhile, have almost completely evaporated. In most cases, stars have to wait until a movie breaks even, after which they share in the profits along with the studio.

Sony's Da Vinci Code series, based on the best-selling books by Dan Brown about intrigue and corruption in the Catholic church, shows how these changes have unfolded. These movies star Tom Hanks and are directed and produced by the highly compensated A-list team of Ron Howard and Brian Grazer. The original, from 2006, grossed $753 million and made Sony a $179 million profit. To bring the trio back for 2009's sequel, *Angels & Demons,* Sony agreed to pay Hanks $20 million, Howard $10 million, and Grazer $2.5 million. But that was just a minimum. The trio also split 25 percent of the first dollar gross. If that worked out to be more than their salaries, then they would make even more. That was what it cost to get A-list talent to work on a movie, particularly a sequel to a successful film, in those days. Stars had the leverage and studios had no choice. But the deal turned out to be a disaster for Sony. *Angels & Demons* grossed a disappointing $479 million at the box office, and the studio lost $24 million. The talent, meanwhile, made more than $75 million once their quarter of the first dollar gross was totaled.

Under their contract for *Angels & Demons,* Hanks, Howard, and Grazer were entitled to be paid at least as much on any follow-up. But by 2014, when Sony started work on an adaptation of a third novel by Brown, *Inferno,* that level of compensation was just not possible. *Angels & Demons* had lost money, after all, and the economics of the industry had changed, with plummeting DVD sales and the waning box-office power of stars like Hanks.

After four months of negotiations, Sony reached a deal with the trio's representatives at CAA. They would all take pay cuts: Hanks got $15.4 million up front, Howard $7.7 million, and Grazer just under $2 million. More significant, instead of sharing one-quarter of every dollar that came in, Sony gave them 50 percent of the profits after the production and marketing costs were covered. Hanks would get 26 percent of the profits, Howard 14 percent, and Grazer 10 percent. Only if the movie was a massive success and Sony earned a huge profit could they make as much as they did on the previous film.

Inferno cost $90 million to make, less than half the budget of *Angels & Demons*. Sony was aiming for it to gross just $300 million, in which case it would make a profit of about $50 million. Lynton was still skeptical as to whether it was a good deal, though. "This is getting pricey for what it is," he told Pascal.

He was right. Tom Hanks and the Da Vinci Code brand proved even less appealing than Sony's most conservative estimate. It grossed only $219 million, meaning the studio lost a little money and there was nothing extra for Hanks, Howard, and Grazer.

The crumbling of the modern star system hit Amy Pascal particularly hard. Though she wasn't much like the moguls of Hollywood's golden age — she didn't have their mean streak or megalomaniacal tendencies — she resembled them in one key way: her focus on building a stable of stars.

In the early days of Hollywood, such an approach was much easier because studios signed talent to long-term contracts that forbade them from working anywhere else without the permission of the mogul, who essentially owned them. Since the old star system ended in the 1950s, however, actors and filmmakers have been free agents. Now studios actually had to earn the loyalty of the talent. When they did, they could convince an A-list writer or director to form a production company that had a "first look" deal at a studio. This arrangement didn't guarantee exclusivity, but it meant that in exchange for providing an office on the lot and covering overhead costs, studios could get a first right of refusal on any film that the company developed. If the talent wanted to produce their own projects, giving them more money and creative control, their home studio still got first dibs on their work.

That's why Clint Eastwood has made so many movies for Warner Bros., Leonardo DiCaprio for Paramount, and James Cameron for Fox.

Amy Pascal used this tool effectively throughout the 2000s. She convinced stars like Drew Barrymore and Jennifer Lopez and directors like

Nora Ephron and James L. Brooks to call Sony home. Always a lover of creative talent and skilled at drawing actors and directors into her orbit, she built her business strategy around making Sony their favorite place to call home. Competitors tried to do the same, but nobody was as consistently effective as Amy Pascal.

The *Los Angeles Times* in 2009 pronounced Sony "the most talent-friendly studio in town."

"Whether it's a filmmaker or a movie star, I don't want them to come here and just do one picture," Pascal said. "My goal is to have the kind of relationship where they want to keep coming back."

Publicly, Sony executives would state that they were as interested in franchises as anyone else was. But it clearly wasn't true. "People labeled us a relationship studio," Pascal reflected in 2014. "We were, and it was our strategy."

Of Sony's top fifty movies from 2000 through 2016, more than two-thirds were "star vehicles," in which the talent involved was as big as or bigger than the move title or the franchise. More than one-third, amazingly, came from just two people, the most important stars on Sony's lot and arguably the studio's most significant movie assets after Spider-Man: Will Smith and Adam Sandler. Movies they starred in or produced grossed $3.7 billion from 2000 through 2015, 20 percent of Sony Pictures' domestic total. From 2007 through 2012, an internal analysis found that this duo's movies generated $450 million in profits — 23 percent of everything the motion picture department earned.

No other studio this century was as reliant on just two movie stars for its success. And no other relationship between talent and studio was as consistent and as consistently lucrative for both sides as that of Adam Sandler and Will Smith with Sony Pictures. Their rise and fall illustrate what has happened to movie stars in Hollywood.

IN WEST PHILADELPHIA BORN AND RAISED . . .

A rapper from Philadelphia, known for rhymes that were more light-hearted than hardcore, Will Smith first rose to fame as the second part

of the hip-hop duo DJ Jazzy Jeff and the Fresh Prince. In 1989, he won
the first ever Grammy for rap at the age of twenty. Two years later, he
became the most prominent black star on TV since Bill Cosby, with his
hit sitcom *The Fresh Prince of Bel-Air.* It ran for six seasons and seared
Smith's charismatic persona and resistance-melting smile into the
minds of a generation, along with a couldn't-forget-it-if-you-wanted-
to theme song, written and performed by the star.

Always a hard worker, with a Tony Robbins–esque belief that if he
focused on his goals, he could achieve anything, Smith decided, "I want
to be the biggest movie star in the world." Working with his business
partner James Lassiter, DJ Jazzy Jeff's former manager, Smith focused
on what the highest-grossing movies had in common to see what he
could apply to his own choices — a habit he would continue throughout his career.

His first leading role was in *Six Degrees of Separation,* a low-grossing
adaptation of a Broadway play perhaps remembered best for Smith's
homophobic refusal to kiss another man, forcing the director to im-
ply their lip-locking by filming the back of Smith's head. Soon after,
though, he found his true calling: as the charming hero that America,
and eventually the world, could root for in big action-adventure movies. Smith's evolution to movie star started in 1995, with the buddy cop
movie *Bad Boys,* and quickly hit an apex in 1996 with *Independence Day,*
which, at $817 million, remains his highest-grossing movie and estab-
lished him as a worldwide sensation at just the time when the international market was blossoming. Smith also proved he was immune to
the conventional industry wisdom that foreigners wouldn't embrace
an African American movie star.

By 1999, with the hits *Men in Black* and *Enemy of the State* under his
belt, Will Smith was ready for producing. This move, which most successful stars ultimately make, would allow him to develop his own material and give him more creative control, rather than just perform in
other people's movies. He and Lassiter formed Overbrook Entertainment, named after the high school they both attended, and signed a
three-year first-look deal with Universal Pictures.

To borrow a box-office term, the deal was a bomb. The duo didn't get a single movie made at Universal. "The truth of the matter is, we were novices, and we hadn't learned the business," Lassiter later reflected. "We hadn't learned what it really means to produce movies."

In 2002, they moved their deal to Sony, the studio that made *Bad Boys* and *Men in Black* and, most important to Smith, 2001's *Ali.* Budget concerns brought Pascal and her boss at the time, John Calley, near to killing this boxing biopic. But they eventually worked out a compromise with Smith and the Oscar-nominated, highly respected, but not exactly frugal director Michael Mann to make it for $109 million, still a huge budget for an R-rated biopic. It grossed only $88 million and lost Sony money. But it earned Smith his first Oscar nomination and, true to the Pascal playbook, endeared him to the studio and its motion picture chief, who was willing to take risks for the talent she adored.

"Home is a place where you feel completely comfortable, and you get unconditional support, and Columbia Pictures has been that place to us for many years," Smith and Lassiter declared as they signed the deal. Pascal had proved her loyalty to them "through deeds, not words."

At Sony, Smith joined another former TV star whom Pascal had lured to America's most important and highest-paying form of pop culture at the time — the movies.

COMEDY WUNDERKIND

Adam Sandler was a standup comedian from New Hampshire who, after being discovered by Dennis Miller, made it onto *Saturday Night Live* as a writer and then a performer. While he earned fans for characters like Opera Man and Canteen Boy and his "Chanukah Song," he did not seem destined for stardom in the way that his contemporaries Dana Carvey, Phil Hartman, and Mike Myers were. He was charming, in a low-key and goofy way, but he seemed like a six-year-old in a grown man's body.

As he transitioned to movies, Sandler's first few efforts weren't breakout hits. *Billy Madison* and *Happy Gilmore,* both built around his man-child persona, grossed only $26 million and $39 million, respectively. But they were cult favorites, watched over and over on DVD and cable by frat boys and stoners.

In 1998, Sandler proved he could actually appeal to a broad audience as a romantic lead, playing a lovable loser who woos Drew Barrymore away from a rich douchebag in *The Wedding Singer.* Then later that year, his man-child persona found a huge audience with *The Waterboy,* which grossed a jaw-dropping $186 million. It was the fifth-highest-grossing film of the year and the most successful sports comedy ever, establishing Sandler as a major movie star.

Amy Pascal fell hard for Sandler after seeing him in *The Wedding Singer.* So when Chris Farley, who was set to star in a Sony comedy as an underachieving toll collector, suddenly died, she turned to Sandler. *Big Daddy* was another monster hit, grossing $235 million worldwide, and it turned Sony into a home for the star's new company, Happy Madison Productions.

Unlike Smith, Sandler didn't have grand designs for his career or carefully plotted strategies for his company. He was a smart but easy-going schlub who worked hard for his family and had no pretensions about who he was and why his fans loved him. Realizing early in his career that newspaper critics and reporters looked down on his work, Sandler simply refused to talk to them. The only publicity he would do for his films was on TV, goofing around with fellow comics like David Letterman and Jay Leno on late-night talk shows.

"He wasn't fancy and he wasn't a dinner-party conversation guy. He was more about the money," said a person close to the star.

Being prolific was the name of the game for Adam Sandler. Between 2000 and 2015, he starred in twenty-four movies and produced another thirteen that he didn't appear in. Sandler starred in at least one crude comedy almost every year to satisfy his fan base and studios. But he wasn't afraid to take risks either, starring in a number of ambitious dramas from respected directors, such as Paul Thomas Anderson's *Punch-Drunk Love,* James L. Brooks's *Spanglish,* and Judd Apatow's *Funny People.*

Smith, meanwhile, was more strategic and deliberative in his choices. He starred in fifteen films during the same period that Sandler made twenty-four, and at one point took a four-year break. He produced seven movies that he didn't star in.

Both enjoyed unmatched success throughout the 2000s. After Pascal supported him in *Ali*, Smith starred in two sequels that she badly wanted, *Men in Black II* and *Bad Boys II*. And if they weren't as profitable as they should have been because the studio overspent, that was hardly his fault. He then proved his romantic-comedy bona fides with *Hitch*, his ability to draw big audiences to an inspirational drama with *The Pursuit of Happyness*, and his appeal in an original superhero film with *Hancock*.

Sandler, meanwhile, proved can't-miss in one dumb but endearing comedy after another. *Mr. Deeds, Anger Management, 50 First Dates, The Longest Yard, Click, You Don't Mess with the Zohan, Grown Ups,* and *Just Go with It* all grossed more than $170 million worldwide.

Sony paid both stars handsomely for their consistent success: $20 million against 20 percent of the gross receipts, whichever was higher, was their standard compensation. They also received as much as $5 million against 5 percent for their production companies, where they employed family and friends. Sony also provided Happy Madison and Overbrook with a generous overhead to cover expenses — worth about $4 million per year. To top it off, Sandler and Smith enjoyed the perks of the luxe studio life. Flights on a corporate jet were common, with family members and friends often invited along. On occasion, Smith's entourage and its belongings necessitated the use of two jets for travel to premieres.

Knowing that Sandler was a huge sports fan, Sony regularly sent him and his pals to the Super Bowl to do publicity. In addition to enjoying the best tickets and accommodations, they had a private basketball court to play on, which the studio rented for them. Back at the Sony lot, the basketball court was renamed Happy Madison Square Garden in the star's honor.

When anybody questioned the wide latitude and endless indulgence given to Sandler and Smith, Sony executives had a standard answer: "Will and Adam bought our houses."

Sony wasn't unique in the perks it provided to its talent. Warner

Bros. had vacation villas in Acapulco and Aspen that stars were welcome to fly to on a corporate jet. Universal custom-designed a Tuscan
villa and a white modernist building on its lot to house the production
companies of the directors Robert Zemeckis and Ivan Reitman. But
Sony was consistently among the biggest spenders. An internal analysis by the studio found that from 2007 through 2012, it spent 13.5 percent more on "above the line" costs — industry jargon for stars, directors, and other key creative talent — than the rest of the industry did.

   "Above-the-line costs represent an opportunity to improve margins," the report modestly recommended.

LOSING LUSTER

That was about to become a lot more true, because 2012 and 2013 were
the years when the star business went south for Sony Pictures.

   Many at the studio were already embarrassed by 2011's *Jack & Jill,*
a comedy that was insipid even by Sandler's standards; in the film he
played a man and his twin sister. Sony executives didn't want to make
it, but it was virtually impossible to say no to one of their biggest stars.
And Sandler's instincts had proved right before. He pushed to make
2009's *Paul Blart: Mall Cop,* a Happy Madison production starring
Kevin James, over the studio's objections, and the low-budget comedy grossed a fantastic $183 million. So despite misgivings, Sony went
ahead with *Jack & Jill,* which earned Sandler the worst reviews of his
career (the Rotten Tomatoes rating was 3 percent) and was his lowest-
grossing comedy since the bomb *Little Nicky,* in 2000. Still, it grossed
$150 million globally and wasn't a complete disaster.

   That fate was reserved for his next movie: *That's My Boy.* Originally
titled *I Hate You Dad,* the 2012 movie featured Andy Samberg as the
adult son of a middle-aged loser played by Sandler. The intent was to
balance the star's typical comedic shenanigans with genuine emotion.
Once again, Pascal didn't want to make the film, but Sandler insisted
and even threatened to use one of Happy Madison's "puts," provisions
in its contract allowing it to force the studio to release a film. She reluc-

tantly agreed, but her fears proved right. The $70 million production — a ridiculous cost for a comedy that reflected the star's still-huge paycheck — was a box-office bomb and lost $42.5 million.

That same year, Will Smith returned to the big screen after a hiatus, following 2008's surprise disappointment, *Seven Pounds*. He starred in a sequel that Sony had been dying to make for many years. *Men in Black* 3 was a challenging movie to produce with a mature Will Smith. Now used to being the dominant creative force in his productions, he often demanded repeated changes to scripts and never worked with directors who could wield more power than he did. That was fine for Overbrook-led productions, but it became a challenge on the third Men in Black offering, which was made in a rush, to take advantage of New York tax credits.

The production was a nightmare. The unhappy Smith holed up in his fifty-three-foot-long trailer, which featured a screening room, offices for assistants, and an all-granite bathroom, while multiple screenwriters reworked the script again and again. The creative conflicts between the star, his producers, and the studio were so severe that production was halted for three months to resolve them. Greenlit with a budget of $210 million, *Men in Black* 3 ended up costing $250 million and barely broke even.

Smith was hardly deterred, though. He had something far bigger in mind for his comeback. Aware that "star vehicles" were fading and talent needed to get involved in franchises, he and his colleagues at Overbrook developed a project called "1000 A.E." Working out of a "war room" filled with concept art, the team envisioned a story set a millennium after the late-twenty-first-century destruction of Earth, which had been caused by environmental calamities. Not just a science-fiction franchise meant to reflect contemporary concerns, 1000 A.E. would be a "transmedia universe," featuring storytelling on every platform.

To flesh out that universe, Smith worked with a team of writers to create a 294-page "bible." It provided details about more than a thousand years of history, told across multiple families, planets, and "arks," which had departed Earth with humanity's survivors. As Overbrook's not-too-modest pitch document described it, "Each generation discovers a world that connects with them on a visceral and emotional level — their appetite for revisiting that world is endless and as they grow older, the attraction continues to grow stronger. Star Trek, Star Wars, Indiana Jones, Lord of the Rings and Harry Potter have all reached such stature, and now they are being joined by 1000 A.E."

The document detailed plans for not only the movie and its sequel, but also a live-action television show, an animated series, webisodes and mobisodes, a video game, consumer products, theme-park attractions, documentaries, comic books, an "in-school education program in partnership with NASA," and "cologne, perfume, toiletries, etc." Fans would become so engaged in the 1000 A.E. universe, according to Overbrook, that it could become the center of their online lives. "Since there is no telling what will become of the Facebook model over the next 3–5 years," the pitch document advised, "it is also essential to create a stand-alone AE branded Social Network."

Sony executives had mixed opinions on the commercial potential of the concept, but they needed franchises and they believed in Smith. The biggest concern for Pascal and others was how much Will Smith the movie would have. Envisioned as a father-son adventure story, the script, in some versions, focused entirely on a young character played by the star's son, Jaden. But naturally, Sony wanted its biggest action star to be onscreen as much as possible. Ultimately, Will Smith appeared in the movie, but spent most of it disabled in a spaceship that has crashed on a devastated Earth. He gives advice over a communicator to his son, who's actually mobile and engaged in adventure.

Executives also weren't thrilled with Smith's choice of a director, M. Night Shyamalan, whose once-hot career had cooled with the widely disliked and commercially disappointing *Lady in the Water, The Happening,* and *The Last Airbender* (and would later be revived by *Split*).

As they put together marketing plans for the May 2013 release, eventually titled *After Earth,* Sony executives realized their best bet was a con job. "Conceal Will Smith's injury," read a set of marketing rules that the studio devised for the film. "He's the star that everyone's looking forward to seeing and it's best for moviegoers to assume that he's a part of the action — it'd be disappointing to our audience to discover that he spends the majority of the film stuck in the ship."

"Also," the document added, "M. Night Shyamalan can be polarizing, and should be downplayed everywhere possible."

But no amount of deception could save *After Earth,* at least in the United States, where it grossed a dismal $61 million. Overseas it performed somewhat better, with $183 million, but ultimately the $149 million production lost more than $25 million. There were no sequels, no TV shows, no video games, no perfumes, and no social network. The failure was devastating to Smith, who not only acted in and produced the movie, but also got his first-ever feature screenwriting credit.

In the wake of *After Earth* and *That's My Boy,* the golden age for Will Smith and Adam Sandler at Sony was over. As was happening to production companies all around Hollywood, the annual overhead for Overbrook and Happy Madison was slashed in half, to about $2 million each. The perks also weren't so generous. "The corporate jet wasn't available so much anymore," said a person close to Sandler.

Inside Sony, the conversation was no longer about how to make more money with the stars, but how to stop relying on them. "I think one of the answers to your question about what replaces adam sandler and will smith at the studio is planting commercial writer/directors here," De Luca told Pascal in 2014.

When Will Smith really wanted to star in *Passengers,* a big-budget science-fiction movie featuring two romantic leads who wake up early from cryogenic sleep on a spaceship, the studio had to reluctantly inform his agent that it preferred a younger rising star, Chris Pratt. "That wasn't a comfortable phone call," said De Luca, "because Will had made billions for the studio."

Sandler, meanwhile, wanted Sony to greenlight an adaptation of the board game Candy Land, which he would star in and produce. When the studio proved reluctant, slowing down the development process, Sandler blew up during a "very difficult" conversation with Pascal. "You said yourself that Adam was gonna be angry," Doug Belgrad reassured his boss, "and you said you didn't care you couldn't fix what was really bothering him that he isn't the guy he once was and nobody can make that better for him."

Following their flops in 2012 and 2013, Sandler and Smith each had only one live-action movie left at Sony before they could start searching for more welcoming backers elsewhere. Neither production was an easy one.

Michael Lynton thought that *Concussion,* about a doctor who discovers the danger of brain injuries to NFL players, should be made at a very low cost with a little-known star like Chiwetel Eijofor, who had been nominated for an Oscar for *12 Years a Slave.* Amy Pascal believed it was the perfect movie to get "back on track" with Smith. True, the subject matter was grim, and football isn't popular outside the United States, but an inspirational drama starring one of the world's biggest movie stars still felt like a home run, along the lines of his mega-hit *The Pursuit of Happyness* from 2006. But there was a problem. Smith's agents at CAA initially wanted him to be paid $15 million against 15 percent of the gross — a cut from his quote of $20 million against 20 percent, but still a huge number for such a small movie.

"I don't know what to do with that," Pascal told Lassiter. "You know what kind of movie this is." Pascal thought they should be able to get him for $10 million, but Lynton thought even that was too much. "Let's try $7.5mm," he told her. "He almost got us fired with the last movie."

Lynton lost that battle, as he so often did when it came to the details of moviemaking. Smith got $10 million, though nothing close to the fifteen gross points that CAA had asked for. He would take up to 50 percent of the movie's profits only after Sony made at least $10 million.

That didn't turn out to be an issue. Released a week after *Star Wars: The Force Awakens* in December 2015, *Concussion* barely registered at the box office — proving once again the power of franchises over movie stars. Produced for $43 million, Sony was targeting $135 million in global box office. But it grossed just $49 million, losing the studio more than $25 million.

Sandler's years of enmeshment with Sony also ended with a whimper in 2015. *Pixels* was, like *After Earth,* meant to catapult an aging star into the new world of global franchises. It was based on a two-minute short film about classic video game characters like Pac-Man and Donkey Kong invading Earth, and Sony thought it could become an action-comedy franchise in the vein of Ghostbusters. Some questioned whether Sandler and his costar, Kevin James, were the right match for a video-game-themed movie meant to appeal to younger audiences. But Happy Madison had originally optioned the short film, and executives like Belgrad, who had built their careers alongside the former *Saturday Night Live* comedian, still believed in Sandler.

Lynton pressured his executives over the budget for *Pixels,* looking to keep it to a tight $110 million despite the extensive visual effects involved. Sandler took only $5 million up front, his lowest paycheck on a major production since the 1990s, in exchange for a big cut of the profits.

After attending a read-through, Pascal promised Lynton that the movie, which also starred Peter Dinklage from *Game of Thrones* and Josh Gad, the voice of Olaf the snowman in *Frozen,* would be different from the typical Sandler fare. "It was brilliantly funny and engaging . . . no boob jokes, no poop jokes, the cast was fantastic and classy," she assured her boss. "Its big and insanly commercial."

Critics largely disagreed, though, calling *Pixels* "dimwitted . . . slapdash, casually sexist." American audiences stayed away, but a decent international performance got *Pixels* to a $245 million worldwide gross. That was enough for Sony to eke out a profit of about $10 million — not a disaster but well below its target of $25 million and certainly not enough to give Sandler and the studio the new franchise they desperately needed.

Despite these disappointments, Sony wouldn't abandon the two stars completely. Sandler was still valuable as the lead voice in the hit animated franchise Hotel Transylvania, and Smith was needed to help reboot the dormant Bad Boys series. But the days of building star vehicles around them were over.

Star power throughout Hollywood, in fact, was now fading fast. As studios sped toward a promising future of franchises while trying to shove movie stars out onto the curb, Adam Sandler and Will Smith were two names on a long list of A-listers who faced a diminished and depressing future. What they didn't know yet is that a new future was being plotted for them, and other stars, by a man who had dropped out of college to manage a video store.

7

A Star Is Born

Netflix, the New
Home for Movie Stars

TED SARANDOS WASN'T AN OBVIOUS candidate to revolution-
ize the entertainment business. A journalism major at Arizona State
University who left in 1983 without a degree to manage a video store,
the compact, square-jawed Sarandos was a fast talker with a quick
mind for business. By the late 1990s, he was vice president of product
and merchandising at West Coast Video, which had about five hundred stores. In 2000 he joined Netflix, where his background seemed
to match what the fledgling dot-com needed: someone who could buy
and manage the millions of DVDs it sent in red envelopes to subscribers each month.

As Netflix evolved from mailer of DVDs to the leading video-
streaming service later in the decade, though, its chief content officer
became a power player in Hollywood. The TV repeats and years-old
movies Sarandos acquired were sucking up more and more of consumers' time, causing studio and network executives to wring their hands
over whether the huge checks Netflix wrote were ultimately a drug de-
stroying their health.

One of the beneficiaries was Sony Pictures. The studio made hundreds of millions of dollars annually from the pay channel Starz, an

HBO competitor that aired movies for its cable subscribers. Starz was able to afford that cost in part because it resold the Internet rights to Netflix for about $30 million per year.

Starz ended that deal in 2011, even though Netflix offered to pay more than $300 million annually to renew it. Like other studios and networks at the time, Starz concluded that it needed to endure short-term financial pain in order to kick the Netflix addiction and stop making its content so easy and cheap for consumers to watch without a cable subscription. Not coincidentally, that was the year Sarandos decided to start buying original programming.

If Netflix couldn't count on Hollywood to provide the content it needed, it would start producing content itself. But, Sarandos reasoned, its selection process should be entirely different. Rather than rely on focus groups, subjective comparisons to similar content, and executives' gut feeling, Netflix used data.

House of Cards was an early and compelling example of how well this approach would work. From its database, Netflix could easily see that Kevin Spacey movies had long done well on the service, and many subscribers had watched the director David Fincher's *The Social Network*, a Sony hit obtained through the Starz deal, from start to finish. Finally, the company knew that the British political drama *House of Cards* was also surprisingly popular among its American subscribers.

So when Spacey and Fincher teamed up on an American remake of that series, Sarandos made a huge bet: $100 million for two seasons. The rest, of course, is history. *House of Cards* was a hit. Not measured by the viewership numbers, which Netflix wouldn't release, but by the way everyone was talking about it and the multiple Emmy nominations it earned, including one for best drama series, in its first season. It was followed by *Orange Is the New Black, Bojack Horseman, The Unbreakable Kimmy Schmidt, Master of None,* and *Stranger Things* — shows with a cultural impact that was easily as significant as anything on HBO, Showtime, or FX.

Marvel even got in on the action, taking superheroes too dark to ever turn into a PG-13-rated global blockbuster and releasing them as more violent, less lighthearted Netflix series like *Daredevil, Jessica Jones, Luke Cage,* and the poorly received *Iron Fist.*

As Netflix's original hits piled up, Sarandos became one of Hollywood's most powerful and celebrated moguls. The former video-store manager traveled to the annual Sun Valley conference for the media elite, attended award shows, and hosted his own splashy premieres.

MOVIES SHOW THEIR STRENGTH

When Netflix started as a DVD service in the late 1990s, 80 percent of the content subscribers watched was movies. As it became more of a television company, that number dropped dramatically, until by the 2010s only one-third of total content viewing was movies.

The surprising thing about that statistic is that it wasn't lower. Nearly all of Netflix's movies were a year old or more, and by the time they showed up on the streaming service, they had already been in theaters, on DVD, and available to rent from iTunes. Most TV shows, by contrast, were either original or available to watch for the first time after airing on traditional TV.

But no matter what happened to Netflix's content mix, movies never fell below one-third of what its users chose to watch. "It's incredible how consistent that stayed, especially considering how great television has become," said Sarandos. "People do want to see movies. The art of the two-hour story is different than the sixty-hour series." Still, people regularly complained that Netflix's movie selection wasn't that great and that its algorithms frequently suggested films they had already seen. Sarandos knew they were right and also knew he couldn't do much about it.

Hollywood's entire business model has long been predicated on holding back movies from services like Netflix. In order to maximize revenue, most films are released first in theaters. Three or more months later, they're available to buy or rent from digital stores like iTunes and on DVD or Blu-ray. Several months after that, usually at least eight after debuting in theaters, they start airing on pay cable services like HBO or Showtime. The films then eventually make their way to cable television networks and, finally, to broadcast TV or the bargain bin at Wal-Mart.

Sometimes Netflix could get movies at the same time as the pay cable networks, though as the end of its deal with Starz illustrated, that was becoming increasingly difficult. In most cases, Netflix got films at the very end of the "windows" process described above — years after they first played in theaters.

This convoluted system developed because it's the best way for studios to earn a profit on movies that cost hundreds of millions of dollars to make and market, and to cover their hundreds of millions per year in overhead. The system relies on what economists call "price discrimination" — making sure consumers who want to consume a product the soonest have to pay the most, while those who are unwilling to pay top dollar for it have to wait. The biggest fans, who want to see a movie in theaters and at home, sometimes even pay twice, for a ticket and then again for the Blu-ray.

But to make Netflix's $10 per month service as valuable as possible to current and potential subscribers, Sarandos needed movies sooner. Even when he outbid Starz to get the pay cable rights to Disney movies — uniquely valuable because kids watch them over and over again — Netflix would still need to wait more than six months from the big-screen debut to availability for streaming. The solution, Sarandos concluded, was the same one he'd previously reached for television: Netflix should start making its own movies. And thanks in part to the end of the Starz deal, for which Netflix had been prepared to pay about $1 billion for Sony movies over three years starting in 2012, he had cash to do so.

People called Netflix's move into original programming audacious. It was certainly innovative. Netflix series were the first ones with network quality to be distributed over the Internet. Also, Netflix posted every episode online together, rather than make viewers wait a week for each new one.

But these changes were nothing compared to how Sarandos wanted to transform film distribution. With its original movies, Netflix would ignore Hollywood's "windows" and make movies available to watch online the same day they debuted in theaters — if they played in theaters at all.

Many objected, of course. Motion pictures were made to be seen on the big screen. But Sarandos believed that except for the biggest-budget "event" movies like *The Avengers,* this view was elitist. Most film consumption takes place at home, whether on DVD or on TV. Thanks to rising ticket and popcorn prices and better television offerings on networks and Netflix, theater attendance had been falling for most of the twenty-first century, from 1.57 billion tickets sold in the United States and Canada in 2002 to 1.31 billion in 2016.

When filmmakers complained that Sarandos was degrading their work, the Netflix executive liked to ask them a question: where had they, as children, watched the movies that inspired them to become directors? Most had to admit it was at home, on a VHS tape or a DVD that they played over and over again. For a generation growing up with on-demand viewing, Sarandos argued, that would be even truer. "With the exception of big tentpoles like *The Avengers* or *Suicide Squad,* most every movie I see, I feel like it would have worked better on Netflix," Sarandos said.

Still, landing movies wasn't easy. Netflix's first film was set to be *The Walk,* the director Robert Zemeckis's adaptation of the documentary *Man on a Wire,* starring Joseph Gordon-Levitt as the French daredevil who crossed New York's Twin Towers on a tightrope. Sarandos had an all-but-done deal to release the movie simultaneously on Netflix and on 3D IMAX screens until Zemeckis got a last second offer from Sony. Tom Rothman wanted to use his TriStar label to release the movie traditionally, on IMAX and regular screens, and would spend $37 million making it. So Zemeckis went with the studio, and *The Walk* bombed, grossing only $10 million domestically and $61 million worldwide. Sony lost more than $10 million.

Ultimately Netflix's first release, in the fall of 2015, was *Beasts of No Nation,* a haunting, well-reviewed drama starring Idris Elba as the commander of an African military squadron made up of young boys. Only thirty-one theaters played the film and it was, by box-office standards, a disaster, grossing just $90,000. But the theatrical run was really just to get film critics and awards voters to pay attention.

Sarandos insisted that for Netflix, it was a streaming media hit. "It was probably the more watched independent film of the year," he boasted.

MOVIE STARS WELCOME

It didn't take long for Netflix to establish a steady diet of original low-budget films. Some, like the Paul Rudd drama *The Fundamentals of Caring* and Elijah Wood's *I Don't Feel at Home,* it bought at festivals such as Sundance. Others, like the director Christopher Guest's mockumentary *Mascots,* were backed by Netflix from the start because studios weren't interested. But the true shock to the Hollywood system came with Sarandos's deal in 2014 with Adam Sandler, a major movie star who was struggling with the harsh new realities of the studio business.

As he finished up work on *Pixels,* Sandler was itching to find a home for his latest signature lowbrow comedy, a Western spoof called *The Ridiculous 6.* Sony had already told the star something it never had before: "pass." Paramount developed it for a while, but ultimately didn't pull the trigger. Warner Bros. flirted with it too, but after Sandler's movie *Blended* flopped for that studio in May 2014, Warner said "no thanks" as well.

A few months later, Sandler got word that Netflix, newly interested in movies, had set its sights squarely on him. Using data gathered from Sony movies that Netflix had played through its Starz deal, Sarandos's team knew that even as his box-office power waned, Sandler remained one of the most popular stars on the streaming service. His aging audience might be less likely to pay to see him in a theater, but they still loved laughing at his antics at home.

"We knew he was popular in markets where his movies had never even opened," Sarandos said.

The mid-budget star vehicle, in other words, still worked great for

Netflix. When people went to theaters, they preferred brand-name franchises. But when they were browsing for something to stream rather than pay fifty dollars for a night out, a familiar face doing the familiar shtick was perfect. Movies without massive visual effects were just as enjoyable at home, after all, if not more so. And if the stars had chosen to stretch their wings and you didn't like the movie you clicked on, you could turn it off immediately. You lost a little bit of time, but not any money.

And though there may not be as many fans of Adam Sandler, or any movie star, as there used to be, that didn't necessarily matter to Netflix.

All studios care about is how many people buy tickets or DVDs. They get their money whether you loved the movie or hated it. But Netflix measures success by how many people finish a movie and are satisfied enough to keep subscribing as a result, or who sign up just in order to watch it. Adam Sandler's fan base may have shrunk, but those who remained were loyal and they were global—just what Netflix wanted. Additionally, Netflix wouldn't have to spend millions of dollars on billboards and TV ads to market each film. Its algorithm would prominently suggest each Sandler movie to his fans on their home screen the moment it was available.

So Ted Sarandos and his team started wooing Adam Sandler. They met him at Netflix's office in Beverly Hills, at the Happy Madison offices on the Sony lot, and on the set of *Pixels* in Toronto. Naturally, Sandler was skeptical. He had escaped television twenty years earlier to become a movie star. Wasn't making movies that people would watch on TV, or even on an iPad, a step backward? But Sarandos told him that by working with Netflix, he'd be on the cutting edge of the business, taking his brand directly to the fans on the platform where they preferred to watch him. Instead of begging for a yes from studio executives who were souring on his commercial appeal and often looked down their nose at his juvenile comedy, why not go with a distributor that valued exactly what he had to offer?

To test Netflix's seriousness, Sandler offered *The Ridiculous 6*. Sarandos immediately said he wanted the project to which all the major studios had given a pass. And when the star and his agents worried that if he made a movie with Netflix, studios would view him as the "enemy" and stop working with him, Sarandos signed Sandler to a four-picture deal, during which the streaming service would be the exclusive home for all his new comedies.

Perhaps best of all, after Sony had cut his fee on *Pixels,* Sandler's paycheck at Netflix skyrocketed again, to nearly $20 million per movie. The difference this time is that there were no gross points, or profit sharing, as he had enjoyed in his heyday with Sony. It was one big check up front, and that was that. Because there would be no box office — Sandler's Netflix movies aren't released in theaters at all — or DVD sales, there was no money directly attributable to a movie to share. Sandler would make the same money, whether the film succeeded or failed.

Sandler's first two movies for Netflix, 2015's *The Ridiculous 6* and 2016's *The Do-Over,* in which he and David Spade fake their deaths, were like old times at Sony. Critics hated them, but the company that made them was thrilled. By April 2017, Netflix users had spent more than 500 million hours watching Adam Sandler movies. That same month, his third original film for the streaming service, the show-biz satire *Sandy Wexler,* debuted to less terrible reviews and Netflix signed Sandler to make another four pictures.

"The Sandler deal has been hugely successful," Sarandos declared.

Adam Sandler wasn't the only A-lister to find Netflix willing to embrace the mid-budget star vehicles that the major studios were abandoning. When Brad Pitt, another huge talent who once commanded $20 million for most anything he wanted to do, started shopping a satirical comedy about the U.S. war in Afghanistan, studios weren't willing to offer much more than the planned $30 million production budget. The star, along with his producing partners and director, would have to take little money up front in exchange for a chunk of the profits, should they ever materialize.

Netflix, however, would compensate everyone handsomely up front in order to debut a Brad Pitt drama on its streaming service. It paid $75 million for global rights to *War Machine,* confident that its controversial subject matter and A-list lead would draw attention and engage at

least some subscribers, even if others were put off by the subject matter. The difference between the film's production budget and Netflix's
check was money that Pitt and the other talent would pay themselves.

By June 2016, Netflix got its hands on Sony's other former favorite son, Will Smith. *Bright* was one of the hottest packages to hit Hollywood in a while. CAA offered studios the chance to produce a supernatural cop movie starring Will Smith and directed by David Ayer,
who had made the respected *End of Watch* and had worked with Smith
on the commercially successful, if critically reviled, superhero movie
Suicide Squad. Sony was willing to pay between $40 million and $50
million and Warner Bros., together with MGM, offered a little more,
but Netflix wrote a check for more than $90 million. That was about
twice the production budget of the film, meaning $45 million would go
to the talent as up-front payment.

Though it featured extensive visual effects, *Bright* was based on
an original idea, making its commercial prospects on the big screen
against the latest Marvel sequel questionable at best. That was one of
the main reasons that Will Smith and his partners were willing to go
with Netflix. "I was after the creative freedom, the ability to make really hard-R-rated movies with vision and voice and see them play in
the on-demand world," Ayer said. "You do that as a theatrical release,
and you'd better hit a bull's-eye, some cultural zeitgeist. Otherwise it's
a gamble for studios; it's easier for them to justify $200 million bud-
gets for tentpoles than $40 million to $90 million for the movies I like
to make."

As of this writing, the world still doesn't seem to know what to make
of Netflix's strides into the film business. Brad Pitt's *War Machine* debuted to decidedly mixed reviews, and there's no way to tell whether
it was a success financially. But it certainly didn't make any discernible
impact on the national culture or the conversations about war and politics that it satirized.

The $50 million *Okja,* from South Korea's most famous director,
Bong Joon Ho, and starring Jake Gyllenhaal, debuted to both boos and
a four-minute standing ovation at the Cannes Film Festival in 2017,
signifying the international film community's uncertainty over how

to treat a company that disrespects movie theaters while embracing a beloved auteur. And what about Netflix's biggest gamble: a $120 million-plus drama starring Robert De Niro and Al Pacino and directed by Martin Scorsese called *The Irishman,* which began shooting in 2017?

These developments reveal one certainty: the bonds that movie studios had forged over decades with stars, directors, and other talent were now forever broken. Ted Sarandos had proved that even though he delivered films via Wi-Fi to devices that fit in a pocket, he could build a better home for movie stars than the movie studios themselves.

8

Frozen

Why Studios Stopped Making
Mid-Budget Dramas

AMY PASCAL WAS FURIOUSLY TRYING to save a movie she thought might be the next *Citizen Kane*. She was doing this while getting a mammogram.

Despite the all-day physical exam that she had planned for that sunny November day in 2014, Sony's motion picture chief was busy typing e-mails and making phone calls in a last-ditch effort to hold on to *Steve Jobs*, an unusual biopic about the Apple cofounder that had consumed much of her professional life that year.

Too much, in the eyes of Michael Lynton, who thought she should be devoting her time to finding the desperately needed franchises that could deliver big profits.

But Pascal had a passion for *Steve Jobs*, which had not lessened despite the many frustrating months of trying to move it from script to camera. Despite a modest budget that fluctuated between $33 million and $70 million and the A-plus talent that had orbited it at various times (including the writer Aaron Sorkin, the directors David Fincher and Danny Boyle, and the actors Leonardo DiCaprio, Christian Bale, Michael Fassbender, Scarlett Johansson, and Seth Rogen), Sony could never make the financials work. And so the team behind the movie, led by the powerful and profane producer Scott Rudin, were taking it out to other suitors. After reluctantly agreeing to let it go, Pascal was now having second thoughts. How could she give up on this movie just because the numbers didn't add up on paper? In her gut she believed it could win awards, win at the box office, and be remembered for decades.

This wasn't who Amy Pascal had been for most of her career. It wasn't who she wanted to be for the rest of it. "I just made the worst decision of my career and i will regret it forever," she told a friend the night before the mammogram. "I don't know what I was thinking."

Now Pascal was letting her annual checkup turn into one of the most stressful days of her career, as she tried to find some way to keep Sony involved in the film and regain her sense of pride as a mogul willing to take risks. When Rudin told her that he had to get her on the phone ASAP to discuss the possibility, she needed him to hang on: "In man gram machine," one of the most powerful people in Hollywood informed another.

It was an absurd situation for many reasons. Perhaps most fundamentally, it shouldn't have been so hard for Amy Pascal to make *Steve Jobs* in the first place. Why, any rational person might ask, would a studio that for the past few years had struggled to make money on movies that cost between $150 million and $260 million say no to one that cost as little as $33 million, came with an A-list talent pedigree, was based on a best-selling book, had a good shot at winning awards, and concerned one of the most fascinating men in modern America?

Why, in other words, was it so hard to make a high-quality, interesting, original mid-budget movie for adults?

QUEEN OF THE STONE AGE

Certainly no one in Hollywood had a better track record with these types of films than Amy Pascal. The prior year, *Captain Phillips,* starring Tom Hanks in the true-to-life story of modern sea piracy, had been one of the few bright spots for Sony in a dismal 2013. It grossed $220 million worldwide and generated a healthy profit of about $45 million. Other profitable, Oscar-nominated mid-budget dramatic hits under Pascal's reign at Sony in the 2010s included *American Hustle, Zero Dark Thirty, Moneyball,* and *The Social Network.*

Compare that to the agony of *The Amazing Spider-Man 2,* which cost $260 million and made less than $20 million in profits. Given all that, didn't it make more sense to focus on the movies that cost one-fifth as much and earned more profits?

Michael Lynton certainly didn't think so. When Pascal believed she had come up with the perfect setup for the *Steve Jobs* movie — DiCaprio, Johansson, and Rogen together, at a budget of about $70 million — she urged her boss to sign off. "I would take that bet every-day . . . would you?" she asked hopefully.

"No, not at that number," he shot back. "Still a drama."

What, the moviegoer tired of superhero sequels might ask, is so bad about the d-word? From *Gone with the Wind* through *Sunset Boulevard, The Godfather, Rain Man,* and *Saving Private Ryan,* dramas have long been among Hollywood's most beloved and successful movies. If Sony's movie chief was better at making them than the competition, why not focus on what she did best? Left unsaid by Lynton, but certainly understood by Pascal, was that major studios like Sony couldn't set-tle for hitting singles and doubles when the competition was regularly blasting home runs.

The hundreds of millions of dollars in profits created by one Aveng-ers or Jurassic or Spider-Man film dwarf the profits of *Captain Phillips, The Social Network,* and *American Hustle* combined. And then there are the sequels, consumer products, and other sources of revenue that come along with a hit franchise film. Those movies also require a lot less work, compared to their potential returns. Creating TV ads and billboards, booking screens, and all the other efforts that a studio's staff puts into releasing a film are largely the same, whether it's a drama that might make $50 million or a superhero sequel that might make $200 million. So why not have your team put most of its energy into the latter?

While Sony had a better track record with mid-budget dramas than other studios did, it couldn't change the fundamental economic equation. Although the maximum profits on a drama like *Steve Jobs* are a fraction of those for *Transformers,* the expected losses from a drama's failure are often similar or worse. Even the lamest big-budget super-hero films, like *The Amazing Spider-Man 2,* almost always attract some audience, drawn simply by the visual spectacle and the appeal of brand-name titles. Dramatic films, because they have no built-in franchise appeal and because they are competing with a slew of excellent dramas available to watch or stream on TV, have to be really good. They are, in Hollywood parlance, "execution dependent." When the final result is anything short of wonderful, the box-office returns and studio losses can be abysmal.

That's why the worst box-office scenario Sony projected when greenlighting *The Amazing Spider-Man 2* still called for it to make a profit. For *Steve Jobs* and other dramas, like Cameron Crowe's *Aloha,* Meryl Streep's *Ricki and the Flash,* and Will Smith's *Concussion,* Sony envisioned significant losses if the stars didn't align. The latter three films, in fact, did lose money; even someone with Pascal's track record wasn't immune to losses on mid-budget dramas. Other studios, lacking someone with her expertise, were even more likely to bleed red ink when they strayed from big-budget "event" movies.

In 2016 alone, nearly every mid-budget movie with a hint of drama to it and that was released nationwide flopped. Among them: the Olympic skier biopic *Eddie the Eagle,* the Matthew McConaughey Civil War drama *Free State of Jones,* Tina Fey's *Whiskey Tango Foxtrot,* the Russell Crowe–Ryan Gosling cop film *The Nice Guys,* and the Iraq War gun-running tale *War Dogs. Sully, La La Land, Hidden Figures,* and *Arrival* were the only mid-budget dramas to gross more than $100 million. And that was considered a surprisingly high number because only two comparable films had grossed that much in 2015.

In 2000, even though average ticket prices were 38 percent lower than they are today, nine mid-budget dramas grossed more than $100 million.

The biggest change over the years is just how poorly mid-budget dramas now perform when they aren't hits. In the past, if a major studio put its resources behind a movie, it was virtually certain to gross at least $15 million. But now, with big franchise films sucking up the oxygen in multiplexes and with most of the cultural buzz about interesting dramas centered on television, a new dramatic movie could come and go unnoticed, as if it never existed.

TriStar, Tom Rothman's label devoted to mid-budget dramas that he ran before taking over all of Sony Pictures, released one flop after another, including *Ricki and the Flash, The Walk,* and *Billy Lynn's Long Halftime Walk,* which grossed less than $2 million.

Sony wasn't the only studio whose shrinking number of mid-budget dramas floundered. Fox released the Warren Beatty–directed drama *Rules Don't Apply* to just $3.7 million. Disney's *Queen of Katwe,* an inspirational true story about an African chess prodigy, made a dismal $8.9 million. DreamWorks' WikiLeaks drama *The Fifth Estate* grossed only $3.3 million. And Universal's *By the Sea,* a dramatic love story with Angelina Jolie and Brad Pitt, didn't even make it to $1 million.

"There just is no floor anymore," Rothman ruefully observed to Pascal.

"I know," Pascal replied to her friend. "It's fucked."

These are exactly the types of movies that people claim they want more of, but they rarely get up off their couches to go and see. And in the age of puny DVD sales, most of these films end up losing tens of millions of dollars. No wonder studios make so few of them. Counterintuitive as it may seem, the mid-budget drama — the inexpensive movies that adults regularly complain have disappeared from cinemas — has become the riskiest category of films for major studios.

That's why, before she began desperately trying to save *Steve Jobs* while in her gynecologist's office, Amy Pascal had reluctantly decided to give up on making the movie herself. She had gotten the budget down to $33.5 million after giving up on the team of David Fincher, Leonardo DiCaprio, and Scarlett Johansson, instead settling for Danny Boyle, Michael Fassbender, and Kate Winslet. But still, when her financial staffers ran the numbers, they told her the film would need to gross $100 million worldwide just to break even and $139 million to make a measly profit of $20 million.

Sure, Sony's *Captain Phillips* and *Zero Dark Thirty* and *The Social*

Network had grossed more than that. But they were exceptions in a modern Hollywood littered with mid-budget-drama flops. Betting on repeating that success with *Steve Jobs* would be like putting your money on a single number at the roulette table because it had come up a few times before. Andrew Gumpert, who ran the business side of Pascal's movie operation, urged her to take a different tack: "If ever there was a fact pattern where we should own zero of this film," he wrote, "this is it."

It made sense for Sony to release *Steve Jobs,* in other words, only if somebody else would pay for it. That way, the studio could put its name on the movie, and get the glory associated with releasing it, without having to take any financial risk. Pascal and her team knew Gumpert's analysis could mean only one thing. As Doug Belgrad put it: "We need Megan."

HELP ME, MEGAN ELLISON, YOU'RE OUR ONLY HOPE

If studio lots inspire and impress with the grandeur of their art deco buildings and faux main streets, the main entrance to Annapurna Pictures makes a very different statement. The first sight upon entering its complex of five buildings in West Hollywood is a massive A, on a black background. Like a pointillist painting, it initially appears to be a smooth image, but upon closer inspection, it is made up of tiny distinct images — not dots, but thick rectangular boxes that once held a generation's only way to see *Scarface, The Graduate, E.T.,* or the Look Who's Talking trilogy. It's a work of art composed of several thousand VHS tapes on twenty-seven shelves.

Inside Annapurna's offices are classic movie posters, a vintage arcade machine, and a staff of several dozen who are, with a handful of exceptions, under age forty. All of them dress like they're under thirty. The ultimate Hollywood hipster heaven, some call it.

It's the playground or the business, depending on your perspective, of Megan Ellison, Annapurna's founder, CEO, and raison d'être.

Some view her as a trust-fund baby having fun with Dad's money in Hollywood, others as a desperately needed patron of the arts in a cultural business dominated by the bottom line. She may be best understood as a fallback home of the interesting, original, challenging movies for adults that studio executives like Amy Pascal wanted to make but couldn't anymore.

Ellison's short filmography since starting Annapurna in 2011 is one any studio executive would kill for — if they cared only about reviews and award nominations, not the bottom line. Fourteen films were released from 2012 through 2016, seven of which were nominated for major Academy Awards, such as best actor or actress, director, and picture. *The Master, Zero Dark Thirty, American Hustle, Her, Foxcatcher, Joy,* and *20th Century Women* were all produced thanks to Ellison's money. Studios like Sony handled the mundane but important tasks of marketing and distribution, allowing them to share in the glory of acclaimed films without taking on the financial risk of making them.

They were happy to leave that unpleasant task to the shy, Aston Martin–driving, eighties-rock-band T-shirt-wearing, cinema-loving daughter of the world's fifth-richest man — a young woman who arguably made a bigger mark in Hollywood than any mogul this century before she turned thirty, in 2016.

Amy Pascal especially adored Megan Ellison. The two movies that brought Pascal's studio closest to winning an Oscar this century, *Zero Dark Thirty* and *American Hustle,* were financed entirely and 50 percent, respectively, by Annapurna's chief.

"The kind of movies Megan is helping to make are tough to do, but they're the reason we all got into this business," Pascal said of her young friend. You can imagine Pascal pursuing a life like Ellison's if, instead of being born middle-class in Los Angeles, she had been the daughter of Larry Ellison, cofounder of the Silicon Valley software giant Oracle, who is estimated to be worth $62 billion.

Megan Ellison's parents divorced before she turned one, and she spent her childhood watching VHS tapes at her mother's home with her brother, who would grow up to finance more mainstream, big-budget films, like sequels to *Terminator* and *Star Trek.* From a young age, the introspective, cerebral, and blunt brunette cultivated something of a punk-rock alternative persona but hardly rebelled against her elite upbringing. She raced speedboats with her father in St. Tropez and learned to competitively ride horses on her mother's estate.

Ellison attended the University of Southern California's prestigious film school but dropped out after two semesters and traveled the world. Among her destinations was Nepal, where she hiked the Himalayan mountain Annapurna, for which her company would be named. Upon returning to the United States, she decided that what she really wanted to do was use her wealth to finance movies from directors she admired. Ellison certainly had eclectic tastes: she worshiped John Cassavetes and Robert Altman yet called the Back to the Future films the "greatest film trilogy of all time"; she also had a soft spot for 1980s comedies like Goldie Hawn's *Overboard.*

When she started working in film, in about 2006, Ellison couldn't have known just how big an opening there would be for her business plan, thanks to the coming franchise-ation of the major studios. At the time, she started with low-budget efforts that could charitably be described as learning experiences. After contacting the director Katherine Brooks out of the blue on MySpace, Ellison showed up at a meeting on a Harley-Davidson and agreed to finance Brooks's independent movie *Waking Madison,* which cost about $2 million. It ended up going straight to video. Three subsequent efforts also made little impact among critics or at the box office. But things changed in 2010, when Ellison gained access to a substantial inheritance, estimated to be in the hundreds of millions, if not billions.

She established her own company, Annapurna, which she initially ran out of a trio of multi-million-dollar houses high in the Hollywood Hills — one for her to live in, one for filmmakers to work in, and one for "corporate" offices. Now Ellison had the ability to fully finance whatever she wanted.

She certainly wasn't the first member of the 1 percent who decided to start spreading her wealth in Hollywood. The movie industry has relied on "dumb money" from rich people enamored by show biz all the way back to Howard Hughes in the 1930s. Around the same time that Ellison came onto the scene, Gigi Pritzker, heir to the Hyatt Hotel fortune, Molly Smith, daughter of the founder of FedEx, and Jeff Skoll, employee number one at eBay, were also putting their money into films — primarily original, mid-budget ones that studios were wary of making.

But Megan Ellison stood out. For one thing, she wasn't in it only for the opportunity to become a celebrity. In fact, she actively shunned the spotlight, refusing every single request to be interviewed. "The control freak in me really clashes with the social anxiety in me, which drives me to drink in social situations," she wrote on Twitter. "It's a real lose, lose." She was almost as much of a recluse as Marvel's chief, Ike Perlmutter, when it came to the media. But unlike him, Ellison could often be found at premieres and other events celebrating her films, usually wearing a black suit and quietly talking to the talent while avoiding photographers and press.

She quickly insinuated herself among the crème of the A-list. At one post–Golden Globes party thrown by the giant talent agency William Morris Endeavor and packed with the Hollywood elite, she casually chatted with Leonardo DiCaprio and Jonah Hill before they and other friends headed upstairs for their own ultra-exclusive gathering.

Ellison was also unique in her ability to throw caution to the wind on the most prestigious projects from some of the best filmmakers. Say what you will about her financial acumen — nobody could question her taste. When Paul Thomas Anderson, the director of *Boogie Nights* and *There Will Be Blood*, wanted $32 million to make *The Master,* an exploration of a group akin to Scientologists, Ellison wrote the check after meeting the filmmaker at Jerry's Famous Deli, a famous L.A. lunch spot. Kathryn Bigelow, Academy Award winner for *The Hurt Locker,* needed $45 million to make *Zero Dark Thirty,* a controversial movie about the hunt for Osama Bin Laden? Done. Spike Jonze (*Being John Malkovich, Adaptation*) wanted to make a meditation on technology and love in the future with a simple title, *Her*? It couldn't be more obviously challenging at the box office, but Ellison put up $23 million.

Most independent producers would say they wanted to make a movie but then take many months to cobble together the financing from foreign distributors, lenders, and other sources. Even if their bank balance had many zeroes on the end, they weren't crazy enough to take on all of the risk. Like any savvy investor, they needed to hedge their bets. Megan Ellison wasn't against selling foreign rights and other efforts to make her film investments a little safer. But those decisions often came after the fact. When she said yes, it meant yes right now, backed up by her personal wealth. Many of her movies, unsurprisingly, didn't do well enough at the box office to justify their sizable budgets and likely lost money or made a very small profit at best (since Annapurna is a private company, we'll never know for sure).

Ellison's first real hit was 2012's *Zero Dark Thirty*, which also forged her bond with Amy Pascal. Sony released the picture, which grossed $133 million. It narrowly lost the Oscar for best picture to the blander *Argo*, directed by Ben Affleck.

The next year, when Pascal had another mid-budget adult drama that she wanted to make that seemed too risky for her studio to back, Ellison stepped up to provide half the $40 million budget. David O. Russell's 1970s crime caper, *American Hustle*, was another hit and, once again, came close to winning the Academy Award for best picture for Sony and Annapurna.

ONE FINAL RESTART

So when *Steve Jobs* started crumbling in Pascal's hands, Megan Ellison was naturally the person to turn to. To make an inexpensive movie she believed in, the head of a multi-billion-dollar, ninety-five-year-old studio needed a twenty-eight-year-old to say yes.

At first, Ellison expressed enthusiasm for the movie and deference to the more experienced Rudin. "I have such admiration for you and you make all the best films that I want to be involved with, it doesn't make sense for us to be at odds with each other," she wrote to him. "Steve Jobs was and always will be an important part of my family. He was my father's best friend, he was the witness at his wedding, he is the only person my father has ever truly admired. So this is also incredibly personal for me. It would be a great joy to be a part of shepherding his story."

Relying on the whims of a wealthy young woman, however, was very different from negotiating with a major company. To move forward, everyone involved wanted Ellison and Boyle to meet, and to do so quickly. But just getting them on the phone proved nearly impossible.

"We left messages for her everywhere. And I e-mailed her twice," Pascal told Rudin. "She just broke up with her girlfriend and is quite distraught. But I didn't want to say anything. Maybe that's why she didn't call."

"Well, that's professional," shot back Rudin.

"For a twenty-six-year-old," said Pascal, underestimating Ellison's age by two years.

"How long will she be twenty-six?" asked Rudin. "Four or five more years?"

A few days later, they tried for an in-person meeting in New York. But that turned into a fiasco too when nobody could reach Ellison or her assistant.

"We're in crazy-land here," a furious Rudin, who labeled Ellison a "lunatic," told Pascal. "Danny is literally sitting by the phone in a hotel room with nothing to do in NY but this. She has never returned his call. This is going to flame out in about ten seconds as Megan Ellison is on the verge of costing us the film when Danny says 'fuck it' and moves off this movie."

Ellison and Boyle finally met the next day. "Very interesting discussion about the script and the approach — she 'sees' it like we all do," reported the director. "And of course her own relationship with her dad, as well as his relationship with Steve, made for a great discussion. She's keen."

But the ego-bruised Rudin was hardly assuaged. "Megan 'sees' it. She has a vision," he snorted. "Thank God I can sleep at night now."

And then, two days later, Megan Ellison delivered a very different message. Even she wasn't sure the movie made sense at $33.5 million, and she was just as doubtful about its star as Pascal was. "It would depend on who it was and how much it costs," Pascal reported to Rudin, the young financier had told her.

"When I say say that," the Sony movie chief added, "it means no."

But Ellison wasn't saying no because the numbers didn't work out on a spreadsheet. She was using the same internal compass that used to guide Pascal and so many other studio moguls: "I simply have to do what I feel is the right thing for me and what my gut is telling me," Ellison told Rudin.

"Why did she do this??? Why put us all through this?" an exasperated Rudin asked Pascal.

"I don't know why anyone does anything they do," she replied.

What they couldn't know is that Ellison was about to radically reassess her approach at Annapurna. Rather than let Sony or Warner Bros. get credit for the risks she took with her money, she was building her own independent studio, which would do all the work and enjoy all the glory. She hired a former president of HBO to get her company into the more lucrative TV business, and she hired veteran executives from Fox and the Weinstein Company to make Annapurna a self-sufficient, fully operational studio. It could now release and market its own movies, starting with *Detroit,* the director Kathryn Bigelow's drama about race riots in the 1970s, released in August 2017.

The new Annapurna also signed a deal making it the new home of Brad Pitt's production company, Plan B, which had made the Oscar winners *12 Years a Slave* and *Moonlight,* and had agreed to spend $50 million on a biopic of Dick Cheney with the director of *The Big Short,* Adam McKay.

Megan Ellison was still a patron of the arts, betting big sums on daring, original films for adults. But her days as fairy princess who made dreams come true for studios that wanted to release original dramas without taking a financial risk were over. Now that Annapurna was releasing its own films, studios like Sony would be forced to narrow their vision even more to the "safer" big-budget franchise movies.

END OF THE ROAD

When Ellison pulled out of *Steve Jobs,* Amy Pascal knew it meant only one thing: "We are fucked. Or at least in a fucked situation."

Under pressure from Rudin and from Boyle's and Sorkin's agents to let them find another studio to make the film if Sony couldn't pull the trigger, Pascal reluctantly agreed. She was doing the "fair and honorable thing," she told Rudin. "You know how much I care about making good movies and how much I wanted to make this one." She hoped that nobody else would want to take the risk either, and Sony would get the film back, with time to find other financing or to develop it into a less costly or more potentially profitable picture. "I hope I get another shot to make it wtih you," Pascal wrote at the end of a wistful note to the producer.

But within a few days Universal Pictures, a studio whose 2015 schedule was packed with huge tentpoles and thus had room to take a flyer on one mid-budget drama, had picked up *Steve Jobs.* That's when Pascal went into full crisis mode, e-mailing from her doctor's office in hopes of finding some way to reverse her decision and keep Sony involved in the film.

She offered to find the money after all ("ILL DO IT ALL OF IT" she proclaimed to Boyle, too late) and "cried and acted like an idiot," in her own words, but she couldn't take back her decision. "You . . . love movies and always aspire to greatness," said the Sony production executive Elizabeth Cantillion, trying to console Pascal. "And that's a difficult thing to do right now."

But for Pascal, it was a painful moment of self-reflection. "I am devastated," she wrote to her friend Bryan Lourd, the CAA partner. "Who have I become?" She would eventually decide the experience had left her "without jobs but much wiser." But she was also left with a searing psychological analysis by her old friend and verbal sparring partner Rudin, who questioned what the *Steve Jobs* fiasco said about Pascal and, perhaps, the role of any modern movie mogul:

Why have the job if you can't do this movie? Stop and think about it — you're at a crossroads and you'd be very smart to recognize it . . .

So you're feeling wobbly in the job right now. Here's the fact: nothing conventional you could do is going to change that, and there is no life-changing hit that is going to fall into your lap that is NOT a nervous decision, because the big obvious movies are going to go elsewhere and you don't have the [intellectual property] right now to create them from standard material.

Force yourself to muster some confidence about it and do the exact thing right now for which your career will be known in movie history: be the person who makes the tough decisions and sticks with them and makes the unlikely things succeed. Fall on your sword — when you've lost that, it's finished. You're the person who does these movies. That's — for better or worse — who you are and who you will remain. To lose that is to lose yourself.

But Amy Pascal had already lost herself. Or rather, Hollywood had lost a place for people like her. It certainly didn't have a place for the films she still desperately wanted to make.

Nearly one year later, Universal released *Steve Jobs*. It got good but not great reviews, earned a pair of Academy Award nominations for Fassbender and Winslet, and bombed at the box office, grossing a dismal $35 million worldwide. It lost about $50 million.

9

Trading Places

How TV Stole Movies' Spot
atop Hollywood

IN EARLY 2014, near the end of a fiscal year in which his studio weathered bombs like *After Earth* and *White House Down* and was battered by the activist investor Daniel Loeb, Steve Mosko canceled dinner plans with his boss, Amy Pascal. He was, he said, tired of feeling disrespected.

"There is now a narrative being told that . . . devalues the efforts of myself and others in the tv group," the president of Sony Pictures Television told the co-chairman of Sony Pictures Entertainment, his e-mail filled with ellipses between his thoughts. "I think people in the know understand what we have overcome and accomplished over the past 11 years . . . the more disturbing piece is the personal attack that has been launched at me by people that work in the company for you and Michael to raise your profile . . . I've always delivered for you guys in every way . . . this year alone is going to be off the charts . . . and it's gotten lost in all this bullshit . . . and as I sit here thinking about what i've sacrificed this year to get the company thru a trying year . . . and getting thrown under the bus and treated like the help . . . it's fucked up."

Pascal was aghast at the accusations. "Of all the people in the world to think that I would want to take credit away from you . . . You just can't possibly believe that," she wrote back.

The fact was, Mosko had been stewing for years. Under his leadership, Sony's television business had grown from a small division of the company that made less than half the profits of the motion picture business in fiscal 2002 to one that regularly outperformed movies in the 2010s, earning about twice as much by 2015. And yet he was clearly second banana in the Sony Pictures hierarchy. If Lynton and Pascal were the royal couple, he was a governor in a far-off land who provided most of the kingdom's tax revenue and constantly grumbled about how justified he would be to revolt.

Mosko made little secret of his unhappiness, internally, throughout Hollywood, or, via surrogates, in the press. Among his biggest complaints:

- Mosko's title was president of Sony Pictures Television, while Pascal, who ran the less profitable film business, was co-chairman of the entire studio. Which meant that, technically, he reported to her, even though she, by her own admission, knew practically nothing about television and had almost no involvement in it.
- At Michael Lynton's senior executive meetings, Mosko was typically the only executive present from television, while several from the movie business, with big titles such as vice-chairman and president, got to sit alongside Pascal.
- Because Sony lumped film and TV results together when reporting its earnings, there was no way to demonstrate just how big a part of the studio's success he accounted for. The world, he felt, needed to know because then it would see how successful his team was and how unjustly he was being treated.

Nobody could accuse Steve Mosko of having a modest opinion of himself and his accomplishments. Or of being a gracious team player. But the growth of his business over a number of years, during which Sony's movie unit kept struggling, was undeniable.

Television's new ascendancy over film culturally and economically, after nearly a century during which the dynamic was the opposite, has caused tensions, anxiety, and resentments throughout the entertainment industry. That conflict was more acutely felt at Sony than at most of its competitors, though. It's one of only two studios, along with Warner Bros., where TV shows and movies are made in the same business unit and report to the same boss. At other entertainment companies, the film and television operations were sufficiently separate to keep their conflicts more theoretical. At Sony and Warner, they were a day-to-day reality.

No matter where you look in Hollywood, though, it's impossible to understand what has happened to movies in recent years without understanding what has happened to television at the same time.

WHERE THE REAL MONEY'S AT

For those who pay attention to fiscal reports, it has long been obvious that television is a better business than movies. Networks, particularly cable ones, are far and away the most profitable parts of media conglomerates like Disney, Viacom, and NBCUniversal. At Time Warner, a single network, HBO, regularly earns more profits than its entire Warner Bros. studio, despite generating about half as much revenue. HBO's profit margin, financial-speak for the percentage of revenue that becomes profit rather than covering costs, is about 33 percent. Throughout most of modern history, movie studios have considered it a good year when their profit margins exceed 10 percent.

Nonetheless, film has long been the higher-profile, more prestigious business, while TV, the workhorse of the bottom line, never got respect. As far back as 2009, before the age of "peak TV," television accounted for 32 percent of Warner's revenue but 50 percent of its profits, thanks to hits like *Friends, ER,* and *Two and a Half Men.* But to the outside world, it was mostly known as the home of popular movie brands: Batman, The Matrix, and Harry Potter.

Studios produce television, just as they do movies, but they don't actually air it. Instead, they sell it to networks or, more recently, to streaming services, which are looking for content. So while *The Big*

Bang Theory plays on CBS, it is Warner that earns hundreds of millions of dollars of profits from selling the show — including new episodes to CBS and repeats to TBS, where it airs twenty-two times per week.

Some networks, like HBO, produce many of their own programs. But Sony doesn't own any networks in the United States (save for a stake in GSN, formerly known as the Game Show Network), so all of its shows appear on channels owned by other companies. It gets little public acclaim for hits like *Outlander* on Starz or *Masters of Sex* on Showtime.

In fact, for many people Sony Pictures is probably more closely associated with *Zero Dark Thirty,* which Megan Ellison's Annapurna financed and the studio released for a fee in the tens of millions of dollars, than with *Wheel of Fortune* and *Jeopardy!,* which Sony actually owns. Those TV shows have made total profits of $2 billion and $1 billion, respectively, over their decades on the air. Even in Hollywood, most people would be surprised that by the mid-2010s, while film and TV revenues were roughly even at Sony, profits from the small-screen business were substantially higher.

But with the dawn of the golden age of television at the same time that movies devolved into franchises and then cinematic universes, TV's status within Hollywood started to evolve. It was no longer the boring workhorse that could be easily dismissed. It became the "new black baby," to borrow an unfortunate phrase from Amy Pascal. *Mister Robot, Game of Thrones, Legion, Orange Is the New Black,* and *Transparent* gave TV cultural prowess to match what it had long enjoyed financially.

These shows didn't just arise because TV executives had an epiphany and decided that they should stop producing crap, however. It was, as Michael Lynton has astutely observed in interviews, a product of technological change. When a television show could be watched only on the night and at the time a network scheduled it, and only if there was nothing else on that you wanted to watch, it was all but impossible to produce complicated serialized stories. With the exception of soap operas, nearly all shows were made to be enjoyed as a single hour or half-hour, with no context that couldn't be summarized briefly in a "previously on." Procedural series like *Law & Order* and *Murder, She Wrote,* in which one crime was solved per episode, ruled in drama, while sitcoms like *Home Improvement* and *Roseanne* regularly topped the ratings.

This setup was necessary because it was unreasonable to expect most people to watch every episode every week and because shows made most of their money in syndication, the repeats that air at 6 or 11 p.m. on weekdays or during the day on weekends, when someone flipping the channels might catch a random episode.

TECHNOLOGY LEADS TO GREAT TV

That situation began to change with the advent of whole seasons of a show offered on DVD. Early binge viewers in the early 2000s would skip entire seasons of *24* or *The Wire* when they aired and then catch up later, sometimes in just a few days. DVD sales, a new and fast-growing source of revenue for studios that produced TV, started to give them a reason to make shows that were better enjoyed several episodes at a time. TV viewing changed even more dramatically with the debut of TiVo, followed by the generic DVR, which by the late 2000s made it impossible for most people to miss a show they wanted to watch, and ridiculously easy to watch multiple episodes in a row.

To make themselves valuable to viewers, and thus charge cable and satellite companies like Comcast or DirecTV as much money as possible to carry them, cable channels started running engaging, original, attention-grabbing shows that took advantage of DVR viewing. This was the era when the occasional great show like *The Sopranos* or *Dexter* on premium cable networks like HBO and Showtime blossomed into dozens of terrific serialized shows for adults on seemingly every cable network, from AMC's *Mad Men* to FX's *The Americans* to Syfy's *Battlestar Galactica.*

Next came Netflix, which changed "binge watching" from an exercise in delayed gratitude, as you waited for the DVD or for episodes to pile up on a DVR, into the default mode for viewing. At first, subscribers binge-watched some of the hundreds of past seasons of network series for which Netflix had bought streaming rights. This altered the economics of serialized shows, which in the past had never made much money from repeats, because who wants to watch a random episode of *Mad Men* at 11 p.m.?

But on Netflix, where you can watch every episode in order and on demand, heavily serialized shows worked brilliantly. Netflix paid Lionsgate, the studio that produced *Mad Men* for AMC, $77 million, or $850,000 per episode. It wasn't long until Netflix and its competitor Amazon started making original series, designed from the ground up to be binged. With the exception of sports programming, the age of television as appointment viewing was now dead.

These technological and financial changes revolutionized television, but they had a huge impact on the movies too. As we've seen, mid-budget dramas and star vehicles were already severely challenged at the box office because the rise of foreign markets and the decline of DVD sales made franchises a more popular and profitable option. But now films had to compete for attention more directly with TV. Watching *The Wire* used to be a difficult endeavor. You had to make sure you were in front of your TV every Sunday night at the appointed time, and if you missed a single episode, you were screwed, unable to follow the story line for the rest of the season. It was much easier to hop in the car and head to the multiplex. But by the 2010s, spending time and money at the multiplex to see a movie that *might* be good was more burdensome and risky for most average adults than staying at home to binge a TV show they already knew they loved.

Hollywood executives, affluent and educated cultural connoisseurs themselves, knew firsthand what the problem was because they gorged on the surfeit of TV shows aimed directly at people just like them. When even Amy Pascal put down her phone and stopped talking about movies every Sunday night to watch *Homeland,* what are the odds the average person was going to leave the living room to see a big-screen drama?

Studio chiefs started openly fretting that higher-quality television was keeping viewers out of theaters and damaging their business, as evidenced by a 7 percent drop in ticket sales between 2009 and 2015 despite a 4 percent increase in the U.S. population. "All of us are looking for ways to make sure this isn't the time when theatrical moviegoing really does go away," the head of Universal Pictures ominously warned in 2011. It wasn't only their bottom line that was threatened. The better TV got, the harder it was for movie executives like Pascal to hold on to Hollywood's best talent. Better TV attracted better actors, writers, and directors.

One major movie star after another, frustrated by how difficult it was to get a great original film produced and lured by the growing respect for television, made the once unthinkable decision to move to the small screen: Meryl Streep and Robert De Niro and Dwayne Johnson and Halle Berry and Jonah Hill and Matthew McConaughey and Emma Stone, to name just a few.

"I'm getting sick of everyone's TV shows," Pascal fumed after learning that Tom Hardy, the star of *Dark Knight* and *Mad Max: Fury Road*, might be unavailable for a Sony movie because he was busy with *Taboo*, his series for FX.

LIFE OF A SALESMAN

Amy Pascal wasn't used to losing talent, audiences, or an entire genre of programming to a guy like Steve Mosko. She and Michael Lynton differed in temperament and which side of the brain they used to make decisions, but they were both sophisticated members of the cultural elite who never questioned that their careers would be all about utilizing their impressive intelligence and taste.

Mosko, by contrast, was a hard-working, glad-handing salesman with working-class roots, whose unlikely rise to the top was the result of his drive to do whatever it took to win at whatever it was he was doing. With his beefy, intimidating physique, slicked-back hair, and faddish rope bracelets, Mosko was unmistakably different from the stylish Pascal and the rumpled but refined Lynton. If Pascal's passion was making movies and Lynton's was solving problems with his intellect,

Mosko's was to never stop making the next sale, rising to the next level, and grabbing another brass ring. He was Hollywood's version of a super-successful Willy Loman, a man to whom attention must be paid. Which made sense, because television was for many decades Hollywood's more proletarian business. Its successful executives were dealmakers, not tastemakers.

Steve Mosko started his career about as far from Hollywood as one can be while still technically working in the entertainment business. Born in 1956, he grew up in a Baltimore suburb as the third of seven children to a father who worked in construction and a homemaker mother. He earned money in high school as a janitor and truck driver. After majoring in communications at the University of Delaware, Mosko decided to take a stab at the TV business, inspired by a high school visit to the set of the local teen game show, *It's Academic*. But with no relevant skills, experience, or connections, he found it wasn't an easy field to break into, especially from Baltimore. He ended up selling ads for the local AM radio station, WITH, which was, as he recalled, "so bad, the [general manager] said that if he turned his radio around and played it out his window so that people down on the street could hear it, our numbers would double."

But Mosko, who loved to gab and could charm anyone around a conference table, over drinks, or on the golf course, was a gifted salesman. Soon he jumped to television, becoming general manager of stations in Baltimore and Philadelphia. And then in 1992 he moved to Los Angeles to become an executive at Columbia TriStar Television Distribution, which had only a few years earlier been acquired by Sony, along with Columbia Pictures. Mosko was in Hollywood now, at a major studio, but in the most decidedly unglamorous part of it. Not only was he not involved in movies — he didn't even make TV. The closest he came to sexy was selling the cheesy syndicated series *V.I.P.*, starring Pamela Anderson, along with repeats of *Mad About You* and *Seinfeld*.

The super-salesman rose through the ranks once again and by 2001 was president of the unit now called Sony Pictures Television. It was not an auspicious time to be promoted, though. He got the job at the same time that Sony decided to stop producing for broadcast networks like ABC and Fox, which at that time aired almost all of the original programming on TV. Because the broadcast networks were increasingly making their own shows and squeezing outside suppliers like Sony, and because the Japanese parent company had never bought or launched a real network of its own, its production business was floundering. So Sony's U.S.A. chief, Howard Stringer, decided to shut it down, laying off more than fifty people. It seemed that Mosko's job would still be primarily made up of selling network repeats, game shows, and soap operas to independent stations like the ones he used to work at. He had risen to the top just as the coolest part of the job was taken away.

But the coolness would soon return, thanks to cable. As channels that had never aired original series before started looking for distinctive programming that would make them "must-watch" in the age of DVRs, Mosko discovered a new class of networks he could sell shows to. And because cable channels were still largely viewed as "beneath" the more established television studios like Warner Bros., Sony could afford to compete for their business on its smaller budget and with its lower stature. So Mosko, cautiously at first, returned his studio to the production game.

Sony made a groundbreaking police drama, *The Shield,* and the Glenn Close legal drama *Damages* for FX; it made *Huff,* about a psychiatrist with issues of his own, played by Hank Azaria, for Showtime. Then came the series that would change Mosko's career, Sony's fortunes, and the way audiences around the world viewed television: *Breaking Bad.*

THE $400 MILLION TV SHOW

When Sony's television executives first told Michael Lynton about their plans for *Breaking Bad,* there was a pause, like a record scratch in a movie, as the studio chairman looked up from his desk with a mystified look on his face. "That is the craziest and worst idea for a television show I have ever heard," he told Mosko's TV production chiefs Jamie Erlicht and Zack Van Amburg.

Without the benefit of hindsight, you certainly can't blame him. Who, anyone in their right mind would probably ask, would want to watch a show about a depressed, middle-aged chemistry teacher who decides to make money for his family before his imminent death from cancer by cooking crystal meth?

This was 2006, many years before *True Detective* and *Stranger Things.* Sony was just inching its way back into series production. Television was still primarily a broadcast network game, and offbeat, daring programs were virtually nonexistent. In a year when 24 won the Emmy for best drama series, it was pretty difficult to imagine that a show like *Breaking Bad* could draw an audience.

But AMC, a network formerly called American Movie Classics, which in the mid-2000s was known primarily for endless repeats of not-so-classic films like *Speed* and *Predator,* decided it needed to take some risks to remain relevant. So it rolled the dice with *Mad Men,* a cerebral show about advertising set in the 1960s, and on *Breaking Bad.*

Lynton rarely expressed any passion for individual movies or TV shows, but he also rarely stood in the way when his creative executives felt it. "Hey, guys, it's your career," he told Erlicht and Van Amburg. "If you really think this is that great, you should go ahead with it."

In reality, it wasn't a show Lynton had reason to give much thought to. Shot in New Mexico to take advantage of that state's generous production tax credit and made without visual effects or major stars, it wasn't particularly expensive to produce. And even if the Sony Pictures CEO's prediction was wrong and *Breaking Bad* was a success, it didn't seem there was a meaningful amount of money to be made. Sony executives initially projected it would earn a profit of $19 million over four seasons. Which was fine, because that was the cable television business in the mid-2000s. But it was insignificant compared to the profits from, say, a Spider-Man movie. Or so everyone assumed.

Breaking Bad wasn't initially a hit in the ratings, averaging fewer than two million viewers for each of its first four seasons, which aired between 2008 and 2012. But it was a critical favorite and beloved by the viewers who watched Bryan Cranston's slow transformation from Mr. Chips to Scarface. It was buzzy, beloved programming, which was exactly what AMC wanted, as it kept paying Sony for more episodes.

It was also exactly what Netflix wanted: a binge-worthy show that lots of people had initially missed on television and wanted to catch up on, to see what the big deal was. The streaming service paid around $800,000 per episode for the repeat rights to *Breaking Bad*. That was not only a financial boon to Sony; it also improved the ratings, as more people caught up and wanted to see the rest of the story of its main character, Walter White. The fifth and final season of *Breaking Bad* averaged 4.3 million viewers and the finale, in September 2013, drew an audience of more than ten million people. It beat all of the scripted shows on broadcast networks that night.

The buzz was now deafening, and *Breaking Bad*, widely hailed as one of the best television series ever, became a must-own, even in the age of waning DVD sales. It was a huge hit in home entertainment, both in the United States and around the world, where Netflix streaming and a Spanish-language remake had earned it a following.

In late 2013, when Sony launched the final season of *Breaking Bad* along with the complete series on DVD and Blu-ray, they sold 100,000 copies and 27,000 copies, respectively, in the first week alone — a big number that made it the only television series among the ten top-selling video discs in the United States. By 2014, *Breaking Bad*'s profit from DVD and Blu-ray sales alone had reached $215 million, a number that dwarfed all of Sony's other shows except the nine-season mega-hit *Seinfeld*.

Home entertainment was the biggest but not the only source of money that poured into Sony's coffers from *Breaking Bad*. Thanks to Netflix, AMC, and a consumer products business that brought in millions (Walter White–inspired cooking apron, anyone?), the total profits grew much bigger.

Even Amy Pascal was amazed.

"ML told me tonight thAt breaking bad is gonna make 300," she wrote to the chief financial officer of her motion picture group. "Jesus is that true[?]"

In fact it was low. By 2016, the ultimate profit from *Breaking Bad* was estimated at more than $400 million. That made it the second-most-profitable piece of entertainment content Sony had made in the twenty-first century, behind only the original *Spider-Man.*

CULTURE WAR

By the end of its run, *Breaking Bad* had become not just one of Sony's most profitable projects ever, but also one of its most prestigious. It won the Emmy Awards for best drama in 2013 and 2014, the same years Sony narrowly lost the best picture Oscars for *Zero Dark Thirty* and *American Hustle,* continuing a winless streak that dates back to 1987's *The Last Emperor.*

Television was now Sony's most important business culturally as well as financially, which made it even more awkward that the leaders of the studio had so little involvement in it. But as TV became so prestigious that the people Amy Pascal was close to in the film business started working in it, she began to dip her toes into the waters too. Rather than bring her closer to Mosko, though, it made things worse between them.

In 2013, Sony produced a pilot based on an idea of Pascal's. *The Vatican,* about power politics inside the Catholic Church, was going to air on the premium cable network Showtime. Pascal enlisted one of the biggest movie directors in Hollywood, Ridley Scott, to helm the pilot for less than his normal fee, and she went to Europe to visit the set, something Mosko himself rarely did.

The Sony TV chief scoffed, to anyone who would listen, at Pascal's efforts to get involved in television, predicting her lack of experience and lax approach to costs would fail her. And indeed, despite the involvement of Scott and the star Kyle Chandler, who was in high demand after *Friday Night Lights,* Showtime didn't pick up the pilot to the series — due largely to conflicts between the network and the A-list movie screenwriter Pascal had enlisted to script it, Paul Attanasio. For Pascal the experience was a "disappointment," the kind of thing she was used to in the unpredictable movie business. But TV executives were not so willing to brush aside the unsuccessful first effort of a woman they viewed as an arrogant interloper.

"Wow, is Pascal having an impact on television!" said NBC's president, Robert Greenblatt, in a sarcastic e-mail.

"Jeez zzz what did I ever do to mr.Greenblatt," she replied, after Mosko forwarded the note to her. "How awfully rude." In her view, she was only helping Mosko when and where her relationships proved useful, and she didn't deserve scorn for lending a hand. "I have never ever gotten in your business except to be helpful to you and you know that," she told him. "I resent that anyone would think otherwise."

Regardless of fault, the bonds between TV and movies at Sony were so poisoned that cooperation was nearly impossible. And any efforts by the film side to attempt rapprochement were viewed with hostility by those in TV, largely because these efforts arose only when television was gaining the upper hand in pop culture. "Oh, *now you* want to work with us?" Team Mosko seemed to be saying, as the wall between the two businesses rose even higher.

This was a shame, because Sony was well positioned to become a leader in a time of blurred lines. As projects that started life as movies, such as *Fargo, Westworld,* and *Lethal Weapon,* became hits on TV, having both businesses under the same roof could have benefited Sony. But little sharing of ideas occurred between executives in different divisions, and no directors or writers who worked on Sony movies flowed seamlessly to Sony television shows, or vice versa.

Even the direst of circumstances were viewed as a zero-sum game, in which one side could benefit at the other's expense. When the hack nearly brought down Sony Pictures in late 2014, executives in the television unit started whispering to the press that they were blameless victims of the motion picture group's incompetence in greenlighting *The Interview,* which apparently sparked the hackers' ire.

"With SPE's leadership standing by the movie as hackers' threats grew more brazen, the resentment among Sony's TV constituency also grew," read an article on the Hollywood industry website Deadline, ideas clearly planted by sources in Sony Television. "In private conversations, some of them express anger at being dragged into a controversy they had no part in."

Lynton was well aware of Mosko's unhappiness, in particular how much he chafed at having a rank lower than Pascal's. But status and titles mattered little to Lynton, and he never resolved the issue. "Steve Mosko is actively campaigning to be made [chief operating officer] of SPE," he complained to Nicole Seligman, president of Sony Corporation of America, a friend and a fellow Harvard graduate who was previously a high-powered attorney in Washington, D.C. "Steve/COO? Oy," she replied.

The cool, cerebral, and sophisticated CEO had little in common with the salesman-to-his-soul television chief, and though they didn't openly feud, they didn't hide their distaste for each other. It was common knowledge in Hollywood that Mosko didn't respect his boss. He was said to be particularly peeved after the investors' day in 2013, despite the fact that Lynton boasted about a "significant shift in emphasis" from film to TV. To Mosko, they were empty words that his boss didn't really believe. If he did, the TV chief figured, why did Lynton specifically praise Pascal as "one of the most diligent and effective executives in the business," with an "unparalleled creative vision," but when discussing television, tell the crowd only about what "we" had accomplished, with no mention of his top TV executive?

Lynton's words certainly weren't equitable. But Mosko's reaction was yet more proof that even on a day that couldn't have been more important to Sony Pictures, he viewed every word through a "movies vs. television" lens.

Some inside the company encouraged Lynton to push back against his ambitious TV chief. They noted that most of Sony Television's profits came from cable channels it owned in other countries, particularly the Hindi-language Sony Entertainment Television, a powerhouse in India. In fiscal 2012, Sony's networks generated $238 million in profits, compared to $220 million from television production.

Foreign networks were perhaps the only business in which Sony Pictures proved willing to make significant investments in the twenty-first century, and those investments paid off. Starting at just $12 million in fiscal 2002, network profits skyrocketed over the next decade. That business reported to Mosko, but he was not as intimately involved in it as with production and sales, which were more directly related to his background.

David Goldhill, the president of GSN, was a Lynton ally who warned him that "your tv guy is very political and spending a lot of time cultivating the press. Growth in tv profitability has been mostly india and gsn, and you're directly responsible for both. Credit going to the wrong place." He told Lynton, "You . . . shouldn't be positioned as the film guy forced to turn to his tv genius to bail him out. Insiders always know the truth but there's a reason political execs pull this shit." Lynton agreed with Goldhill, as evidenced in his short response, decipherable only to Hollywood insiders: "And Bruce Rosenblum tried this."

Bruce Rosenblum was proof that Sony's internal feuds and Steve Mosko's resentments weren't unique. For Lynton and others like him, Rosenblum was like a character in one of Aesop's fables, warning of the dangers of television executives whose egos grow too big. Rosenblum had been the head of television at Warner Bros. Between 2010 and 2013, he and the heads of film and home entertainment competed to succeed that studio's CEO as he prepared to retire. Most in Hollywood thought the job was Rosenblum's to lose, since TV was Warner's most profitable and consistently successful business. But like Mosko, Rosenblum was a salesman whose public politicking for the job put off his more refined boss, Time Warner's CEO, Jeff Bewkes. In the end, Bewkes chose the home-entertainment chief, Kevin Tsujihara, a fellow Stanford MBA. Rosenblum left soon after and didn't find another job as powerful as running Hollywood's largest television studio.

Rosenblum's fate more aptly foreshadowed Mosko's than anyone may have realized at the time. Although Sony wasn't yet looking for a new CEO, there was no question Mosko would be gunning for the position once it opened up. He had earned it, he and his supporters believed, and more important, television had earned it.

But when Mosko's contract expired in 2016, Lynton had a different fate in mind for him. As he had done with Pascal a year prior, he told his top television executive that it was time to go, and didn't renew his deal. But unlike his decision concerning Pascal, this one wasn't about performance. It was simply about a personality conflict. Lynton believed Mosko's ego had grown so large as to be more of a hindrance than a help to his studio.

And unlike Pascal, Mosko was not given a multi-million-dollar production deal to stay at Sony.

Isolated and atrophied cultures often change much more slowly than the world around them, and the way studios like Sony treated their television businesses was the perfect example. By 2016 it was undeniable that TV generated the bulk of Hollywood's profits and its cultural cachet, but still, Steve Mosko was never going to be treated with the same amount of respect as Amy Pascal. Yes, he was ambitious and conniving and a samurai master of corporate politics, but the same could be said for half the film executives in Hollywood who were never kicked to the curb so long as they remained successful.

Part of the reason the movie business was struggling throughout the 2010s was that its leaders couldn't adjust to the fact that they were no longer the center of the pop-culture universe, around which all other media orbited. Movies still had an important place, of course, but they no longer had the first and foremost claim on the best talent, the critics' acclaim, and the audiences' attention.

Success in film now would mean accepting its diminished position in the world and a carefully thought-out assessment of what movies can still do that television and streaming can't.

PART 2

Where Hollywood Is Headed

10

The Terminator

Disney, the Perfect Studio for the Franchise Age

FOR YEARS, DICK COOK had been trying to get his hands on one of Disney's animated classics.

The head of the Walt Disney Company's film studio for most of the 2000s wanted more branded movies to release, and what better source than his studio's beloved collection of cartoon hits, many of which seemed ripe for live-action remakes? But the men who ran Disney animation, Walt Disney's nephew Roy and then *Toy Story*'s director, John Lasseter, kept telling him to get lost. *Snow White* and *Pinocchio* and *Cinderella* were classics for a reason, and they would not let their legacy potentially be sullied by a live-action film they couldn't control.

After years of lobbying, Cook finally got his colleagues in animation to let him have a crack at one of Disney's less iconic films of yesteryear, *Alice in Wonderland*. Well known but never listed among the studio's greats, it was a low-risk way to let the live-action studio, which was struggling to find an identity, try something new with something old. *Alice,* directed by Tim Burton and released in 2010, succeeded beyond anyone's expectations or imagination, grossing $1 billion globally. And it kicked off a wave of animation remakes, all hugely successful, that has come to define Disney's live-action movie brand.

It also provided the final piece of a puzzle that no one previously thought could be found: how can a Hollywood studio be consistently hugely profitable? For more than a century, moviemaking has been seen as a business of inevitable highs and lows; good years have a few more hits than misses, and bad years have a few more misses than hits. But Disney proved that it's possible to create release slates on which almost every movie is a hit, generating profits beyond anything seen in Hollywood before. It has done that with one word: *branding*. Nearly all of Disney's films fit into a narrowly defined brand that supports big-budget franchises, such as Marvel superheroes, Star Wars space adventures, Pixar and Disney animated family films, or live-action remakes of animated classics.

If Sony Pictures is the textbook example of a movie studio suited to the early 2000s, Disney is the exemplar of our modern franchise film era.

Its dominance is hard to overstate. Beginning in 2013, Disney has ranked number one or number two at the box office every year, despite consistently releasing fewer movies than the other five major studios. Of the forty highest-grossing films released between 2013 and 2016, eighteen came from Disney. Its profit margins over that period sky-rocketed, from the roughly 10 percent other movie studios maxed out at, to nearly 30 percent, a previously unimaginable high.

It was easy for competitors to snipe that anyone could dominate the movie business when they were releasing the third Captain America, a sequel to *Finding Nemo,* or the first new Star Wars movie in a generation. But the consistency of Disney's success, from *Frozen* to *Iron Man 3* to *Maleficent* to *Guardians of the Galaxy* to *Inside Out, Rogue One,* and *Beauty and the Beast,* is unprecedented in modern movie history. In a single two-month span in 2016, it released three blockbuster hits, the animated *Zootopia,* the live-action remake of *The Jungle Book,* and the Marvel superhero blowout *Captain America: Civil War.* Together, they grossed $3.1 billion. That's more than every Sony release, combined, grossed in 2014, 2015, or 2016.

In Hollywood today, the simple truth is that there are two types of movie studios: Disney, and those that wish they were Disney.

Understanding why studios have turned so aggressively toward franchises, sequels, and superheroes and away from originality, risks, and mid-budget dramas takes more than an appreciation for the financial pressures faced by executives like Michael Lynton and Amy Pascal. Just as Olympic swimmers can't help but pace themselves against Michael Phelps, Sony and its competitors have for years been jealous of and frustrated by Disney. Hollywood is a herd industry. Its executives are constantly looking out the side window or at the rearview mirror and asking, "Why aren't we doing *that*?"

For those peering at Disney, *that* means slashing the number of movies made per year by two-thirds. It also means largely abandoning any type of film that costs less than $100 million, is based on an original idea, or appeals to any group smaller than all the moviegoers around the globe.

Disney doesn't make dramas for adults. It doesn't make thrillers. It doesn't make romantic comedies. It doesn't make bawdy comedies. It doesn't make horror movies. It doesn't make star vehicles. It doesn't adapt novels. It doesn't buy original scripts. It doesn't buy anything at film festivals. It doesn't make anything political or controversial. It doesn't make anything with an R-rating. It doesn't give award-winning directors like Alfonso Cuarón or Christopher Nolan wide latitude to pursue their visions.

Though Disney still has flops, it has fewer than any other studio — fewer than anyone ever dreamed was possible in a business that has for decades seen more failures than successes and has been compared to riding a roller coaster. Disney has, in short, taken a huge chunk of the risk out of a risky business.

Many in Hollywood view Disney as a soulless, creativity-killing machine that treats motion pictures like toothpaste and leaves no room for the next great talent, the next great idea, or the belief that films have any meaning beyond their contribution to the bottom line. By contrast, investors and MBAs are thrilled that Disney has figured out how to make more money, more consistently, from the film business than anyone ever has before. But actually, Disney isn't in the movie business, at least as we previously understood it. It's in the Disney brands business. Movies are meant to serve those brands. Not the other way around.

Even some Disney executives admit in private that they feel more creatively limited in their jobs than they imagined possible when starting careers in Hollywood. But, as evidenced by box-office returns, Disney is undeniably giving people what they want. It's also following the example of one of the men its CEO, Bob Iger, admired most in the world: Apple's cofounder, Steve Jobs. Apple makes very few products, focuses obsessively on quality and detail, and once it launches something that consumers love, milks it endlessly. People wondering why there's a new Star Wars movie every year could easily ask the same question about the modestly updated iPhone that launches each and every fall.

Disney approaches movies much like Apple approaches consumer products. Nobody blames Apple for not coming out with a groundbreaking new gadget every year, and nobody blames it for coming out with new versions of its smartphone and tablet until consumers get sick of them. Microsoft for years tried being the "everything for everybody" company, and that didn't work out well. So if Disney has abandoned whole categories of films that used to be part of every studio's slates and certain people bemoan the loss, well, that's simply not its problem.

Iger, himself a fan of such decidedly non-Disney fare as *Spotlight,* winner of the Oscar for best picture in 2016, has a clear-eyed view of what his company is doing. "There's a difference between being a moviegoer," he said in his office, in late 2016, "and running a really successful movie business."

JUST ANOTHER STUDIO

For most of the 2000s, Disney looked similar to any other studio. Still partly inspired by a 1991 memo from Jeffrey Katzenberg, then its studio chairman, to focus largely on "singles and doubles," it released as many as thirty films per year, in all genres, for all audience groups, and at all budget levels. Only occasionally did it swing for the fences with a would-be tentpole, like the computer-animated *Dinosaur* of 2000 and the World War II adventure film *Pearl Harbor* of 2001, which was directed by Michael Bay and starred Ben Affleck.

Some years it was number one at the box office and some years it was number six, but there was little remarkable or special about Disney's studio. In fact, some Disney executives admired the more consistent success of competitors like Sony, which under Amy Pascal seemed to simply do a better job of picking hit movies at a time when that was the most important skill.

The only thing that really made Disney distinct was its animation studio. But this was not the era of *Snow White* or *Sleeping Beauty* or even 1990s hits like *The Lion King*. Disney Animation had fallen on hard times, and the 2000s were filled with forgettable duds such as *Treasure Planet, The Emperor's New Groove,* and *Home on the Range.*

Perhaps its biggest asset, which in hindsight seems remarkably underutilized, was the studio's brand name. Universal and Paramount didn't mean anything to consumers, but Disney signaled that a film would be kid-safe and family-friendly. However, only about half of Disney's releases in the early 2000s placed the company's name above the title. And most of those were lower-budget, goofy fare, like Tim Allen's Santa Clause series, Anne Hathaway's *The Princess Diaries,* or inspirational sports films like *Remember the Titans.* Not safe for anybody over thirteen who wasn't dragged in by a kid, in other words.

Much of the rest of the studio's output came from the Touchstone label. Launched in 1984 with the mermaid romantic comedy *Splash,* Touchstone encompassed pretty much any and every type of film not appropriate to be labeled as Disney. Action movies produced by Jerry Bruckheimer, such as *Armageddon* and *Con Air,* were Touchstone movies, as were *Pretty Woman,* the Coen brothers' *O Brother, Where Art Thou?,* Wes Anderson's *The Royal Tenenbaums,* the Jodie Foster thriller *Flightplan,* and an adaptation of the beloved sci-fi/comedy book *The Hitchhiker's Guide to the Galaxy.*

These are all films, notably, that the Disney of today would never release.

Even Tim Burton's *The Nightmare Before Christmas,* now consid-

ered a Disney animated classic, was released under the Touchstone label in 1993 because it was considered too scary to use the parent company's brand name.

The remaining films came from Miramax, the lower-budget "indie"
label run by the brothers Harvey and Bob Weinstein. Disney bought
Miramax in 1993, at the height of the mania surrounding hits pouring
out of the Sundance Film Festival. Miramax was for years a reliable
source of Academy Award winners like *Shakespeare in Love* and movies that, when made cheaply, could be hugely profitable, like *Good Will
Hunting* and *Pulp Fiction*. But by the 2000s, Miramax was venturing
into more expensive territory and faced big losses on movies that failed
to deliver the necessary returns, such as Martin Scorsese's historical
epic *Gangs of New York* and the Ben Affleck thriller *Reindeer Games.*

Still, it was unimaginable that Disney would ever get out of the
Touchstone and Miramax businesses. This was an era when most films
made money, thanks to booming DVD sales, which meant that big and
broad slates made sense. And at a time when movie stars were critical
to box-office success, you could hardly expect them all to want to make
Disney-branded kiddie fare. Touchstone films gave Disney's slate
"breadth and depth," the studio chairman Dick Cook said, in 2004.
"You can't eat vanilla ice cream every day. You still want chocolate and
strawberry too."

A takeover by vanilla began with a movie that initially seemed the
opposite of innovative, evolutionary, or even interesting. *Pirates of the
Caribbean* was one of a pair of films Disney made in the early 2000s
with the aim of exploiting corporate synergy between popular theme-
park attractions and movies. The other was *The Haunted Mansion.*
Walt Disney Studios' chairman, Dick Cook, had started his career in
Disney's theme parks and pushed the idea. But most people at the
company thought *The Haunted Mansion,* which starred Eddie Murphy,
had more of the ingredients of a mainstream hit.

The other film was a riskier endeavor. The pirate genre had been
dead since the 1995 flop *Cutthroat Island,* and few thought an adaptation of a parks attraction, featuring singing audio-animatronic figures, was likely to revive it. And in the lead role was Johnny Depp,

best known for offbeat fare such as *Chocolat* and *What's Eating Gilbert Grape.* He hadn't yet achieved movie-star status in America, let alone around the world. Executives throughout the company expressed their concern to Cook, who had just taken over the studio as *Pirates* got going in 2002. Even the CEO, Michael Eisner, sent him e-mails questioning whether making the film was a good idea.

But the affable Cook, who began his career operating steam engines and monorails at Disneyland in 1970, firmly believed he knew what audiences wanted from the company. He was prepared to expand the scope of Disney-branded films with *Pirates,* which is why he gave the project to Bruckheimer, best known for PG-13 and R-rated action movies with plenty of sex and violence, to produce.

Still, nobody was prepared for just how different *Pirates of the Caribbean: The Curse of the Black Pearl* turned out to be.

Disney's president of production, Nina Jacobson, told Bruckheimer and the director, Gore Verbinski, to "try very hard to get the PG," urging them to "steer clear of things like language, sex, and significant amounts of blood" that would earn a PG-13. But as she and other executives saw footage of intense and sometimes scary violence, including stabbings, they started to realize a PG rating was unlikely. As they saw more and more of Depp's performance, they also realized it would be anything but bland, vanilla fare. Rather than play a traditional yo-ho-ho, swashbuckling pirate, he made his villain, Jack Sparrow, into a fey, seemingly drunk blowhard wearing mascara and eyeliner — the persona was based on the actor's rock-and-roll idol, Keith Richards. The raw footage making its way back to Disney headquarters was "very, very out there" compared to what Jacobson and others had been expecting.

Many on the Disney lot were concerned about the movie, but the company didn't exercise nearly as much hands-on control over its films then as it does today. That was partly because it had several dozen movies on its slate at a time and partly because A-list talent had more power at the box office then, and thus more leverage in the creative process. By naming Bruckheimer producer, Disney had essentially made him CEO of *Pirates of the Caribbean* and was at best his partner and certainly not his boss (unless they wanted to go through the costly and embarrassing process of shutting down the production). If Bruckheimer and his hand-picked director and star were making a violent, creatively edgy *Pirates* movie, Disney would have to find a way to live with it.

Making it a Touchstone release was a possibility, but that was complicated by the fact that *Pirates* was an attraction at a Disney-branded theme park. And internally, some executives were starting to feel that the Disney brand name needed to expand to include PG-13, a rating used for more and more of the most successful films of that era, like *Lord of the Rings* and *Spider-Man*. Many families felt fine about allowing children as young as seven or eight to see them. And so Cook was convinced. If Disney theme parks could have all sorts of different attractions, he figured, perhaps the Disney film label could too. The PG-13 rating on *Pirates,* he said, was akin to the height restrictions and health warnings on rides like Space Mountain and the Tower of Terror.

Pirates of the Caribbean: The Curse of the Black Pearl was a massive hit in 2003. Its combination of action, comedy, and a mesmerizing performance by Depp, which earned him an Academy Award nomination, pulled in $654 million of ticket sales worldwide. It was not only the number four movie of the year. It was Disney's highest-grossing live-action film ever, under its own label or Touchstone's.

For Disney executives, it was like a river had parted. Finally they could get the benefit of their company's brand name — signaling to families that it was a safe and wholesome film, in line with the values of Walt Disney himself — without having to sacrifice the action, adventure, and interesting performances that were the hallmarks of most successful movies in the 2000s.

Cook still had some rules for Disney-branded movies: no cursing, no drugs, no sex, and no blood. But fantastical action and adventure now had a green light. Which meant that teenagers, young adults, and even middle-aged people who wanted to enjoy the movies they took their kids to could now consider releases from Walt Disney Pictures. For the first time, Disney live-action films could appeal to everyone.

Not long after that, studio executives were screening an early cut of

National Treasure, a Bruckheimer-produced adventure movie starring Nicolas Cage as a code-breaker seeking a pile of loot, the location of which is hidden in the Declaration of Independence. *National Treasure* was intended to be a Touchstone release. But during the screening, with *Pirates* on his mind, the studio's marketing president, Oren Aviv, leaned over to Cook and asked, "Is there any reason this can't be a Disney movie?"

Cook thought for about five seconds. "Nope," he replied.

Bruckheimer had to be convinced that making it a Disney movie wouldn't necessitate watering down the movie or alienating the young adults who loved Cage's action flicks. But he was won over and *National Treasure* was another huge hit, grossing $348 million and becoming the second-highest-grossing live-action film ever under the Disney label, behind only *Pirates.*

All of a sudden the Disney brand was thriving, regularly outperforming Touchstone at the box office and in terms of profitability. Which led the company's new CEO in 2005 to ask a simple question: why don't we make more of what works and less of everything else?

"AN AWFUL BUSINESS"

Bob Iger became CEO of the Walt Disney Company in October 2005, after several years of corporate drama and weakened financial results that resulted in the departure of his predecessor, Eisner. Many dismissed Iger, a former TV weatherman, as a lightweight, an empty suit who had reached the top not because he was most qualified, but because he was the least controversial among the company's top executives — the lowest common denominator.

Certainly, among those who ran Disney's movie business, Iger wasn't taken too seriously. Unlike Eisner, who in 1984 came from Paramount Pictures, Iger had no experience in film. He was purely a TV guy who had come to Disney in 1996 when it purchased the ABC network, where he was president.

But Iger, who had a bachelor's degree in television and radio from

Ithaca College but talked and thought like an MBA, was smarter and more ambitious than many gave him credit for. He decided right away to try to smooth over the corporate feuds that had festered under Eisner and to improve the company's weak bottom line of the past few years. Both missions ended up having a dramatic impact on the movies Disney made.

On the first front, Iger made it his priority to heal Disney's rift with Pixar Animation Studios, the hugely successful company behind *Toy Story, Finding Nemo,* and *Monsters, Inc.* Though Pixar was an independent company in the San Francisco Bay Area, Disney marketed and released all of its movies under a multi-year deal, according to which the two companies equally split all costs and profits.

Eisner and the chief of Pixar, Steve Jobs (who ran the animation studio simultaneously with running Apple), were both men of monumental egos. Rather than try to work together as that old deal was wrapping up near the end of Eisner's tenure, they took to sniping at each other in the press about which side needed the other more.

Iger, a technology nut, had great admiration for what Jobs had accomplished since taking over Apple for the second time in the late 1990s and then revolutionizing the music business with the iPod and iTunes. He was also more clear-eyed than his predecessor about the need to revive Disney's own struggling animation unit. Iger had no prior involvement in it and thus no personal stake in how it was perceived. And so he started a rapprochement soon after becoming CEO by making Disney the first company to sell movies and TV shows to be watched on Apple's new video iPod. And then, in January 2006, he bought Pixar for $7.4 billion, bringing the world's most respected animation studio into his company and also tasking its creative heads, John Lasseter and Ed Catmull, with fixing Walt Disney Animation Studios, which had been lagging behind Pixar throughout the 2000s.

It turned out to be a smart deal. Disney benefited from the future success of *Cars, Toy Story 3,* and *Up,* not just at the box office, but also in its consumer products and theme-park businesses. And though it took several years, Catmull and Lasseter eventually did turn around Walt Disney Animation Studios by applying the Pixar strategy of having directors honestly critique one another's ideas and reworking films in production as many times and for as long as necessary to make them excellent. By the mid-2010s, Disney Animation was regularly outperforming Pixar, with successes like *Frozen* and *Zootopia*.

But the company could release only one or two animated movies per year. That wouldn't fundamentally turn around its studio, which when Iger took over was coming off a disastrous year. It had made a profit of only $207 million on revenue of $7.6 billion — a margin of less than 3 percent. Among the reasons for the weak performance were two Touchstone flops: *A Lot Like Love,* a romantic comedy with Ashton Kutcher, and director Wes Anderson's *The Life Aquatic with Steve Zissou.*

In fact, Walt Disney Studios had posted weak results in 2001 and 2002 as well. In 2003 and 2004, its margins of 8 percent were solid for the movie industry, but hardly impressive to anyone who wasn't used to the generally poor return on investment that movies had long offered. The television business that Iger came from, for example, had a profit margin of about 20 percent at the time.

Soon after taking over, Iger began to analyze Disney's businesses one by one, on the basis of "return on invested capital," the profit made on every dollar invested. There were troubles throughout the company, but the movie studio stood out the most. And within the studio, it was Touchstone and Miramax that returned the lowest profits, with average margins in the low single digits. "That's an awful business. Awful," Iger concluded. The solution, he believed, was obvious. Disney-branded movies consistently returned the biggest profits, particularly in the wake of *Pirates of the Caribbean* and *National Treasure.* And so he started asking how quickly his studio could pump up production of Walt Disney Pictures films and abandon everything else.

But Iger didn't parachute in and start giving orders at the studio. Others in the movie business, including Disney veterans, warned him that such changes would be viewed suspiciously, especially coming from an outsider. They asked how the company would support its worldwide distribution infrastructure if it slashed the number of pictures that came out each year. Who among Hollywood's A-list stars and directors would want to make "Disney" movies, which despite *Pirates* and *National Treasure* still carried a stigma as bland kiddie fare, instead of the interesting, more mature movies that Touchstone had long specialized in? And what kind of signal would it send to the artistic community if Disney pulled out of Miramax and stopped making the kind of indie films that wowed critics and won awards?

The longer a person had worked in the movie business, the more likely he or she would tell Iger that his idea couldn't work. It never had worked. Studios released lots of different movies for lots of different people. At the time, that's what the market dictated. Most insiders could not imagine that this would change. Some also questioned whether Iger's plan to make fewer movies, all of them big ones, was wise. Katzenberg's 1991 memo had warned of the dangers of big bets that, when they failed, could derail the financial performance of the entire studio in a given year. A broader, more diverse slate was designed to help balance out the bottom line when some films flopped.

But with international markets starting to grow in importance and the video iPod signaling that home viewing on digital devices would soon take off, Iger correctly surmised that big "event" movies were needed to draw people into theaters. He loved the 2006 hit *Little Miss Sunshine,* which Miramax's competitor Fox Searchlight bought at Sundance, but he wondered how many years longer people would go to theaters to see that type of film, rather than wait to watch it at home. Iger surmised that major studio movies would have to become "must see" offerings, and Disney's job was to make them so, even if it was difficult and even if some of those big swings lost a lot of money along the way. This conclusion matched the results of research that Cook and his team of executives were doing at about the same time. They found that movies costing more than $100 million to make were less risky than those with smaller budgets — a counterintuitive conclusion indeed.

Iger had the support of his board of directors, who wanted higher and more consistent profits from the movie studio. He also had the backing of other divisions of the company that wanted the kind of popular intellectual property that Disney-branded movies provided. *Pearl*

Harbor didn't sell toys, and there was never going to be a *Pretty Woman* attraction at Disneyland. But *Pirates of the Caribbean* and *National Treasure* and, later, the princess film *Enchanted* were brands the rest of the company could use, as were most of the studio's animated features.

Nonetheless, the changes weren't quick. Due to the long period of time it takes to develop scripts and then shoot and edit a film, Iger couldn't really force changes on Disney's release slate until 2008 at the earliest. Rather than give notes on scripts and footage or other meddling, Iger was more strategic, trying to effect change via intermittent but ground-shaking strategic moves, such as the Pixar acquisition.

Miramax was already in the midst of a revolution when Iger took over. The Weinstein Brothers had been feuding for years with Eisner and Cook over how much money they were allowed to spend making movies or on business investments, as well as creative latitude. One of the biggest points of conflict came in 2004, when Disney blocked Miramax from releasing the director Michael Moore's controversial *Fahrenheit 9/11*, about the current president, George W. Bush, before the election. It was released instead by Miramax's competitor Lionsgate and grossed a staggering $119 million, still the record for a documentary.

Bob and Harvey Weinstein left Miramax in March 2005. Iger was by that time CEO-designate, and he and the board of directors pushed to shut down Miramax, figuring the money would be better spent on Disney tentpoles that could potentially create a windfall. The art-house division in its best recent years had eked out only a small profit. But Cook fought adamantly to save Miramax. Like many in Hollywood, he disagreed with Iger's view that a film studio should be run solely to maximize the return on investment. He thought benefits that couldn't be measured on a balance sheet were important to the long-term vitality of a studio and its industry, such as fostering creative relationships, finding new talent, and winning awards.

Miramax brought Disney all of that, he argued, and shutting it down would send a distressing signal to Hollywood and mature moviegoers that the company didn't care about them. And so he and corporate management agreed on a compromise. A veteran studio executive named Daniel Battsek was put in charge of a severely slimmed-down

Miramax. He had only about $300 million to spend annually on six to eight movies, instead of the more than $600 million that the Weinsteins used to make close to twenty films a year.

As many in Hollywood suspected, though, the mini-Miramax was just an evolutionary step. Despite winning the best picture Oscar for 2007's *No Country for Old Men,* Miramax enjoyed few hits under Battsek and became increasingly out of place in Iger's franchise-focused Disney empire. Cook had to fight each and every year to save it from Iger and the board's desire to make it disappear. Not until 2009 did Iger finally put Miramax on the auction block, eventually selling it to a group of investors for $663 million.

Phasing out Touchstone took time as well. The label had a backlog of adult movies in the works, and studio executives didn't want to announce that they were killing their brand for original and more mature pictures until they had perfected a new slate focused on Disney-branded movies. "There was still some stigma for Disney live-action movies, and if you just made an announcement that's all we were doing, agents and talent managers might not bring us cool projects anymore," said one executive who worked for the studio at the time.

Slowly but surely, however, Disney made fewer Touchstone movies. It released seven under the label in 2005 and 2006, but just three or four in 2008, 2009, and 2010. By 2011, Disney had stopped making Touchstone movies. Its last one was *You Again,* a forgettable romantic comedy starring Kristen Bell and Sigourney Weaver that grossed a weak $32 million. Disney kept the Touchstone label alive for the next few years only as part of a deal to release movies made and fully financed by Steven Spielberg's DreamWorks Pictures, such as the hits *Lincoln* and *The Help.* But DreamWorks was in the mid-budget movie business and, unsurprisingly, most of its productions flopped, including the Vince Vaughn comedy *Delivery Man* and the video-game adaptation *Need for Speed.* By 2016, nearly defunct, DreamWorks raised new money to stay alive and moved to Universal Pictures. Its departure from Disney marked the official and final end of Touchstone, a death barely noticed in Hollywood or elsewhere.

As Miramax and Touchstone withered, Disney's release slate shrank year by year, just as Iger had believed was essential. The studio released thirty movies in 2005, then twenty-one in 2007 and 2008, and just ten by 2013 — a direct contrast to the old strategy of Katzenberg and so many others in Hollywood, which was to flood the market and count on a few major hits emerging from the morass. Iger believed that more successes would come from more refined concentration. "When you're releasing a new film every two weeks, no wonder the returns are so low, because there's no focus," Iger observed.

Culling the slate was one thing, but as Iger and Disney learned the hard way over the next few years, building it back up with hits was a more challenging task. Until 2012, in fact, Disney's slate was not noticeably better on a consistent basis, save for the addition of Pixar, which released successes like *Cars, Wall-E,* and *Toy Story 3* every year.

Iger and Cook still believed the Disney live-action label was key to powering better returns. Sequels to *Pirates* in 2006 and 2007 were indeed huge hits. However, much like Sony's *Spider-Man 3,* they displeased many fans and left the series in a creative funk.

Apart from those two movies, the Disney live-action label was largely a mess for nearly a decade after Iger took over. Under the CEO's mantra of fewer, bigger movies, the studio spent well over $100 million each on films stuffed with visual effects and meant to appeal to a broad array of moviegoers around the world. Many came with well-known titles, whether from Disney's rich lore or elsewhere, and carried a PG-13 rating. All were designed to spawn franchises. They were, in other words, attempts to replicate the success of *Pirates of the Caribbean.* And nearly all of them failed.

Some were merely disappointments that didn't match the studio's lofty ambitions. Those included *Tron: Legacy,* an updated version of Disney's 1982 cult classic; *G-Force,* Jerry Bruckheimer's team of special agent rodents; and *Prince of Persia,* starring Jake Gyllenhaal in an adaptation of the hit video games.

More Disney live-action movies in this period, however, were outright disasters that lost hundreds of millions. Among the mega-flops were *Mars Needs Moms,* a motion-captured adaptation of a best-selling children's book; *John Carter,* the Pixar director Andrew Stanton's take on the classic science-fiction stories; *The Lone Ranger,* in which Bruck-heimer and Depp attempted to update the hero of the Old West; and *Tomorrowland,* a preachy science-fiction story starring George Cloo-ney, which shared a name with an area in Disney theme parks.

"All of the characteristics of the movies as Disney tentpoles were right, but they just weren't good enough," Iger told me about the string of disappointments. "What we learned is we have to be more selective in what we make and we have to demand more perfection." Together, those flops signaled that although Disney under Iger knew what it wanted to do with its movie business, it was still struggling to figure out *how* to do it.

In 2009, the CEO attempted to shock the system with another big move. Firing Dick Cook caused jaws to hit the floor throughout Hol-lywood. After thirty-eight years at the company and seven atop its stu-dio, Cook was one of the most beloved personalities at Disney, ad-mired by his staff and the entire entertainment industry.

The ostensible reason for the ouster was that Cook ran the studio too much like a silo, refusing to cooperate with other divisions as much as the CEO wanted. Four days before he was fired, in fact, Cook had refused to tell corporate executives that at the company's D23 conven-tion (Disney's version of Comic-Con), he was planning to bring out Depp, Miley Cyrus, and the director Tim Burton to wow fans.

But top executives also believed Cook was fundamentally part of the old guard. Yes, he was popular with employees and creative talent like Depp. But the suits who ran the Walt Disney Company believed he just wasn't the right person to make the radical changes Iger wanted to see in the movie business. It was a classic clash between someone who believed he was a staunch defender of a brand and the bottom-line-focused bosses who believed success could be measured entirely in numbers.

And so the fifty-nine-year-old Cook was pushed aside and replaced with the slicker, more corporate-friendly head of the Disney Channel, Rich Ross. Ross's two-and-a-half-year tenure atop Walt Disney Stu-dios was a disaster — a sign that although Iger had a clear strategic vision for where the movie business needed to go, he still wasn't sure how to get there. It was one thing for a "disruptor" like Iger to shake up the movie studio from afar, and quite another to put such a person in charge. Ross replaced most of the studio's top executives and in short order soured relationships with movie theaters, producers, and others. It was too much change, too fast.

The studio's finances would have been hit hard by this too, if not for Iger's next ground-shaking move: his $4 billion acquisition of Marvel in 2009.

Executives at the studio had long thought Marvel would be a great fit. Aware that Disney was leading the way in an age when branding mattered more for movies, they held blue-sky discussions about what assets they would love to add to their portfolio, if feasibility wasn't an issue. At one such meeting in the mid-2000s, held in the seventy-year-old "Hyperion bungalow" on the lot, a group of thirty to forty people threw out a handful of names, including Marvel, DC Comics, and Lucasfilm, the owner of Star Wars. It was a pie-in-the-sky exercise. Or so they thought.

When Iger surprised the industry, and most people at his own company, by purchasing Marvel, he also brought much-needed relief to its movie business. Beginning in 2012, all of Marvel Studios' big-budget superhero pictures would be released by Disney, taking up two slots per year on its slimmed-down slate. That meant Ross and his team would have to conjure up two fewer Disney-branded films each year.

The first Marvel movie released by Disney was *The Avengers,* which grossed $1.5 billion and offered a preview of just how successful the new division would be.

A COLLECTION OF BRANDS

Iger's original vision had been to focus his movie studio on one brand: Disney. But now it was home to several brands, including Pixar, Disney Animation, Marvel, and the live-action business. The job of the studio chairman was no longer to be an agent of change, but a parental figure who could keep the different divisions, with their distinct personalities, happy and working together harmoniously.

Rich Ross was certainly not the man for that job, and amid increasing dissatisfaction at the studio, Iger fired him in 2012. His replacement was Alan Horn, a longtime president of Warner Bros. who was much more similar to Cook than Ross in gravitas, knowledge, and the respect he garnered throughout Hollywood. With nothing at stake as to how the studio used to be run, he was fully onboard with Iger's vision. This included fixing the Disney live-action label.

A hint of how to do that had emerged at the beginning of Ross's tenure, with a movie greenlit near the end of Cook's: *Alice in Wonderland*. People inside and outside the company weren't sure if it had succeeded so spectacularly because it starred Depp, because of Burton's unique style, or because it was the first major digital 3D film after *Avatar* had made the technology popular worldwide.

Disney executives suspected something else: perhaps, due to the company's legacy of animated hits based on them, fairy tales were a unique Disney asset. Perhaps *Alice in Wonderland* succeeded in large part because in people's minds the title perfectly matched the name of the company releasing the film. That theory was put to the test with another adaptation, one that wouldn't raise too many eyebrows among defenders of the animated tradition because it offered an alternative take on a classic tale.

Maleficent told the story of Sleeping Beauty through the eyes of its villain, played by Angelina Jolie and given a new and sympathetic backstory. It was a troubled production, with cost overruns, reshoots, and extensive changes in the editing room. The end result was still muddled, and many inside the company figured it would bomb. But the 2014 release was a huge success, overcoming bad reviews to gross $759 million.

Finally, after so many years of flops and missteps in an attempt to figure out what made for a successful Disney live-action movie and how to replicate the success of *Pirates of the Caribbean,* the company had an answer: comb through its library of animated fairy tales and start remaking them, with a modest twist to update them for modern sensibilities.

It couldn't be that simple, could it?

But it was. *Cinderella,* which retold the story of the peasant turned princess while making her less of a passive participant in her own life, was a hit in 2015, grossing $543 million. *The Jungle Book,* which dropped the original's unsettling colonialist themes, was a blockbuster in 2016, with $967 million. *Beauty and the Beast,* which added a new backstory and songs, was a juggernaut in 2017, outgrossing *Alice* with $1.26 billion. Executives were now confident that, just like Marvel, they had a brand that couldn't miss. Upcoming remakes — *Mulan, Dumbo, The Lion King* — all seemed like surefire hits.

By then, Disney also had bought yet another brand once just a dream for employees brainstorming in a bungalow: Star Wars. Iger's $4 billion purchase of Lucasfilm in 2012 had been his second acquisition in three years that shocked Hollywood. Even executives at 20th Century Fox, which had released all six Star Wars movies for Lucas, didn't know it was coming. But Disney — with its theme parks, consumer products business, and successful track record of integrating Pixar and Marvel — had advantages no competitor could match.

The purchase price had been based on Disney's assumptions about how much money it could make releasing three new Star Wars sequels (episodes VII, VIII, and IX) in 2015, 2017, and 2019; Lucas had begun work on them. Soon after the sale, however, the company realized it had more than enough ideas to support the release of Star Wars movies annually and to create a sci-fi cinematic universe much like the one that was raking in profits for Marvel. And so while 2015's episode VII, titled *The Force Awakens,* was a blockbuster, with ticket sales of more than $2 billion, 2016's spinoff *Rogue One* was also a huge hit, grossing more than $1 billion and proving you really couldn't go wrong when a film had "Star Wars" in the title.

Under Horn, Disney's studio was a collection of production houses, each with a specialty and each overseen by a formerly independent producer who now did that job inside the company. Feige made the Marvel superhero films, Lasseter ran animation, Kathy Kennedy was in charge of Lucasfilm's Star Wars stable, and Sean Bailey made the Disney live-action fairy tales. All of them did their own thing, while Horn's centralized marketing and distribution team put the productions into theaters and maximized their profits.

Combined, the results were astronomical. Disney's motion-picture profit margin reached 21 percent in fiscal 2014, 24 percent in 2015, and 29 percent in 2016. Bob Iger was hailed on Wall Street as a hero. "The biggest change," he told me in his typically blunt style, "is that people now look at movies like a real business."

Other studios tried to follow suit. Warner not only finally gave its DC superheroes, like Batman and Wonder Woman, their own cinematic universe, but tried to get into the animation remake business itself, since the fairy tales on which Disney had based many of its animated classics were in the public domain and thus fair game.

But without the Disney brand, fairy-tale movies proved far less appealing to audiences. Warner's *Pan,* a new origin story for the boy who could fly, starring Hugh Jackman, was a bomb in 2015, and its *King Arthur,* the character whom many people know from Disney's *The Sword in the Stone,* was a disaster as well. Warner's own attempt at a *Jungle Book* remake, meanwhile, was delayed to 2018 amid worries at the studio it couldn't measure up to Disney's hit.

Brand wasn't the only advantage Disney had over its competitors. The frustrating fact for the rest of Hollywood was that Disney's franchise movies were rarely bad. Sure, there was little chance of a surprise hit like *Gravity* or *Straight Outta Compton* emerging from Iger's company, since it took so few risks. But nearly every Marvel, Star Wars, and fairy-tale movie thrilled fans and got solid marks from critics.

That kind of consistent quality was unheard of in Hollywood. Iger attributed it to the studio's tiny slate. Typically, production presidents at a studio oversee a dozen or more films annually. Feige, Kennedy, Lasseter, and Bailey each had a literal handful. They were heavily involved in every movie they made, meaning there was no excuse for mediocre results.

Time was also not an issue at Disney. At Sony, and most other stu-

dios, moving the release dates of movies around was dangerous because it affected the promised profits for a fiscal year. But with its
movie studio succeeding at such a high level, Iger could afford to let big
productions slip when needed, and to spend substantial sums on reshoots. For example, episode VII of Star Wars was originally supposed
to come out in the summer of 2015, but was pushed back six months
into the next fiscal year when it became clear that a heavily rewritten
script wouldn't be ready in time. Likewise, early cuts of *Rogue One* were
clearly flawed. When Kennedy and Horn determined that six weeks of
reshoots, at a cost of tens of millions of dollars, would be needed to fix
it, Iger didn't blink.

Inspired in large part by Lasseter and Catmull's philosophy at Pixar
— that nobody would remember if a movie was late, but everyone
would remember if it was bad — Iger took a quality-over-quantity approach that his company's success afforded. "We're playing by different rules and we're going to continue to," the CEO said succinctly.

By 2016, the company was making its last attempts to color outside
the lines of its brands. That year saw it release *The Finest Hours,* an $80
million story of a real-world Coast Guard rescue, and *Queen of Katwe,* a
low-budget tale about an unlikely African chess champion. Both were
well reviewed and had inspirational themes that perfectly fit the Disney brand. Iger politely referred to such films as "brand deposits," figuring that even if they couldn't make as much money as Star Wars or
Cinderella movies, they reflected well on the company in the minds of
audiences worldwide.

But good feelings about Disney weren't worth the $75 million that
Disney lost on *The Finest Hours,* or the millions more on *Katwe* when it
grossed a measly $10 million at the box office. By the end of that year,
no "brand deposits" were on the Disney slate anymore. Audiences
would accept new stories from Disney, it seemed, only in the form of
animation, as evidenced by hits such as *Inside Out* and *Moana.*

Executives in Bailey's live-action group were now focused almost
entirely on adapting animated classics, even though everyone knew
they would eventually run out of material. "We'd like new ideas to

come from the live-action Disney studio too," Iger admitted, describing it as perhaps a long-term aspiration rather than a short-term mandate. "They have not found their stride there yet, but they will."

There certainly wasn't any urgency. Between animation, live-action fairy tales, Marvel, and Star Wars, Disney had a collection of the industry's best brands at a time when that defined success in the motion picture business.

Conventional Hollywood wisdom said that fickle audiences would lose interest in any or all of those franchises, which would fade to obscurity, much as Friday the 13th and Planet of the Apes had in the past. But those series didn't have teams of producers backed by the world's largest media company, whose sole job was to keep them vibrant. And if anything did start to falter, well, Disney had reserve ammunition. Its purchase of Lucasfilm brought it another well-known movie brand, one it wasn't initially sure what to do with.

At any other studio, Indiana Jones would be rushed to the front burner and turned into the industry's next cinematic universe. But Disney had no need to hurry. After a few years of pondering the matter and working out a deal with the producer Steven Spielberg, executives finally decided sure, why not go for it? And so it scheduled a reboot of Indiana Jones for July 2020, three weeks after its latest Pixar production and four weeks before a Marvel superhero movie.

11

The Producers

Creativity Meets Franchise Management

FOR EVERYONE IN HOLLYWOOD who's not at Disney and therefore doesn't enjoy a self-perpetuating cycle of box-office dominance, success has become tenuous and tricky.

Since they don't own and control Marvel or Star Wars, other studios get their hands on intellectual property with big-screen potential however they can, and then often rely on a new breed of filmmakers — of a sort — to make them successful.

They're typically not directors, the creative forces who used to wield the most power in Hollywood, but rather producers and writers who sit in between studios and their most valuable franchises. By keeping one movie after another after another in a cinematic series on track, on budget, and creatively consistent yet fresh, they serve what has become one of the most important roles in modern Hollywood.

At one such operation, the lobby is covered not with classic movie posters and coffee table art books, like producers' offices of yore, but rather with a giant mural that reads WELCOME TO BRICKSBURG. Made out of Legos, the wall-spanning work of art also includes space for visitors to post their own creations with conveniently provided plastic bricks. On a warm summer day in 2016, previous guests had marked their presence with a pirate ship, a space shuttle, a dinosaur, pyramids, and a castle.

Technically speaking, this seemingly drab, two-story office building in the center of Los Angeles is the headquarters of Lin Pictures, where the man for whom the company is named tries to package and sell movie and television ideas, as so many other former studio executives before him have done in the second act of their careers. But the Bricksburg Chamber of Commerce, another catchy name for the building, is something Hollywood has never quite seen before. It's a combination production company and animation studio built around a single toy and movie brand: Legos.

Though the animation work is completed in Australia, directors and artists here do the conceptual and design work on films like *The Lego Batman Movie, Lego Ninjago,* and *The Lego Movie 2,* part of what Lin and Warner Bros. hope will be a never-ending series of new movies. A cinematic universe, that is, made out of tiny plastic bricks. Bizarre as it is to see a franchise-focused digital animation studio grafted onto an old-fashioned production company — or is it the other way around? — the Bricksburg Chamber of Commerce shows what it will take to succeed as a moviemaker in the Hollywood of the future.

From a purely artistic standpoint, directors still rule moviemaking. They are in charge of the creative process on a set, and by guiding the cast and crew and deciding how each scene is shot, they leave a signature clearly evident in the final product. Nonetheless, directors' overall power in Hollywood has diminished considerably as the industry has shifted to a franchise model, in which the cinematic series is more important than any single movie within it.

There used to be well over a dozen A-list directors working in Hollywood at any given time who could get most any movie they wanted greenlit at any studio where they chose to work. Today there are only three: Steven Spielberg, James Cameron, and Christopher Nolan. In the franchise age, directors increasingly resemble hired hands who are brought in to helm a single sequel or spinoff but aren't integral to the brand. The fourteen Marvel Studios films released through 2016, for instance, had eleven different directors.

The model is similar to that of a television series. Directors come and go for different episodes and are valued largely for their ability to maintain the tone of the series and bring their installment in on time and on budget. In TV, the power has traditionally lain with writers and producers — many of whom serve both roles — who work on every episode, maintaining long-running story arcs and the consistency and coherence of story lines and characters.

As more and more films are created as part of a cinematic universe, moviemakers are adopting a similar model. It's the producers, or writer-producers, who create and manage cinematic universes. Directors work in partnership with them and are expected to exercise their creativity within a predetermined set of parameters. A groundbreaking director's bold new creative vision is not what anyone is looking for in the ninth Fast & Furious movie or the sixth Mission: Impossible.

To understand how filmmaking really works in Hollywood today and what hope there is for creativity and originality within the franchise-driven model, we have to meet the new A-list: producers and writer-producers who are managing and creating cinematic universes.

In some ways they are like corporate brand managers, tasked with keeping a product line running smoothly. But none came to Hollywood to become the show-biz equivalent of the vice president in charge of Pampers for Procter & Gamble. They love movies and they profess to be as tired as anyone of the sameness of so much that Hollywood offers. They see themselves as creatives within a corporate system, trying to inject original ideas and personal vision into the franchise films that studios want them to keep pumping out for audiences. Once you know the people behind Lego, X-Men, and an upcoming series of films based on Hasbro toys, it becomes a little tougher to dismiss their work as the cynical, derivative corporate ploys they often look like from the outside.

This chapter goes behind the scenes of those three franchises to look at how they're made and how the producers and writers behind them try to do their jobs while keeping their creative souls intact. The work of people like Dan Lin, Simon Kinberg, and a room full of writers led by Akiva Goldsman is helping define what kind of films we get in the coming years and whether the franchise age can, despite so many forces pushing in the opposite direction, be a creatively vibrant one.

THE MBA

Before he became the mayor of Bricksburg, Dan Lin was on a very traditional Hollywood career path. Lin immigrated to the United States from Taiwan at age five, and though he learned about America from watching TV and movies and had a particular love for John Hughes films like *The Breakfast Club,* he wasn't thinking about a career in Hollywood. Like so many immigrants and middle-class kids, he didn't even know such a thing was possible.

In his senior year at the University of Pennsylvania's Wharton School of Business in 1993, however, Lin heard the alumnus Chris Lee give a speech, and it changed his life. Lee was a top production executive at Columbia Pictures and one of the very few Chinese Americans in the upper echelons of Hollywood. That was the first time Lin learned about jobs that melded business and creative skills.

After working as a consultant, Lin started on an MBA at Harvard and spent the summer after his first year interning at Warner Bros., for the president of production, Lorenzo di Bonaventura. In addition to performing menial tasks like packing picnic baskets for concerts his boss attended at the outdoor Hollywood Bowl, Lin served as a translator during meetings with the Chinese action star Jet Li, who was in the studio's *Lethal Weapon 4*. Those meetings also allowed him to interact with the movie's producer, Joel Silver, and gave him enough experience and exposure that di Bonaventura invited him to come back, once he finished his MBA, as a "creative executive," the lowest rung on the studio ladder, just above assistant.

It was not an obvious move for someone graduating from Harvard Business School. A career counselor warned Lin, who would be making less than $50,000 in his new job, that he would be the lowest-paid member of his graduating class by a long shot. Lin gave himself three years to succeed in Hollywood, after which he would return to a more boring business career if things didn't work out.

But he never had to. The baby-faced Lin, who with his full head of hair and penchant for hoodies and T-shirts barely looked thirty even well into his forties, rose to become a senior vice president of production. He worked on a number of movies but made his biggest mark with *The Departed*, Martin Scorsese's Oscar-winning film of 2006, which Lin helped to adapt from a Hong Kong film released in 2002.

During Lin's time at Warner, the entertainment business was already becoming more corporate, and he concluded that the job he was heading toward, president of production, was not nearly as fun as it used to be. The pressure to produce globally successful franchises was starting to mount, and the more freewheeling, risk-taking culture of studios like Warner Bros. was fading. Perhaps counterintuitively for a Harvard MBA, Lin wanted some degree of creativity and unpredictability in his career. It was why he had gone to Hollywood rather than sticking with management consulting. So he opted out of the executive path to become a producer. And it seemed he had a key to stability in his pocket: he was going to produce a new slate of superhero movies featuring the characters from Warner-owned DC Comics.

The studio's *Superman Returns* had been a dud in 2006. Chris Nolan had successfully revived Batman with 2005's *Batman Begins* but had not yet made his blockbuster sequel, *The Dark Knight*. Warner wanted to refresh Superman and bring its other prominent superheroes, like Wonder Woman, Flash, and Aquaman, to the big screen for the first time. Lin's plan, which he presented to the studio management in a PowerPoint deck, was to kick off a series of DC movies by presenting all of the characters together in a Justice League film. Then, once audiences were familiar with them, each would each get an individual movie.

Warner signed off on the idea, giving Lin the first movie for his newly formed company, Lin Pictures, to produce: *Justice League: Mortal*. George Miller, of *Mad Max* fame, was going to direct it, with a cast of young newcomers. Armie Hammer, later known for *The Social Network* and *The Lone Ranger*, would play Batman, and Adam Brody, of

The O.C., would play Flash. The film was set to shoot in 2008, for release in 2009. Lin's plan called for a new solo film for Superman to follow soon after, then films for other key DC superheroes, after which a Justice League sequel would be released in 2012 and every three years thereafter.

Though Lin and Warner were unaware of it, this was the opposite of the plan being hatched at the time by Marvel Studios, which would introduce its superheroes in a series of solo films, starting with *Iron Man* in 2008, before bringing them together in *The Avengers* in 2012.

If it had succeeded, Lin's plan for DC movies would have made his studio immediately competitive with Marvel in the superhero cinema world. But that was not to happen. Just months before shooting was to start in Australia, *Justice League: Mortal* was delayed by a strike by the Writers Guild of America. By the time the strike ended, Warner executives had gone cold on the film due to its huge budget and concerns that audiences might be confused by a different version of Batman than the one played by Christian Bale in *The Dark Knight.*

So Lin now had to start his producing venture from scratch, a difficult task as the 2010s dawned and studios were cutting back their slates and focusing more on branded movies. He quickly produced one film that he had first developed as an executive, a fourth Terminator, but the 2009 release performed only decently at the box office, and fans hated it, so no sequels followed. A trio of low-budget pictures, the horror movie *The Box,* the kids' film *Shorts,* and the Ricky Gervais comedy *The Invention of Lying,* all performed poorly.

But a new version of *Sherlock Holmes,* starring Robert Downey Jr., was a hit that year. It seemed that Lin had found his first franchise as a producer; a successful sequel quickly followed in 2011. But the Sherlock movies were based less on the core appeal of the character than the charismatic performance of Downey. Once he became busy starring in a Marvel movie nearly every year, plus occasional passion projects like *The Judge,* the Sherlock series came to a halt.

Lin's toughest year as a producer came in 2013. He hoped that year's reboot of *Godzilla,* for which he had helped to acquire rights, would kick off the new franchise his company needed, but instead it resulted in the darkest moment of his career. The financier Legendary Pictures booted Lin and his fellow producer, Roy Lee, from the project, alleging they had not done enough work to earn the millions that the duo claimed was rightfully theirs. Lin, who rarely betrayed any strong emotion, particularly anger, felt severely wronged. He and Lee sued Legendary, but the case was in court for two years and the legal bills were substantial.

With his company short on hit films and no TV show on the air yet, Lin had to move his family to a rental house and lay off his top executive in order to stay afloat.

Lin Pictures might have met an ignominious end, if not for *The Lego Movie*. The project had initially come Lin's way as a Warner executive, when Roy Lee had pitched him to make a film based on Bionicle, a Lego sub-brand with characters that resembled the Transformers. Lin wasn't interested, but he met with a Lego executive and ended up discussing a bigger idea. After seeing his young son Miles play with Legos and invent his own worlds, Lin thought he could use the brand to make a movie with broader themes about invention and creativity.

Executives inside Warner and throughout Hollywood mocked the idea of a film based on a toy set that lacked characters or a story. They thought at best it would be a "hand tugger," the type of movie that little kids have to drag their parents to see. But as Lin developed the movie for several years, he stuck with his belief that the Lego title would attract a broad audience if it married two qualities: a subversive sense of humor that appealed to adults and an action-adventure story full of physical humor for kids. By linking brand to big idea, it drew upon his skills as an MBA and as a Hollywood producer. Lin also found a way, with his Australian animation studio, to make the movie for the bargain-basement price of $60 million and signed Phil Lord and Chris Miller, who had shown their ability to playfully subvert a brand in Sony's hit 21 *Jump Street,* to write and direct.

Lin forged deals to feature a variety of characters, many not owned by Warner, to appear in the film in Lego block form, including Batman, Gandalf from *The Lord of the Rings*, the Teenage Mutant Ninja Turtles, and Chewbacca from Star Wars. Those satirical portrayals, as well as a

surprise live-action scene featuring Will Ferrell, were funnier than anyone expected but still gave depth to the story, about a painfully ordi-
nary guy who saves the world by discovering his creativity.

The movie got extremely high marks from preview audiences, and
as its debut, in February 2014, approached, Warner upped its internal
estimates for the opening weekend from $30 million to $40 million to
$50 million and, finally, $60 million. That was still short of the actual
opening gross: $69 million. *The Lego Movie* ultimately grossed $469
million worldwide and was hugely profitable, giving Lin and his company the financial break they needed, thanks to his share of the revenues.

But it was the week before *The Lego Movie* opened that the major
transformation of Lin Pictures really began. The chief executive of
Warner Bros., Kevin Tsujihara, called Lin and asked whether he had
more ideas for Legos. Lin replied that he did and almost immediately
sent the studio a plan. It was in fact the presentation he had prepared
for the DC movie franchise seven years earlier. "I literally just put the
Lego name on it and revised a few of the details, but all of the notions
were the same," Lin later explained.

Warner itself was in need of franchises, as the Harry Potter series
had just ended and the Hobbit trilogy was about to expire too. So the
studio quickly approved Lin's plan, asking him how many follow-ups
he could make, and how soon. They quickly decided that, just as Lin
had originally planned for follow-ups to *Justice League,* spinoffs featuring individual characters should follow *The Lego Movie,* after which a
proper sequel would be released. *Lego Batman,* featuring an obnox-
iously hilarious version of the Dark Knight, was the first spinoff, after
which would come a movie about a group of goofy Lego fighters called
Ninjago. These would be capped by *The Lego Movie 2.*

Lin and his team had been given wide latitude to make the first Lego
movie however they wanted. But now that it was a franchise, and Tsujihara had publicly touted Lego as one of the studio's three pillars, along
with DC and the Harry Potter spinoff *Fantastic Beasts and Where to
Find Them,* it would be tougher to keep the series fresh. "Everyone
wants to get their hands on it," Lin observed. So he convinced War-

ner to fund the creation of Bricksburg, arguing that the movies needed their own creative culture away from the corporate studio lot. Most important, Lin wanted to keep the idea of a child's freewheeling play at the core of every movie and allow Lord and Miller, who remained as producers, and the new directors and animators to let ideas run wild, without scaring executives who thought they knew what a Lego movie was supposed to be.

The result is a building filled with purposely planned whimsy, including a yellow slide connecting the two floors on which animators work and a hidden room, furnished with a phonograph, a light bulb in a glass human head, and a chandelier made of branches, that's accessible only via a bookcase opened by yanking on *The Illustrated Works of Sherlock Holmes.*

Lin works with the studio executives at Warner headquarters in Burbank and the animators in Australia, trying to protect the creatives working in Bricksburg from corporate and technical concerns. His job is twofold: to keep a project on schedule, so Lego movies don't disappear from public attention for too long, and to keep his team creatively invigorated, so that their work feels fresh but also in line with the culturally savvy attitude and turbocharged visuals that audiences expect from the franchise.

Pixar had taken many years to develop its unique culture, but Lin had to bootstrap one in a hurry with Bricksburg. Inevitably, perhaps, it feels a bit affected, but also endearingly earnest. "We're trying to keep a sense of creative chaos, because that's what was so successful in the first movie," Lin said in "Another Room," his name for the hideout behind the bookcase. "But the chaos is hard to scale, particularly because the stakes are so much higher now."

The first offering from Bricksburg, *The Lego Batman Movie,* demonstrated that, if anything, it was working better as an engine of creativity than as a source of big profits for Warner Bros. The movie grossed $301 million, a solid result but well below the $469 million that *The Lego Movie* generated.

But there was no denying that *Lego Batman* was something different. Its outwardly obnoxious but inwardly lonely protagonist was the funniest superhero seen onscreen perhaps ever, and the film earned overwhelmingly positive reviews. For a spinoff created on a high-pressure schedule and featuring two franchises in the title, that's no easy feat.

KING OF THE X-MEN

Simon Kinberg's office is nothing magical to look at. With the exception of a pile of *Deadpool* DVDs sitting on a table, there was almost no hint on a summer afternoon in 2016 that it's the creative home base for 20th Century Fox's most important film franchise, the X-Men.

While Bricksburg is a physical manifestation of the cinematic universe at the heart of Dan Lin's career, Kinberg works out of an office the size of a child's bedroom inside an old bungalow on a faux suburban street on the Fox lot. The X-Men cinematic universe, it turns out, can be found only inside the head of the skinny, neurotic screenwriter with spiky gray hair who works there.

According to the cliché, a movie writer spends most of her time hacking at a keyboard in a coffee shop or a poorly lit apartment while bemoaning Hollywood's lack of interest in her original idea. Or he is lamenting over an arrogant director's unwillingness to let him spend time on the set where actors are speaking his words.

Simon Kinberg hasn't written an original screenplay in more than a decade. And he is on set virtually every day for the movies he writes. Nobody has spent more time on the sets of Fox's superhero movies over the past five years than he has. Understand him, in fact, and you can understand some of the most important themes of the recent X-Men movies, hidden beneath the sound and fury of superpowered mutants battling over the fate of the world. You might even see these adaptations of Marvel's most famous superhero team as personal stories of his.

People have referred to Kinberg as a showrunner for the films he writes and produces, and the comparison is apt. In television, showrunners are combo writer-producers who serve as the chief creative authority over a series, writing key episodes during the season and over-seeing the rest. They are the people with the overarching vision that connects each episode.

Kinberg has written the last two X-Men movies, *Days of Future Past* and *Apocalypse,* and at the time we met, he was working on a third. He also wrote the 2015 reboot of *Fantastic Four* and served as producer of the hit X-Men spinoff *Deadpool* and upcoming ones, including *X-Force* and *New Mutants.* All are based on Marvel characters that Fox controls under a licensing deal signed several years before the comic book company went bankrupt and more than a decade before Marvel Studios started making its own movies.

Though he works with a variety of filmmakers and Fox executives, Kinberg is the sole person to whom the studio entrusts near-total creative control and the one individual who takes credit for every success and gets the blame for every failure.

"I have a profound, almost insane amount of freedom, where they trust me to make these movies until we fuck up consistently," he says with both pride and a fear that's particularly salient on this Tuesday, just two weeks after *X-Men: Apocalypse* opened to good but not great box office and a decidedly mixed reaction from critics and fans.

The idea of a screenwriter as creative chief in the movies was unthinkable until very recently. Screenwriters were considered a dime a dozen, which is why big movies so often had four or six or more of them working on a script until it satisfied the lead actors, the studio, and the director, the ones who were really in charge.

On the first two X-Men movies, there was no question that the director, Bryan Singer, was the creative visionary. He helmed the 2000 original and its 2003 sequel and was set to do 2006's number three until he left Fox to direct *Superman Returns* for Warner Bros., which caused a squabble between the two studios. Directors led most key studio franchises in the first decade of the 2000s. Paramount's Transformers franchise belonged to Michael Bay, and Warner Bros.' Dark Knight trilogy was under the purview of Chris Nolan.

The success of Marvel Studios changed that, as it did so many things in Hollywood. When it proved that fans would turn out for, and even preferred, multiple related superhero movies appearing in the same year, the idea of putting a director in charge went out the window, because each film required a director's near-total attention for two years.

Simon Kinberg was suited for the world of screenwriter-as-franchise-master because he had long approached his profession with a mind equally attuned to the industry's commercial needs and his own creative desires. The son of a writer-producer who met his wife, an assistant director, while working in England, Kinberg was born in London but spent most of his childhood in Los Angeles, where his father worked largely in TV miniseries before becoming a film professor.

Kinberg grew up in Hollywood but was largely repulsed by it. His father had been only moderately successful and had "complicated feelings" about his profession. Many of Kinberg's friends at the private school he attended in the 1980s were the children of film-industry professionals who were snorting drugs and getting divorced and generally doing whatever was necessary to turn their kids into the future protagonists of a Bret Easton Ellis book.

He learned to love movies nonetheless, both by watching classic black-and-white films from his father's youth on their Betamax deck and going to the local theater for personal favorites like *Beverly Hills Cop, The Terminator,* and *The Empire Strikes Back,* which he saw more than twenty times.

But Kinberg figured he would be a "real" writer. He wrote short stories while studying English at Brown and, afterward, during off-hours from his menial job in New York in the mid-1990s. He wasn't successful at getting anything published, though, and when friends suggested that his stories, which were driven more by plot than character or point of view, read like screenplays, he decided to see whether the comparison was valid. Despite the milieu of his youth, Kinberg had never read a screenplay.

At the dawn of the Internet, it was almost impossible to find screenplays online, so Kinberg spent hours reading them in an archive at Lincoln Center, which was close to his apartment. He was intrigued by the scripts and felt he had an intuitive understanding of how they worked, as he used a notepad and pencil to reverse-engineer the structure of each one he read. This, he figured, might be a better path for his career than short stories, not because he felt the need to express himself on the big screen rather than the printed page, but because it was easier for him.

And so Kinberg enrolled at Columbia Film School and quickly found he was right. By his second year, an original script of his about grave robbers in nineteenth-century New York caught the attention of producers teaching a class, and they helped him submit it to professionals in L.A., landing him an agent, a manager, and relationships with young executives, which helped kick-start his career.

That script was never made, but his meetings led to a connection that led to his first paid job, writing a horror movie for Warner Bros. By the end of his second year, Kinberg had a career as a writer-for-hire in Los Angeles and started missing classes at Columbia.

To finish his degree, he decided to write a thesis script that might also sell in Hollywood. *Mr. and Mrs. Smith* was inspired by a girlfriend who told Kinberg that he was a great partner when there was conflict and tension in the relationship, but a bad one when things were calm. Upon reflection, Kinberg saw that the critique was accurate. It also inspired a big movie idea, about an unhappy pair of married spies whose love is rekindled when they are hired to kill each other. "Almost everything I've written from scratch has some really personal, emotional component to it," Kinberg reflected in his office years later. "It just manifests itself as superheroes and spies."

Kinberg tried pitching *Mr. and Mrs. Smith* to every studio in town twice, once on his own and once with the help of the producer Akiva Goldsman, who liked the idea. When nobody bought it, he decided to simply write the script, finish his Columbia degree, and see if anyone would buy the final product.

He eventually found a small company that was interested and got his big break when it signed Nicole Kidman, then one of the hottest actresses in Hollywood, to star. That started a seven-year process during which Brad Pitt signed on, Kidman dropped out, Angelina Jolie replaced her, and an epically long production and series of reshoots became a paparazzi sensation, once word leaked out that the stars had become a romantic couple.

Kinberg got to spend more time on set than most first-time screenwriters could dream of because the producer, Goldsman, was also a writer and protected him. And because the director, Doug Liman, liked to experiment with different versions of a scene and didn't always get along with his stars, Kinberg learned how to interface with high-maintenance filmmakers and actors as he performed endless rewrites on set.

Mr. and Mrs. Smith was a huge hit when it was released in the summer of 2005 and accelerated an already healthy career for its screenwriter.

Over the next few years, Kinberg did uncredited rewrites, often at the last minute and on set, for movies including the action sequel *Charlie's Angels: Full Throttle,* the comedies *Night at the Museum 2* and *Date Night,* the Tom Cruise–Cameron Diaz flop *Knight and Day,* and Fox's first *Fantastic Four,* which did decently at the box office but earned little love from comic book readers. Now working regularly at Fox and also friendly with Avi Arad and Kevin Feige at Marvel, who produced the X-Men movies, Kinberg was hired to co-write the third film in the series: *X-Men: The Last Stand.* The experience was "complicated" for him, since he got to adapt the story *Dark Phoenix,* beloved of comic book readers — but despite its box-office success, fans scorned the resulting movie.

Perhaps most notable, Kinberg was on set in Vancouver for most of the shoot of *The Last Stand,* working directly with Ratner and the stars Hugh Jackman, Halle Berry, and Patrick Stewart. When he served a similar role on his next film, *Jumper,* also directed by *Mr. and Mrs. Smith*'s Liman, Kinberg requested and received a producer credit for his work. He also signed a multi-year producing deal with Fox. He wanted to make on-set work with talent a core part of his career and not something he did as an adjunct.

"I learned on *Jumper* I can do both of these things and they are fulfilling to me in different ways," he reflected. "Producing is less lonely than writing and I enjoy being with people solving tangible problems. Perhaps not as much as living in my imagination, but I enjoy it."

Under that deal, he was asked to help the studio reboot the X-Men franchise in 2011, since *The Last Stand* and a 2009 spinoff focused on Jackman's Wolverine character had disappointed fans and Marvel Studios had by now set a new standard for superhero universes.

Together with Singer, who also produced, and the director, Matthew Vaughn, Kinberg helped shape *X-Men: First Class,* which featured a new origin story with a young cast. It didn't do as well at the box office, perhaps because the franchise had lost momentum in the public compared to *The Avengers,* but it was well received by fans and critics and gave Fox confidence to make more superhero movies more frequently.

Kinberg was charged with making it happen. The studio needed an architect for its superhero universe, and he was the most obvious candidate. So he wrote and produced *X-Men: Days of Future Past,* spending every day on set with Singer, who returned to direct, and becoming as close as anyone behind the camera to the cast, all of whom he knew from *The Last Stand* and *First Class.*

Days of Future Past was shot in Montreal in 2013, a difficult year for Kinberg, as his marriage was falling apart. He considered himself "a very optimistic person, especially for a Jewish writer," but splitting with his wife of fourteen years was a painful experience, and he felt hopeless. Stuck rewriting the script at the same time, Kinberg turned it into a therapeutic process, injecting the comic book story he was adapting with a subplot in which James McAvoy's Professor X has lost hope and has to be convinced that he and his team can still make a difference.

Kinberg rewrote a key scene between McAvoy and Stewart, who play the character Professor X at different ages and briefly meet, thanks to time travel. Kinberg worked on the scene while at the airport on his way back to Montreal, after telling his two young sons about the divorce.

"It's not their pain you're afraid of, it's yours," Stewart's character says to McAvoy's character in that scene. "And as frightening as it can be, their pain will make you stronger if you allow yourself to feel it, embrace it. It will make you more powerful than you ever imagined. It's the greatest gift we have: to bear pain without breaking. And it's born from the most human power: Hope. Please, Charles, we need you to hope again."

Days of Future Past achieved in 2014 what the franchise hadn't enjoyed since *X2* in 2003: a blockbuster hit at the box office, at nearly $750 million, that also thrilled fans. The franchise was back on track, and the studio now wanted Kinberg to help it pump out multiple superhero films every year. There were now so many that he couldn't write or be on set for them all, though he would remain as the creative overseer.

He wrote and produced 2015's *Fantastic Four,* a reboot that proved to be a debacle both creatively and at the box office. Reshoots attempting to salvage the film only made it worse, particularly when the costar, Kate Mara, wore a wig that didn't remotely resemble her hair on the original shoot.

The studio blamed the director Josh Trank's erratic behavior on set. But Kinberg, speaking a year later, said that as the studio's superhero showrunner, he bore some responsibility. He was particularly remorseful that he made the movie about how powers are a psychological burden, almost like a disease. *Fantastic Four,* he concluded, should have been more playful, with a pop science-fiction feel. "You can blame execution when you miss by a little bit," he said of *Fantastic Four,* which grossed only $168 million. "But when you miss by a mile, you have to look at what's broken in the DNA."

Things turned out much better for the X-Men in 2016, though not in the way anyone expected. *Apocalypse,* the sequel to *Days of Future Past,* featuring the core superhero team, did well but not great. The low-budget spinoff *Deadpool,* however, was massive, grossing $768 million on a budget of just $58 million. It later became the first superhero flick nominated for a Golden Globe for best picture.

The idea for an R-rated spinoff, featuring a loud-mouthed antihero who mocks other X-Men, had been in the works for a decade. Kinberg's biggest contribution came in supporting its greenlight, helping with reshoots that enhanced the movie's romantic relationship, and turning a series of unconnected scenes into an action montage. Nonetheless, its success was a boon to Kinberg's superhero cinematic universe. By late 2016, Ryan Reynolds's character, Deadpool, was a key part of the writer-producer's burgeoning plans for the X-Men movies, which Kinberg hoped would soon reach a cadence of two or three films per year, matching Marvel Studios.

Speaking from his home in the Hollywood Hills, where he was writing the first draft of 2018's X-Men movie, which would retell and perhaps redeem the Dark Phoenix story line from 2006's *The Last Stand*, Kinberg said he was preparing for an even bigger step. He planned to direct the film. It was a big step for a writer, but perhaps also a natural one, since no one knew the X-Men franchise, characters, or cast better.

Many screenwriters have a "one for them, one for me" philosophy, in which they balance assignments to write sequels or comic book adaptations with their own new creations. Kinberg hasn't written an original screenplay since *Mr. and Mrs. Smith*. He briefly considered doing so in early 2016, when a flu knocked him out for nearly a month and he lost fifteen pounds from an already thin frame. "Maybe I need to take a break," he said to himself, "and write something from scratch."

So Kinberg sat down over a weekend and started brainstorming ideas. The latest issues on his mind had to do with love and loss, pain, jealousy, and anger. He started thinking about how to work them into a movie and soon he saw it: they would be the themes of 2018's *X-Men* sequel, now called simply *Dark Phoenix*.

"The truth is that I find myself in these movies, I'm not writing them on an assembly line," he said. "My brain is always living in these stories, even when I think I may die from the flu."

THE WRITERS' ROOM

As movies were increasingly being managed like corporate brands and run like television shows, it was perhaps inevitable that those two forces would meld.

That's exactly what Simon Kinberg's former mentor, the writer-producer Akiva Goldsman, has been doing in a new phase of his career.

On a soundstage on the Paramount Pictures lot where the TV show *Glee* used to be shot, the bald, glasses-wearing Goldsman, who won an Oscar for *A Beautiful Mind,* gathered a group of ten eclectic screenwriters in 2016 to imagine a new cinematic universe that could spawn a never-ending series of movies.

The room was filled with whiteboards, TV screens, and toys that would look familiar to anyone who watched TV in the 1980s, with names like G.I. Joe, M.A.S.K., and the Micronauts. The writers sitting at a square table were brought there not just by Paramount, but by its corporate partner, the company that made those toys, Hasbro.

Goldsman and his writers, a group that included the Pulitzer Prize–winning novelist Michael Chabon and the *Guardians of the Galaxy* writer Nicole Perlman, were charged with creating the framework for a "Hasbro cinematic universe," one that could weave together a new lineup of movies that might also sell a few million new toys.

The task, as Goldsman described it, was "universe building," and that term is essential to understanding moviemaking in Hollywood today. On the biggest and most important films, it's no longer just about the writer who comes up with the story and the director who translates it visually. Today, the design of the overarching fiction, the cinematic universe in which all of the films will take place, is the beating heart of the creative process.

And behind most cinematic universes, of course, is a brand — most frequently one that can sell a lot of consumer products. Just as the Marvel cinematic universe was created to sell more toys, Hasbro partnered with Paramount on its planned series of movies for the same purpose. It's exactly the same reason why there were cheesy after-school cartoons in the 1980s featuring the same characters. But like nearly everything unsavory about TV from the past, that strategy is now migrating to the big screen.

It thus made perfect sense to also borrow the key creative process of television production: the writers' room. In TV, a team of writers brainstorms overall story arcs for a season and then works together to outline the key plot points of each episode. Only then do individual writers go off to script an episode.

Hasbro, with its plan to make a series of films that would overlap and fit together in a larger story line, wanted a team of writers to do the exact same thing for them. "Movies and TV have inverted in their most essential values . . . including that which was most endemic to television: the ongoing stories and character arcs which are best addressed by the writers' room," Goldsman explained.

Goldsman's bosses were equally enthusiastic about the writers' room, though for a very different reason. "It allows us to activate our brand more effectively and do much more long lead planning when you've got writers coming up with multiple ideas for movies all at once," Stephen Davis, Hasbro's chief content officer, said. Translation: When you know there's a M.A.S.K. movie coming out in 2020, you can more easily convince Toys "R" Us to put a lot more M.A.S.K. toys on its shelves that year.

It's the most cynical reason possible to make a movie. Which is why Goldsman, if he didn't want his films to feel like tools to help with merchandise planning for toys, needed to go to great lengths to make his writers' room as joyous a place as possible. The Hasbro writers' room was actually Goldsman's second such effort. In 2015, he led a writers' room for the Transformers movies on the Paramount lot, planning out a series of interconnected films that took the robot franchise from an every-two-or-three-years event to an annual occurrence starting in 2017.

Among the lessons he learned was to make the room a safe space designed entirely to juice writers' creativity. So Goldsman got Hasbro and Paramount to create a "writers' summer camp" for his team, with toys, pinball machines, limitless food, artists to turn their every idea into a visual design, and even entertainers to throw themed parties for their families. Writers of the caliber of Chabon wouldn't be attracted just because of the creative challenge of the next G.I. Joe film, but for the chance to "get out of my room and my head and collaborate with gifted, talented people in an environment that was very writer-centric."

After getting schooled by Hasbro experts on the history of the toys and TV shows, Goldsman and his ten writers started sketching out a timeline of their cinematic universe, just as he had already done for Transformers. A chronology was drawn along the whiteboards, detailing the roles characters from each of the toy brands played, from pre–World War II history to the present day and future. The ten ideas the team ended up with were certainly not big-screen versions of the 1980s cartoons. There would be a World War II G.I. Joe movie featuring the origins of that team; a present-day M.A.S.K. film featuring multicultural teens in Detroit who come across the spy team's high-tech gear; and another movie, kept as more of a secret, set in the future. And they would all tie together in a larger story about the conflict between magic and technology.

By the end of three weeks, each writer was assigned to write a treatment, or story summary, for one film. When those were done a few months later, they were collected into a hardcover book, along with visual designs and fake posters for each film, which were distributed to insiders.

If the plan succeeded, it pointed to a new paradigm for filmmaking. Ten movies on Paramount's slate over the next several years would already be planned out. The origins of their shared universe would lie in a combination of corporate imperatives to sell toys and a creative process borrowed from television that put writers and their ideas in charge.

A FRANCHISE-FUNDED HOME FOR CREATIVITY

Dan Lin knows Lego won't last forever. Marvel Studios aside, most franchises ebb and flow in Hollywood, particularly when inevitable creative missteps happen. Despite the overall dominance of cinematic brands, anyone who hitches their career to a single one may end up like Saudi Arabia in an age of declining oil prices.

So when Lin in 2015 received what he described as a "huge check" as part of the settlement of his Godzilla lawsuit, he thought and prayed long and hard about what to do with the money. Ultimately, he decided to apply some of the best practices being applied to cinematic universes and try to harness them in support of originality.

Lin bought an old post office in the Filipinotown neighborhood of Los Angeles, which he intends to turn into a creative hub called Rideback Ranch, named after a cowboy term for riders who support each other. By 2018, it was set to host the offices for Lin Pictures and the Bricksburg Chamber of Commerce, where animators work on the next set of the Lego movies. But it will also have space where writers, directors, and other creative folks are free to work on any idea they want. The producer's idea is to use the freewheeling and collaborative spirit that brought success to *The Lego Movie* and *Lego Batman* to generate new ideas. Some might be one-off films or television shows that when fully developed by the right creative team, would be more likely than an original script written in isolation to get bought by a studio. Others could become the next great franchise.

Lin Pictures wouldn't necessarily own the ideas, but since it's located in-house, it would be part of the process and potentially produce some of them. "It's harder and harder to make original content, and as the business becomes more corporate, creators need to go the other way," Lin said of his plan.

It's an interesting paradox for the MBA whose film career is currently staked on a toy brand. But Lin realizes, as Goldsman does in his writers' room and Kinberg when applying his personal pain to his superhero films, that creativity must be intentional because Hollywood is no longer an industry that naturally encourages it. Left alone, the economic forces of the film business will generate only reboots, sequels, and spinoffs with as little originality, risk taking, and interesting ideas as possible.

Certainly the producer of *The Lego Movie 2* and a pair of Sherlock Holmes films doesn't expect that to fundamentally change. But he knows, as most thoughtful people in Hollywood do, that if taken too far, the cinematic brand strategy could become a self-destructive loop that will leave Hollywood with no new franchises to replace the ones that expire. Some evidence from 2016 suggests that the snake is starting to eat its own tail. Many branded movies, like the *Ghostbusters* reboot and the *Independence Day* revival and the second *Teenage Mutant Ninja Turtles,* fizzled at the box office.

Creativity in Hollywood these days comes in odd forms. It may be a movie about multicultural teens in Detroit wrapped into one meant to revive a 1980s toy brand, or ideas about disappointment and hope snuck into the sixth film in a comic book franchise, or a space for creative collaboration built on the back of a cinematic universe made of toys. But the people who thrive in the movie business today and the near future will be those who can straddle the line between giving studios and global audiences the franchises they demand while cultivating the creativity that cinema needs, in the long run, to survive.

12

The Shop Around the Corner

Amazon Saves the Indie
Film Business

MANCHESTER BY THE SEA WAS the prototypical Sundance sensation: a heart-wrenching drama about human tragedy and finding the will to move past it. Brilliantly executed by the writer-director Kenneth Lonergan and featuring a gut punch of a lead performance by the future Oscar winner Casey Affleck, it seemed certain to stand as one of the best movies of 2016.

It was equally certain to be a commercial challenge. Getting audiences to buy tickets for a dark indie drama was difficult in the best of times. Now, in the age of *Fast and Furious* and *The Avengers* and an endless supply of great dramas on television, it was near impossible.

By January 2016, during the thirty-eighth annual Sundance Film Festival, the prospects for indie dramas at the box office were bleak. The two biggest hits from the prior year's Sundance, the black comedy *Me and Earl and the Dying Girl* and the hip-hop-themed caper *Dope,* had both bombed at the box office despite the certainty among festival attendees that they brilliantly straddled indie and commercial sensibilities.

It had been seven years, in fact, since an indie movie bought at a film festival had broken out at the box office and grossed more than $50 million. In the time since 2009's brutal drama *Precious,* which won

Mo'Nique an Oscar, and 2006's breakout comedy *Little Miss Sunshine* starring Steve Carell, the indie business had turned quite grim.

The genre was strong as late as 2007, when Fox Searchlight's *Juno,* which premiered at the Toronto festival, grossed an astounding $143 million. The same year, Miramax's Oscar winner *No Country for Old Men* took in $74 million and the romantic war drama *Atonement,* from Universal's Focus Features, took in $51 million domestically. These were huge numbers for low-budget movies that tackled weighty topics like abortion, rape, and a grisly murder spree. Perhaps not coincidentally, 2007 was also near the peak of the DVD boom, the beginning of the golden age of television, and one year before *Iron Man* launched the Marvel cinematic universe.

Over the next several years, Disney, Warner Bros., and Paramount scrapped their indie divisions and Universal significantly scaled back. Only Fox, whose Searchlight had long been the most successful studio indie unit, and Sony Pictures Classics, which operated with extremely low overhead and kept its ambitions very modest, stayed in the game. Many independent companies shut down or struggled to stay afloat, and those that remained, like the upstart A24, were tiny operations.

Even the Weinstein brothers started questioning the sanity of the indie film business. After their post-Miramax venture, The Weinstein Company, released just six movies in 2016, down from fourteen the prior year, Harvey Weinstein admitted, "TV at this point of my career is more lucrative and a lot easier to do."

It was becoming so difficult for art-house films to find audiences in theaters that more and more were released directly in the home, where distributors could save on marketing expenses and try to make their money through video-on-demand rentals on iTunes and cable boxes.

So when *Manchester by the Sea* premiered to a standing ovation at the Eccles Theatre in Park City, Utah, there was still reason to be hesitant. So many movies with similarly rapturous responses at Sundance had failed commercially over the past few years. And *Manchester* didn't even have the comedy and youth appeal of *Dope* or *Me and Earl and the Dying Girl,* both of which featured young multicultural casts. In a year when *diversity* was a buzzword, due to the #OscarsSoWhite uproar, *Manchester* was basically a downer about white adults. It seemed a miracle, in fact, when Fox Searchlight, Sony Classics, and other studio players brought bidding for the domestic rights for *Manchester by the Sea* up past $5 million.

Then America's biggest online retailer said it would take the movie for $10 million.

Amazon.com's offer for *Manchester by the Sea* blew the other bidders out of the water. It was a staggering amount of money for such a commercially challenging film. After all, Kenneth Lonergan's two previous movies had grossed only $9 million combined.

But Amazon, whose top entertainment executives had vaulted over seats in the Eccles when *Manchester* ended and sped up a hill in a snowstorm in their SUV to meet with the agents representing the movie, had more than a quick profit in mind. They were building a business. And just as Amazon had done in almost every retail category it had entered and come to dominate over the past twenty-two years, it was prepared to make loud statements and absorb short-term losses in order to do so. For $10 million, *Manchester by the Sea* was quite likely to do both.

Although Amazon Studios, already known for such well-regarded television shows as *Transparent* and *Mozart in the Jungle,* had first signaled its intention to start making movies a year earlier, its purchase of *Manchester* was still shocking. Here was arguably the most cold-hearted capitalist company in American history, one that many blamed for gutting and feeding off the carcass of the book industry, riding to the rescue of the most artistic and uncommercial corner of cinema.

Many Sundance veterans were skeptical of Netflix too, but at least its presence at Sundance made sense. It was a streaming video company, after all, and it had an agenda: to take indie films out of theaters and put them on televisions and iPads, where its chief content officer, Ted Sarandos, thought they rightly belonged. So when Netflix bid $20 million for another Sundance sensation, the slave rebellion drama *The Birth of a Nation,* few were surprised. And most nodded their heads in approval when the producers went with a lower offer from Fox Searchlight, which promised a robust theatrical release. (*Birth* eventually fizzled at the box office, but it's unclear how much of that was simply the challenges facing all indie films versus a specific public relations nightmare involving a past sexual assault allegation against the director, Nate Parker.)

But Amazon made its money selling books and shoes and Kindles, not video subscriptions. And it didn't have a digital-first agenda. In fact, it promised Lonergan and his producers that *Manchester* would enjoy a healthy run in theaters before debuting on its Amazon Prime Video service, which offered an assortment of television shows and films to stream on digital devices along with the unlimited two-day shipping on products that members got for $99 per year.

They were true to their word. Thanks in part to an aggressive and costly marketing campaign, *Manchester* ended up grossing $48 million, making it the biggest hit to come out of Sundance in seven years.

Amazon left the Sundance festival in 2016 with four movies, which together with other acquisitions gave it a lineup of more than a dozen pictures that year alone. Among them was the forty-third movie by Woody Allen, for which it paid $15 million, another staggering price that lured the filmmaker away from Sony Pictures Classics, which had released his prior seven films. Amazon didn't let up in 2017, when it once again made the biggest acquisition of the festival: $12 million for a dark comedy, *The Big Sick.*

Amazon's slate was entirely art-house cinema: original films from critically beloved but rarely commercially successful directors like Spike Lee, Todd Haynes, and Richard Linklater, along with documentaries and quirky intellectual fare, like a cinematic retelling of the time Richard Nixon met Elvis Presley. They were the 180-degree opposite of what major studios were making now — the kinds of movies that, if traditional Hollywood had anything to do with it, would soon become as extinct as silent cinema.

Of all the changes the movie business had seen in the past few years, this was easily the least predictable. The best prospects for a vibrant indie movie scene, one that challenged political and cultural norms and connected defiant and unique voices with fans around the world, now rested with a seemingly soulless digital superstore.

THE ACCIDENTAL STUDIO

Despite his platinum Hollywood pedigree as the son of Frank Price, who formerly ran both Columbia Pictures and Universal Pictures, Roy Price did not seem like a budding creative mogul when he joined Amazon in 2004. A lawyer who had worked as a consultant for Allen & Company and McKinsey & Company and as a mid-level development executive for Disney's television animation unit, he was initially tapped to run Amazon's video-on-demand business. He didn't develop or select shows — he simply allowed people to rent or buy digital copies online, as they could already do on Apple's competing platform, iTunes.

Six years later, though, Price launched Amazon Studios, a new business initially intended to let anyone submit screenplays or short films and then, through a mix of community feedback and expert judging, turn the best ones into feature films or television series.

But amid complaints from Hollywood professionals and difficulties in finding gems amid the heaps of mediocrity, little came of the initiative. And eventually Price, who with his spiked gray hair and leather jackets tried to meld Hollywood cool with Silicon Valley smarts, morphed Amazon Studios into something more traditional. He hired experienced development executives, worked with agencies to solicit scripts from experienced writers, and launched a slew of TV shows in 2013.

The twist was that pilot episodes for a group of finalists were released online for users to watch and rate. Amazon executives, all the way up to Bezos, then used that data to help inform their decisions on the series it decided to make and, as competitor Netflix was already doing, release online all at once for viewers to binge-watch.

After a few initial duds, like the political comedy *Alpha House,* Amazon found an identity with *Transparent,* a groundbreaking show about a transgender woman, played by Jeffrey Tambor, who shocks her family by transitioning late in life. *Transparent* wasn't as broadly popular a hit as Netflix's *House of Cards* or *Orange Is the New Black.* But it generated lots of buzz among tastemakers and critics, and it won awards.

It also gave Amazon Studios an identity as a home for highbrow series aimed squarely at upscale, educated, affluent types. Though it produced kids' programs and more broadly appealing shows like the cop drama *Bosch*, Amazon's standout programs continued to be aimed primarily at college professors and the people who loved them, such as the Golden Globe–winning *Mozart in the Jungle*, about the cutthroat world of classical music.

By the time he decided to start making original movies with professionals (and not trying to find ideas from the general public), Price was doubling down on that strategy. You don't call Ted Hope, after all, if you're looking for the next superhero flick or even a fun romantic comedy. You call him if you're looking to create a digital Miramax.

OLD DOGS, OLD TRICKS, NEW HOME

The title of the blog post was undeniably direct: "I Am No Longer Going To Produce Films For My Living." Producing films, Ted Hope wrote in 2013, "requires me to deliver quantity over quality. Or to not contribute as fully as I like since I won't be fairly compensated. Or to make something that is virtually guaranteed to not have the cultural impact it warrants."

Hope still loved movies, he added, but he believed the system, the film *industry*, no longer made that possible. "I want to make films that lift the world and our culture higher — and our current way of doing things does just the opposite," wrote the middle-aged hipster with black-frame glasses and graying hair.

It was a shot across the bow or an admission of defeat, depending on your perspective, by one of the most respected voices in the world of independent cinema. Over the prior quarter-century, Ted Hope had produced movies and developed close relationships with many of the greatest directors of his time, including Hal Hartley, Ang Lee, Ed Burns, Todd Haynes, Nicole Holofcener, Michel Gondry, and Alejandro González Iñárritu. He was one of the founders of Good Machine, a New York company at the leading edge of the indie film revolution in the 1990s that released movies by those directors and many others and was eventually acquired by Universal and turned into its specialty label Focus Features.

But by the 2010s, the economic underpinnings of Hope's industry were collapsing. Audiences seemed to be shifting away from the type of films he made, and studios were increasingly unwilling to subsidize them. As an independent producer, unless he happened to make one of the ever-shrinking number of movies that scored a big sale at Sundance or Toronto, it simply was no longer financially feasible to do his job.

And so Ted Hope decided to go at it a different way. He ran the San Francisco Film Society, hoping to turn it into "an accelerator, an incubator, for new story forms and new business models around film." But that didn't work out, and after a year, he resigned to run Fandor, a Netflix-like subscription video-on-demand service focused on obscure and independent movies for the cinema lover. But even though it was backed by Chris Kelly, the first general counsel for Facebook, Hope quickly found that Fandor didn't have the resources and organization to build the new digital studio that he believed represented the only possible road forward for independent cinema. "I had completely misconceived what it would take," he later admitted.

Then, in May 2014, Hope met Roy Price at a conference sponsored by *Wired* magazine, and the two stayed in touch through the release of the producer's book, *Hope for Film,* on Labor Day weekend. In some ways, the book, in which Hope talks about his love for obscure independent filmmakers like Jim Jarmusch, Susan Seidelman, and Raúl Ruiz and how he got into the business because he "wanted to make the equivalent of European art films from an American perspective," seemed diametrically opposed to the ethos of Amazon, which sells everything to everybody.

But in the book, Hope also talked about the need for a "complete systems reboot" to fix an indie film business he thought was fundamentally broken, because marketing costs were too high and profit oppor-

tunities were too narrow to allow for experimentation and creative in-
novation. "Instead of thinking of ourselves as media makers who want
to employ new technologies to distribute and market our work, maybe
we should align ourselves with technologists (or at least technology
collaborators) who want to use the existing media to make our work
flourish," he wrote.

Hope had been talking and blogging about the need for big changes
to his business for years, but felt like he was just yelling into the void.
Then, on the Tuesday after Labor Day, Price called him. The Amazon
executive had read *Hope for Film* over the holiday weekend and said
its ethos aligned perfectly with the movie studio he wanted to launch.
The two soon met for dinner in Los Angeles, and by December 14,
Price called to offer him a job as head of production at Amazon's new
movie studio.

Despite the company's longstanding obsession with data, there
would be no audience testing of ideas and no sorting through click-
through rates to figure out which director to work with next. In the
most old-fashioned setup possible, Hope was being hired as a taste-
maker. Price and his boss, Amazon's CEO, Jeff Bezos, wanted a veteran
indie movie producer to decide who they should work with and what
they should make.

It was a once-in-a-lifetime opportunity and Hope knew it. With its
$300 billion-plus market capitalization and its history of investing in
businesses for the long term, Amazon had the resources and proven
fortitude to stick with a new indie studio for the several years it would
take to build. And with its massive database of hundreds of millions of
customers' interests and tastes, it could market movies with precision,
saving money and reducing financial risk. It essentially solved, on day
one, the problems Hope had faced at the San Francisco Film Society
and Fandor.

And as unbelievable as it seemed, coming from a lawyer working
for a dot-com, Price said the exact words Hope needed to hear: that
he wanted to make "bold and visionary" movies and that he wanted
risky, unusual films on Amazon. The company's message to filmmak-

ers, Price told Hope, should be "unless you're afraid your film may not work, we should not be the ones making it."

As he assembled his team, Hope seemed to be rebuilding an art-house studio from the days when major studios believed in them. To run marketing and distribution he hired Bob Berney, who founded Newmarket, the distributor of *Memento* and *The Passion of the Christ,* before running the art-house label Picturehouse for HBO and New Line — and then, after it was shut down, struggling like so many other indie executives to find a stable home.

"We look for something artful. We don't say first and foremost, 'Would this be good business?'" Hope declared of his intentions at Amazon.

Those were words sure to make shareholders shudder. Then again, many had in the past questioned whether it really made sense for the dot-com giant to spend millions to start selling jewelry, providing web-hosting services to businesses, or manufacturing e-readers. Each and every time, Jeff Bezos had shown a willingness to ignore the risk-averse on Wall Street, who cared about short-term returns. In most cases, his instincts had proved correct, as evidenced by the company's domi-nance of so many categories. If anyone had to be taken seriously while pursuing an effort to outdo Hollywood in the riskiest and most rarely profitable category of movies, it was Bezos.

Amazon forced Hope to make only two accommodations for his new venture. One was to accept a boss with a more traditional busi-ness background. Jason Ropell, Amazon's head of global movies, had previously helped license the movies from other studios that the com-pany offered to its Prime subscribers and had launched Prime Video in Europe and Japan.

The other was that although Amazon was willing to debut movies in theaters, it wouldn't keep them there long. With the company's first release, Spike Lee's political satire about gun violence, *Chi-Raq,* Price didn't insist it be available simultaneously on the big screen and on-line, as Netflix was already doing with its films. But Lee's movie was in theaters only thirty days, in December 2015, before it became available to buy or rent from Amazon and other digital retailers. Thirty days after that, Amazon Prime subscribers could stream it on TV, a tablet, or a phone for free.

Only 305 theaters played *Chi-Raq*, since most major chains refuse to play movies that aren't available exclusively on the big screen for ninety days, and it grossed a modest $2.7 million. Still, Amazon's strategy of advantaging digital viewership at the expense of cinemas made obvious sense since it was, after all, a digital company. Why make movies if they weren't going to disrupt the traditional system in favor of the Internet?

But just a few months after *Chi-Raq*, Amazon executives had given up on the strategy of rushing movies from theaters to the Internet. As Hope and his team moved to buy the hottest movies, like *Manchester by the Sea*, and work with directors like Woody Allen, they found they had to promise a long playtime in theaters. The filmmakers they wanted to work with demanded it.

And when the company started looking at what people watched most on Amazon Prime, it discovered that a theatrical run first made a big difference. I spoke to Bob Berney about this, in the sleek corporate offices of Amazon Studios in Santa Monica, a beach city adjacent to Los Angeles. Balding and clad in a T-shirt from the famous Alamo Drafthouse Cinema in Austin, Texas, he told me, "Our customers wanted the awareness of the theatrical release to guide them on what to watch."

Hope, in fact, believed that making audiences wait to see his films online was a smart way to prove the films had value. If something was good, he figured, people should have to work a little to get it. "There's no convenience to the theatrical experience," he observed. "So it's a first measure of whether you've succeeded in reaching a passionate audience."

This was the exact opposite of the logic employed by Netflix, where Sarandos figured that convenience was the key to get more people to watch movies. But even Ropell, who seemed less likely than the indie veterans Hope and Berney to be swayed by the romantic notions of filmmakers, was convinced Amazon shouldn't follow its primary competitor's lead and try to change the way theaters do business and customers find movies. "We're trying to deliver high-quality films to the platform and going to war [with movie theaters] may not result in what we want to do," the bearded, buff Ropell said, choosing his words carefully. "This is a very traditional business grafted onto a new one."

That everyone in the corporate food chain, up to Price and even Bezos, was convinced of the need to work with theaters on their terms and not put their movies on Amazon Prime until five months after they debuted on the big screen proved the company was all-in on art-house movies. It was, in fact, the core of Amazon's strategy. Rather than serve everyone everything they might want, as Netflix was doing with its mix of Adam Sandler comedies, Will Smith action flicks, and some indies, Amazon wanted to build a distinct identity for its Prime Video service.

By making a particular kind of movie, everyone at Amazon figured, they would build an identity for their service, one that made it noticeably different from what almost everyone else in Hollywood was doing. Sure, many people wouldn't be interested in the weird, depressing, or simply outré works that it was releasing, but at least those who were into it would love it. Amazon executives distinctly didn't want a studio that was as bland as the company's selection of USB cables.

"We don't want something that 80 percent of the audiences eventually gets around to watching," said Hope. "We want the thing that 20 percent of the audience is so passionate about, they'll break up with you if you don't feel the same way. We want to inspire an urgent need to see."

In addition, the people who go to art-house movies tend to be upscale, well-educated people who live in cities and who like to shop online. If the ultimate goal of Amazon's movie business was to attract, retain, and engage Prime subscribers, it only made sense to draw people who would buy the most computers, books, and Kindles online.

"They are often very good retail customers," Price said sheepishly. "So that's not a bad thing."

FLOPS? NO BIG DEAL.

Amazon's first slate of movies was by and large a collection of the latest works by established indie veterans whom Hope or Berney had known for decades. In addition to Lee and Allen and *Manchester*'s director Lonergan, there was Whit Stillman, whose costume drama *Love & Friendship* was a modest hit for Amazon, and Nicolas Winding Refn, whose horror drama *The Neon Demon* was a bomb.

Refn's experience on *The Neon Demon* was instructive as to how surprisingly simple Amazon's approach to picking movies is. A Dane known for stylized work that bends genres, he had one prior hit in the United States: the action movie *Drive,* starring Ryan Gosling, from 2011. His other films were beloved by cineastes but barely seen in the United States, even in art-house theaters.

Refn earns his living by directing commercials, including a widely viewed ad for Lincoln that starred Matthew McConaughey. But his passion is movies, ones that he writes and directs and over which he has total creative control. Cobbling together money from European distributors, and even kicking in $500,000 himself, he raised $5.5 million in 2015 to make *The Neon Demon,* about a young model, played by Elle Fanning, who enters the metaphorically and literally nightmarish world of Los Angeles fashion.

Berney had worked at FilmDistrict, the company that released *Drive,* and soon after starting at Amazon, he called Refn and asked to see his latest work, which was still being edited. Berney and Hope flew to Denmark, saw a cut of *The Neon Demon,* and within two weeks signed a deal to be the movie's U.S. distributor.

To Refn, a new media company with a massive streaming platform that was equally committed to a theatrical release and run by veterans of the indie scene whom he knew and trusted was almost unbelievable luck. "They're like the kings in the seventeenth century — they have become the true patrons," Refn said over lunch at a trendy L.A. organic restaurant, wearing sunglasses and a shirt unbuttoned halfway down his chest.

At a basic level, he went with Amazon simply because with such a poor box-office track record, he needed a patron willing to take a big risk. But he was also savvy enough to know that much of the value in his movies lay in giving fans a way to pore over them dozens of times in search of hidden meanings. So digital streaming was critical, as it is for most indie movies whose directors are realistic about the superhero-dominated state of the multiplexes. "I wanted to get into the Amazon business because they were the first company to present an answer in this new ecosystem," Refn said. "I wanted to jump into the future before the future was created."

It was a good bet. Critics were divided on *The Neon Demon,* but had a lot to say about it, and people who saw it loved it — some even sent Refn pictures of their *Neon Demon*–inspired tattoos. But there weren't nearly enough of them. *The Neon Demon* was one of 2016's biggest bombs at the box office, grossing just $1.3 million in its nationwide release. For any normal Hollywood distributor, be it Fox Searchlight or the Weinstein Company, that would have been a disaster, with a loss in the tens of millions of dollars once marketing costs were included.

Amazon certainly wasn't pleased with the outcome, but it could easily absorb the blow. Price had explicitly stated, in fact, that he didn't care about the losses or profits on any particular film. Amazon was building a slate of movies that would give its streaming service an identity and would engage passionate fans. On that count, at least, *The Neon Demon* could still be a win. "I think that it's going to be a success on Prime," said Berney. "But if we were a small company, we wouldn't be able to ride it out for a year."

Hope, perhaps even more boldly, was willing to declare the movie a success soon after its miserable theatrical run because of what it told audiences about Amazon Studios. "We don't measure success by an individual film," he said. "Audiences are built by a consistent supply of quality goods in an environment they trust. That ultimately alters people's behavior."

In the long run, Ropell admitted, he wanted hits just like any movie company. But because Amazon had ambitions much broader than each picture's bottom line, failure was measured very differently. "The only thing that would be unacceptable," he said, "would be if we were making films that weren't high quality."

"AWFUL" IS A MATTER OF PERSPECTIVE

January 2017 was a notable turning point for the movie business. With *Manchester by the Sea,* a dot-com company had earned a best picture Academy Award nomination for the first time. Two months later, it won for best actor and best screenplay.

Amazon threw some of the most extravagant, star-studded parties around the Oscars and Golden Globes that year, and Bezos became a regular presence on the Hollywood cocktail circuit, sipping champagne in a tuxedo while hobnobbing with moguls and stars. It was all a sign that Silicon Valley was encroaching on Hollywood's turf and gaining a more dominant place in popular culture, as it had already done in so many other areas of our lives, from communication to journalism to cars.

But in a few years, it may be remembered best as the moment when Amazon proved it could do what Hollywood no longer could: provide a sustainable, supportive home for interesting, original indie movies.

Hollywood studios, which made movies in order to make money from movies, simply couldn't justify using their parent companies' funds to let indie darling James Gray re-create a doomed voyage up the Amazon River and Gillian Robespierre portray a fractured family in 1990s New York. As Bob Iger had said about Miramax: "That's an awful business. Awful."

But Amazon didn't make movies primarily to make money from movies. It used movies to draw attention, to increase engagement, and to dominate people's time and digital behavior so they would ultimately buy more stuff from the company.

The solution Ted Hope had long wanted, one that would keep feeding intelligent moviegoers and the culture at large with truly artful cinema, had finally revealed itself. All he needed was a company that, at its core, couldn't care less about movies.

13

Apt Pupil

China's Shifting Relationship
with Hollywood

AS HOLLYWOOD SOUGHT NEW SOURCES of money in recent years to help fund the risky, original movies it wouldn't make itself, it didn't just look north to Silicon Valley. It also turned east, to China.

It was a big change, since for many years Hollywood had been using China simply as a new market in which to make more money from its biggest films. But by the mid-2010s, proposals from Chinese companies eager to put their own money into Hollywood arrived with increasing regularity on studio doorsteps. In one such proposal, in 2014, a Chinese conglomerate announced itself eager to invest in Sony Pictures' *Amazing Spider-Man 2,* promising to help increase box office in the world's second-largest movie market in exchange for a small piece of the movie's profits and the chance to have its name listed as a producer.

"We focus much more on the strategic value of our cooperation in Spiderman, and hope this will work out for both parties," wrote Yuan Zhou, the head of motion pictures for China's powerful Shanghai Media Group, in broken English. "We do believe SMG could be Sony's close friend and strategic partner in China market, and this relationship can lead to much greater success with the fast growth and opening up of our market."

Sony executives were intrigued but certainly didn't feel they needed such a deal to make their next Spidey blockbuster a hit in China. Deciding the financial terms weren't in Sony's favor, the business affairs chief, Andrew Gumpert, made a succinct recommendation to Michael Lynton and Amy Pascal concerning the proposal: "NO THANKS!"

The Amazing Spider-Man 2 went on to gross $94 million in China, its best foreign performance by a factor of more than two. A visual-effects-heavy 3D sequel, featuring a well-known superhero, was exactly what Chinese moviegoers loved, and Sony's bet that it didn't need a partner to succeed there proved correct.

Two years later, though, things had changed. After years of white-hot growth, the Chinese market was cooling. Hollywood tentpoles, while still popular, no longer owned the top of the box-office charts. A local family movie, *Monster Hunt*, had hit number one at the box office in 2015, and a romantic comedy fantasy, *The Mermaid*, was topping the charts in 2016, with more than twice as much box office as the number two film, Disney's *Zootopia*.

Sony, with its shortage of "event" films, was feeling the pain particularly intensely. It was number six among major studios at the 2015 box office in China, even worse than its fifth-place showing in the United States. Its biggest production of 2016, the female-led reboot of *Ghostbusters*, wasn't even released in China, due either to censors' concerns about its supernatural themes or bureaucrats' belief that the franchise was too old to be recognizable to audiences there (the Chinese government almost never gave reasons for its decisions on whether and when to import Hollywood films).

So in September 2016, Sony signed a deal with a new Chinese partner. Wanda Group, a massive conglomerate led by China's richest man, Wang Jianlin, would invest in a series of upcoming Sony productions and get involved in order to "highlight the China element in the films." Wanda would also use its online ticketing platforms, theme parks, and theaters to promote Sony movies and try to give them a leg up over the competition.

The American studio bought out by the Japanese twenty-seven years ago was, in short, giving up a piece of its business to China in order to gain a foothold in the new center of power for the global entertainment business. And it was hardly the only Hollywood giant to do so.

Wanda's Sony deal was just a small example of its monstrous hunger to devour anything and everything it could find in Hollywood. It started by acquiring AMC, now America's biggest movie theater chain, in 2012, for $2.6 billion. In 2015, it bought Legendary Pictures, which made the monster movies *Godzilla* and *Pacific Rim* and co-financed *Jurassic World* and *The Dark Knight,* for $3.5 billion. Everyone in Hollywood thought it was an absurd and unjustifiable price for such a small company. Many speculated that Wanda may not have even understood that Legendary was only a passive investor in *Jurassic World* and *The Dark Knight* and didn't produce or own either film.

But the Chinese conglomerate was undeterred. The head of Wanda had so many meetings in Hollywood that soon everyone in the entertainment business knew who "Chairman Wang" was. Whenever he met with the heads of studios and production companies, he almost immediately asked what it would take to buy them out and then acted annoyed when, because these entities were part of large public companies or had private investors, they couldn't make a deal right there on the spot. In 2016, though, Wanda nearly bought a 49 percent stake in Paramount Pictures, the 103-year-old studio behind *The Ten Commandments, Top Gun,* and *Transformers.* The sale fell apart at the last second, due to a boardroom battle at Paramount's corporate parent, Viacom.

Other Chinese companies, meanwhile, were investing in slates of movies from numerous studios and new ventures formed by former studio executives.

Hollywood was going Chinese.

It was a remarkable moment. Twenty-five years earlier, China was interesting to Hollywood only as a place where toys and T-shirts based on its biggest titles could be cheaply manufactured. It was of no use as a box-office market because China had few movie theaters and the government didn't allow Western movies in anyway.

In the 2000s, however, things changed dramatically. As the government shifted China's economy from one based on manufacturing for export to one based on domestic consumption of goods and services, movies became one of the prime growth drivers. Like so many foreigners before them, Chinese audiences went crazy for Hollywood films, particularly big-budget franchise ones, and as the government allowed more of them in, theater construction grew at a frenzied rate. By 2014, eighteen new screens were being built every day.

In 2005, the highest-grossing Hollywood movie in China, *Harry Potter and the Goblet of Fire,* grossed $11.7 million. In 2017, the eighth Fast & Furious film grossed $392 million there. Total box-office sales skyrocketed from $248 million in 2005 to $6.6 billion in 2016. It was already the number two movie market in the world, and experts predicted that sometime before 2020, it would surpass the United States to become number one.

Still, between censorship, import quotas, and blatant manipulation by the government and its partners, it wasn't an easy market in which to make money. And American studios took home only 25 percent of every box-office dollar earned in China, compared to 55 or 60 percent in the United States, where they also made money from DVD and television sales that barely existed in the world's most populous nation.

Nonetheless, the growth of China was a godsend for Hollywood. Virtually every dollar made there was a found one, and it came just as other sources of money were collapsing. "When studios greenlight a movie, it used to be about, 'What are the DVD sales going to be?'" observed Rich Gelfond, who as CEO of the giant digital-screen company IMAX works with just about every movie studio in the world. "As DVDs fell off, it was replaced by the question, 'How's the movie going to do in China?'" The strategy paid off big-time. Some American films, including the video-game adaptation *Warcraft* and the last two sequels in the Fast & Furious series, made more money in China than they did in the United States.

Concerns about Chinese audiences and regulators started to affect how movies were made and, in some cases, whether they were made at all. And so it really wasn't that big a change when billions of Chinese dollars started flowing into American movies. Instead of indirectly controlling Hollywood by forcing studios to anticipate what would make money in their country, the Chinese were starting to take direct control.

And there was little doubt that this was just the beginning. Though his ambitions for Paramount were thwarted by American corporate infighting, Wanda's Wang was desperate to get his hands on one major studio or another. He declared there was "no ceiling" as to what he would pay. In Hollywood, a town that invented slogans like "In space, no one can hear you scream" and "Go ahead, make my day," a new one emerged in 2016: "China is now the wallet. And Hollywood is the factory."

The future of Hollywood is in large part being written by China. And the story of the Chinese movie business is critical to understanding how that happened.

STARTING AS TOURISTS

Rich Gelfond went to China because he didn't have any other options. He ended up on the ground floor of a market explosion bigger than any bang in an Arnold Schwarzenegger movie and a chase for dollars unrivaled by any high-speed dash at the end of a Tom Cruise film.

A few years after he and a partner had taken over IMAX, whose business was screening nature documentaries on its giant screens in museums and science centers, the short, fast-talking, long-haired Gelfond was still struggling to find ways to grow the business. He had a long-term vision that IMAX would become part of the Hollywood system, screening real movies and generating sizable box office. But he had a chicken-and-egg problem: no studio was interested in making movies for IMAX if the company was only in museums, and no multiplex wanted to install an IMAX screen if it would be able to show only documentaries about space shuttles and hummingbirds.

In the late 1990s, Western movies were just starting to be shown in China for the first time in years. After 1978's *Superman* was released in the country in 1986 and then hastily withdrawn one month later, due to criticisms that the character was "a narcotic which the capitalist class gives itself to cast off its serious crises," Hollywood was banned for nearly a decade. Then in 1994, the State Administration of Radio, Film, and Television (SARFT) started allowing "the 10 best foreign movies" each year to play in the small number of theaters that existed in large cities like Beijing and Shanghai. Harrison Ford's *The Fugitive* was the first. It was followed by other entertaining, largely mindless action movies like *Speed* and *True Lies*.

For all of the 1990s, though, movie exports to China were little more than an interesting experiment for Hollywood.

Box-office grosses there were in the low millions at best, in large part because its 1.26 billion people had only about two thousand theaters in the year 2000, compared to seven thousand in the United States, whose population was less than a quarter of the size of China's. And because the Chinese government took such a huge chunk of each box-office dollar, the studios were lucky to earn even $1 million per film.

China was also politically treacherous. In the wake of 1989's Tiananmen Square protests and massacre, the government was sensitive to any Western content that could fan controversial political beliefs. Disney's plans to expand into the country were set back years because in the United States it had released Martin Scorsese's *Kundun*, about the Tibetan spiritual leader the Dalai Lama, who has long been at odds with the Beijing government.

But political sensitivities were good news for IMAX, Gelfond figured. The documentaries that played on his screens wouldn't offend a ninety-year-old nun, let alone a Communist official. And so he set his eyes on China. The country was ripe for more screens, and he wanted IMAX to lead the way, figuring its benign content would be more help than hindrance there, unlike the situation in the United States.

But expanding into a country where the government controlled everything and few Western retail businesses were present was a hazy path at best. So in the late 1990s, Gelfond hired a lobbyist in Beijing to introduce IMAX to the politicians who could open the gates it would need to pass through. "There were no Western entertainment companies in China, so I literally had dinner with top officials in the state council," Gelfond recalled in his New York office in 2016. "I would ask each of them for their advice on how to get into China and how to succeed in the long run." The answers were ones that every Hollywood company would need to learn as they tried to gain a foothold in China in the 2000s.

Make China feel important and look for "win/win scenarios," they advised him.

Forge partnerships with local businesses, they said, and whatever you do, don't lecture them on the right way to do things. Even if they were novices at capitalism, the Chinese wanted to feel like equal partners. To show respect, they said, Gelfond should take most meetings himself, rather than send an underling who was in charge of "China relations."

And make clear, with every decision, that you are here for the long run, they insisted. The last thing the Chinese wanted was a new generation of colonialists seeking to extract some money and then head back home. The capsule message, Gelfond recalled, was simple: "Don't come in like an outsider looking to make a quick killing, which was the U.S.'s reputation around the world."

For movie studios, this would not prove an easy pill to swallow. Studios were used to being dominant in every relationship because they had the movies that people were dying to see and theaters were dying to show. But as Gelfond was learning, acting self-important in China was a quick way to get sent back across the Pacific. Patience and deference were key, even when dealing with opaque government bureaucracies that wielded their power in a seemingly arbitrary manner.

IMAX wasn't that important, at least not yet, and Gelfond had no trouble following the Chinese bureaucrats' advice. He moved his Asian headquarters from Singapore to Shanghai in order to demonstrate his commitment to the country and partnered with Shanghai Film Studios to make a documentary about panda bears. He also became intimately familiar with flight schedules across the Pacific as he avoided dispatching subordinates and traveled to China multiple times per year to personally conduct meetings. Over the next twenty years, he would make the trip more than fifty times. "We made it clear we were following what they were saying and doing a long-term thing," he said.

IMAX was able to build a few screens at science centers in China, but its first big reward came in 2002, when it signed a deal for its first commercial theater, in the hub of Beijing, People's Square.

At the same time, Gelfond's many years of lobbying in Hollywood were also starting to bear fruit. His company debuted its first "real" film in its giant-screen format: a digital remaster of the 1995 Tom Hanks space drama *Apollo 13*. In the United States, it played at the museums and educational institutions that had IMAX screens, but in China, the timing was perfect for it to play in a commercial location.

The initial results weren't stellar, but they were good enough for IMAX to grow steadily in China, making deals for two theaters here and five there. After the import quota was doubled to twenty movies per year in 2002, studios saw a steady growth in their business too. China wasn't a massive market yet, but it was a notable one. By 2009, the disaster movie *2012* and the second Transformers film were setting records by grossing more than $65 million each. Total box office in the country reached $908 million, nearly 10 percent of the combined total of $10.6 billion from the United States and Canada.

Then came *Avatar*.

THE TURNING POINT

James Cameron was perhaps the only Western filmmaker who was a well-known name in China in 2009. His 1998 epic, *Titanic,* was not only the highest-grossing movie in the world at the time, at $2.2 billion, but its $52.7 million gross in China was a record that stood for more than a decade, until *Transformers* and *2012* surpassed it.

His next film, *Avatar,* was easily the riskiest of the twenty-first century, with a budget of $310 million and new digital 3D technology, which had never been used in a commercial movie before. It opened on December 18, 2009, in the United States and most foreign countries and quickly became a smash, with audiences fascinated by the ground-breaking visual effects portraying the richly drawn alien world of Pandora and its motion-captured inhabitants. By January 7 of the next year, it had grossed $1 billion worldwide, before it even opened in China.

In the world's most populous nation, though, *Avatar* wasn't a hit. It was a phenomenon. Despite the biggest snowfall in fifty-four years and freezing temperatures, people waited in line to see it for as long as six hours, and the movie broke a record for the biggest weekday opening ever in the country. Tickets, which usually cost a few dollars, were being scalped for as much as a hundred dollars. Whereas Westerners saw Cameron's story as a standard, perhaps preachy, allegory about racism and environmental destruction, the movie struck a culturally resonant chord in China, where developers' forced appropriation of property was a hot topic at the time.

But, as Gelfond noticed, the biggest reason for *Avatar*'s Chinese success was digital 3D. In China and other developing nations, going to the movies was not just a fun way to enjoy some pop culture. It was an opportunity for an emerging middle class, suddenly flush with cash, thanks to the country's supernova economy, to experience luxuries they may have never dreamed possible while growing up in a poor rural village. Much like Americans going on a foreign vacation, Chinese moviegoers wanted to see something spectacular, something that would blow their minds and be worth bragging about when they got back home. And they didn't mind spending a little extra money to do it.

There could be no better news for IMAX, which charged more for its superior cinema experience. Cameron had worked with IMAX to develop the 3D technology he used in *Avatar* and designed the movie to be best viewed on its screens. The film was a hit for IMAX all over the world but a game-changer in China.

Avatar grossed $204 million in China, more than tripling the previous record set by *2012*, and $25 million of that came from IMAX. This number can truly be appreciated only when you consider that the company had just thirteen screens in the country at the time. Each one grossed more than $2 million over the several months that the government let the film run.

210 THE BIG PICTURE

One of those screens in Beijing even shut down for an afternoon as senior government officials used it for a private viewing of *Avatar*.

Within months of the debut of *Avatar*, IMAX signed a deal to open a hundred new theaters in China. Many more followed. "*Avatar* was far and away our biggest success there," Gelfond said. "It was an overnight turning point." Other 3D IMAX hits followed, including *Alice in Wonderland, Clash of the Titans,* and *Iron Man 2.* Total box office in China surged by 61 percent in 2010, to $1.47 billion. The next year it hit $2 billion. In 2012, it rose to $2.7 billion.

Though audiences in the West grew tired of 3D after it was used for seemingly every "event" movie, many with cheap and poorly produced effects, the Chinese couldn't get enough. In 2012, the government even agreed to let in an additional fourteen foreign movies per year, but only if they were in 3D or formatted for IMAX screens.

That deal also nearly doubled the maximum amount of box-office receipts a foreign studio could keep from their movies in China, from 13 to 25 percent. China was now a major, fast-growing source of revenue, and as DVD sales plummeted, studios increasingly focused on it. For the first time, decisions were being made with the Chinese market in mind. Chinese audiences couldn't understand and weren't interested in most American dramas, comedies, or other mid-budget films. They wanted big-budget films full of visual effects that could be understood even without subtitles and would make moviegoing an event worthy of their time and money.

Chinese audiences also preferred brands they knew and trusted, ones that made moviegoing a safe experience and one with the same patina of luxury they got in an Apple or Hermès store. And so Hollywood pumped out more and more branded franchise films. Americans sick of yet another Transformers or X-Men movie couldn't blame just Hollywood anymore. They would have to blame China too.

The Communist giant didn't just affect which movies were made, but also how. In 2011, a bankrupt MGM was looking to sell off movies it no longer had the resources to release, including a remake of the Cold War–era film *Red Dawn,* about American farm kids who repel a Soviet invasion. To make the film more politically relevant when it was shot in

2009, the filmmakers replaced the Soviet invaders with Chinese ones. But by 2011, post-*Avatar,* no distributor would risk buying a movie that would offend the Chinese government. Not only would *Red Dawn* be impossible to play in the world's fastest-growing movie market, but angry government officials could punish companies that released it elsewhere, as they had done to Disney with *Kundun.*

The filmmakers used digital technology to erase every Chinese flag and military symbol in *Red Dawn* and replace them with those of an Asian country nobody cared about offending: North Korea. These changes eventually allowed the movie to find a U.S. distributor (though it didn't do very well at the box office) and also spurred a minor backlash among those who feared it was a sign that American companies were kowtowing to political pressure from an authoritarian government for the sake of dollars.

The fact was, however, that by 2011 studios were already falling over each other to make nice with China.

THE STUDENT BECOMES THE MASTER

The prior year, Sony had worked with the state-owned China Film Group to produce a remake of *The Karate Kid* starring Will Smith's son, Jaden, along with Jackie Chan. China Film contributed $5 million of a $40 million budget and helped steer the film, shot in its country, so it wouldn't ruffle any government feathers. A slightly different version was even put together in the editing room for Chinese release. The bullying sequences and a kiss between young characters were shown in the rest of the world but cut from the Chinese version.

To get *Men in Black 3* released in China, Sony trimmed several minutes from the 2012 film, deleting a shootout and its aftermath at a restaurant in New York's Chinatown. After the gunfight, characters played by Will Smith and Tommy Lee Jones mind-wipe Chinese American bystanders, a moment some thought could be interpreted as a comment on China's censorship of the Internet.

A villain was cut from *Pirates of the Caribbean: At World's End* for its China release because the native actor Chow Yun-fat played him — possibly suggesting negative things about Chinese character, which might displease government officials.

Sometimes studios added content in an effort to please Chinese audiences and officials. For 2013's *Iron Man 3*, Marvel worked with a Chinese production partner to add four minutes of footage, including two scenes featuring a doctor and his assistant played by Chinese actors and a news report on the superhero playing with Chinese schoolchildren. Reaction to the additions was largely negative in China, however, because it was so obviously superfluous and featured blatant product placement for a local energy drink. For 2016's *Passengers,* Sony cut a glimpse of Chris Pratt's bare backside to satisfy Chinese censors and added a scene of the star talking to a robot bartender in Mandarin.

Soon it wasn't rare at all to see Chinese stars like Fan Bingbing and Angelababy showing up in major Hollywood movies such as *X-Men: Days of Future Past* and *Independence Day: Resurgence.* Sony even put out a call to talent agencies for a Chinese actor to include in its planned reboot of the family movie *Jumanji.* What was the role? That wasn't clear yet. "They want to have a Chinese component. They don't necessarily know what it is," said a talent agent.

Still, trying to please Chinese government officials who decided which movies were allowed in under the quota, when they would be released, and how censorship rules would be applied was an impossible task. SARFT, its subsidiary China Film Bureau, and the state-owned China Film Group, all of which controlled the fate of Hollywood movies in the country, didn't play by a consistent and predictable set of rules. Rather, they based their actions on their own interests at a particular moment.

So when American movies started taking up too much of the box-office receipts in 2012 for the government's liking, China Film decided it would be best to open *The Dark Knight Rises* and *The Amazing Spider-Man* on the same day, in a successful bid to limit their total returns. They'd force the two superhero pictures to compete. "We hope those protective measures will be able to create a space for domestic movies to survive and grow," said the deputy head of the Film Bureau, describing this decision to the *People's Daily*.

Chinese bureaucrats turned to this gambit whenever locally made movies started falling below 50 percent of the country's total box office. In 2015, the government released three American animated movies, *Inside Out, Hotel Transylvania 2*, and *The Peanuts Movie*, all within a month of one another, forcing them to fight for the same family audience. At other times, the government used one of its precious quota spots to import an American movie everyone knew would do no business in China. Sony's remake of the musical *Annie* grossed just $500,000 in the country, and Fox's *Eddie the Eagle*, a low-budget comedy about a hapless would-be Olympic skier, made just under $1 million.

When it wanted to boost a particular local film, China wasn't above stealing money from Hollywood. Box-office numbers were always somewhat questionable and difficult to audit in China, but at times it seemed these figures were blatantly manipulated. In September 2015, it was critical to the government that a propagandistic film, *The Hundred Regiments Offensive*, succeed at the box office; it portrayed a battle, in 1940, during which Communist armies defeated Japanese occupiers. And so, few in Hollywood were surprised when moviegoers who swore they saw the Hollywood sequel *Terminator Genisys* posted photos of the tickets they were given, which said *Regiments* instead. Some pictures even showed the word *Terminator* handwritten over a printed *Regiments* ticket. It was clear people were seeing *Terminator* but their box-office spending was being attributed to the Chinese movie.

But American companies had no leverage over the Chinese government and no real way to protest, unless they were willing to put billions of dollars in annual revenue at risk. "I never even thought about China ten years ago," said Adam Goodman, the former head of production for Paramount Pictures. "Now we're at a point where Hollywood can't exist without China."

And so by 2015 a race was apparently on as to which studio could best insinuate itself into powerful Chinese interests. For its fourth Transformers movie, in 2014, Paramount partnered with a pair of Chi-

nese companies on a slew of local marketing and promotional partnerships. These included a reality show to cast four roles in the film, weeks
of local shooting during which stars frequently were photographed on
social media, and separate premieres in Hong Kong, Shanghai, and
Beijing. One real estate firm even sued when the film didn't include the
expected twenty seconds of footage of one of its properties. But Paramount got results. *Transformers: Age of Extinction* grossed $320 million
in China, a record at the time.

By the next year, studios were starting to recognize an even easier
way into China's good graces: let it put money into films. China Film
Group invested in the fantasy movie *Seventh Son,* the action sequel *Furious 7,* and Adam Sandler's *Pixels* in 2015, providing about 10 percent
of the production budgets in exchange for a stake in worldwide revenues. While studios often allow outside investors to put money into a
slate of films, doing so on a one-off basis is rare, particularly for surefire
hits like the seventh Fast & Furious movie. Although no explicit quid
pro quo was stated in the deals, nobody was surprised when all three
films got favorable release dates in China and performed well there —
even *Seventh Son* and *Pixels,* which fizzled in most other countries. *Furious 7* beat the Transformers record, grossing $391 million in China.

In some cases, the Chinese box office completely transformed films'
financial outcomes. *Warcraft,* an adaptation of the hit video game from
Wanda-owned Legendary Pictures, bombed in the United States and
most foreign countries. But it made more money in China, $221 mil-
lion, than it did everywhere else in the world combined. If Americans
see a *Warcraft* 2 on their multiplex marquee in a few years, it will be entirely due to demand in China. The United States will be treated merely
as a foreign adjunct, where the film might pick up a few extra dollars.

As movies were being transformed by China, IMAX was too. In
2015, Gelfond's company established a separate Chinese subsidiary.
When it held a public IPO, it raised nearly $250 million. By late 2016 it
had 371 screens open in China, with contracts to build 381 more. That
was 45 percent of the company's worldwide total. One of the advan-
tages of the public stock listing, Gelfond noted, was that a number of
IMAX's top investors were now Chinese state-backed companies. "If

they screw with us," he said of the government, "they screw with themselves."

FUNDING THE FUTURE OF HOLLYWOOD

On a sunny September day in Beverly Hills, Adam Goodman was
in a hotel suite, eager to talk about his new company. But the silver-
haired, baby-faced executive had to wait until his partner and financier
finished smoking a cigarette on the balcony. Very few people in Hollywood except actors still smoked, but now that everyone was doing
business with the Chinese, the town's moguls had to get used to the
habit again.

Goodman's résumé was as American as they got in the movie business. After starting his career in his hometown, Chicago, as a production assistant on movies by John Hughes, the director of *The Breakfast Club* and *Ferris Bueller's Day Off*, Goodman made his way to L.A.,
where in 1996 he started as an assistant at Steven Spielberg's Dream-
Works studio. He quickly became a favorite of the director of *E.T.* and
Jurassic Park, and by 2004 Goodman was the company's president of
production. Next came a similar job at Paramount Pictures, where
Goodman oversaw hits, like films in the Star Trek and the Transformer
series, but eventually took the blame for a bad run at the box office and
was kicked out the door.

At any other time in the history of Hollywood, Goodman would
have followed the well-established path for ousted production chiefs:
setting up shop as a producer and using his long-developed connections to make movies for studios, including his former employer. But
by 2016, studios had slashed spending on outside producers, and anyone who wasn't contractually connected to a big hit franchise was
struggling.

Goodman also knew from his time at Paramount that despite years
of cutbacks, the major studios were still bloated, slow-moving institutions. Their only idea for adapting to modern consumer preferences
and financial pressures was to search desperately for the next block-

buster cinematic universe that could make them a rival to Disney. Paramount in particular was having a hard time because, like Sony Pictures, its troubled parent company did not invest much in it for many years.

Goodman initially called his new production venture Dichotomy, because he wanted to focus on two types of films: big-budget blockbusters and "micro-budget" movies. The first type undeniably generated bigger profits when they succeeded because global audiences loved them. Micro-budget movies, meanwhile, had no stars, lavish sets, or impressive visual effects, and could be made for a few hundred thousand to a few million dollars. If well executed, such a film could be the next *Paranormal Activity,* a horror sensation that was one of Goodman's proudest successes at Paramount. And if they turned out poorly, studios could release micro-budget movies directly on DVD and video-on-demand, losing little money due to the films' minuscule cost.

Since studios were reluctant to cut producers like Goodman in on the action on franchise films and didn't believe in his vision for micro-budgets, he would need outside money to help fund the movies he wanted to do. Just a few years ago, that would have been impossible if his father wasn't Larry Ellison. The only sources of money for movies had been Warner Bros., Disney, or Paramount.

But now, it was obvious what he would have to do: look to China.

Over the prior few years, the trickle of Chinese money into Hollywood had turned into a torrent. At first, this move seemed strategic: for example, Wanda's purchase of AMC Theatres was a way to consolidate the global exhibition business. Then it got more interesting: Chinese investors funded new companies run by Jeff Robinov, the former production chief of Warner Bros., and Dick Cook, the former chairman of Walt Disney Studios. They invested in Steven Spielberg's new company, Amblin Partners. They also started putting money into individual films, including sequels to *Star Trek* and *Mission: Impossible,* and committing hundreds of millions of dollars to fund a portion of nearly every movie made at Lionsgate and Universal Pictures.

Some viewed Chinese investors as the latest "dumb money" to hit

Hollywood. It is no doubt true that financing movies is not the smartest way for any investor, from anywhere in the world, to earn the best returns. Others had a different theory — that some wealthy Chinese individuals and businesses were seeking to get their money out of China, where an autocratic government could still steal anyone's wealth at any time, for any reason. Certainly Hollywood had long been a destination for legal money laundering. But those who worked most closely with the Chinese knew that the biggest reason for these investments was a form of reverse-colonialism. After more than a decade as a place for Hollywood to make money, China wanted to turn the tables.

The United States had already proved the power of pop culture to help establish a nation's global dominance. Now China wanted to do the same. The Beijing government considered art and culture to be a form of "soft power," whereby it could extend influence around the world without the use of weapons.

Over the past few years, locally produced Chinese films had become more successful at the box office there. But most were culturally specific comedies and love stories that didn't translate anywhere else. China had yet to produce a global blockbuster. And with box-office growth in that country slowing in 2016 and early 2017, hits that resonated internationally would be critical if the Communist nation was to grow its movie business and use it to become the kind of global power it wanted to be.

So Chinese companies, with the backing of the government, started investing in Hollywood, with a mission to learn how experienced hands there made blockbusters that thrived worldwide. Within a few years, they figured, China would learn how to do that without anyone's help. "Working with a company like Universal will help us elevate our skill set in moviemaking," the head of the Chinese entertainment company Perfect World Pictures said, while investing $250 million in a slate of upcoming films from the American studio.

Getting there wouldn't be easy. One of the highest-profile efforts to produce a worldwide hit out of China was *The Great Wall,* starring Matt Damon and made by Wanda's Legendary Pictures. The $150 million film, about a war against monsters set on the Chinese historic landmark, grossed an underwhelming $171 million and a disastrous $45 million in the United States. Then, to create another obstacle, Chinese government currency controls established in early 2017 slowed, at least temporarily, the flow of money from China into Hollywood.

But by then it was too late to turn back. As seemed to always be true when it came to Hollywood's relationship with China, the Americans had no choice but to keep playing along. Nobody else was willing to pour billions of dollars into the struggling movie business in the mid-2010s, particularly for original or lower-budget productions.

"This is really one of the first true Chinese movie studios in Hollywood," Goodman said of his new venture, once his partner Zhang Zhou, the vice chairman of the Chinese company LeEco, finished his cigarette. "It's a creative partnership taking the best of where we came from and where they're going."

LeEco is a Chinese electronics giant involved in smartphones, Internet-connected televisions, and electric cars; it also operates an online video service akin to Netflix. The ultra-confident, English-fluent Zhang, whom Goodman called "ZZ," wanted to pair information about consumer behavior around the world, which his firm could gather, with a filmmaking operation that could base its decisions in part on that data and also use the company's platforms to release its productions.

That idea matched perfectly with Goodman's desire to move faster than the old studio infrastructure allowed. His Dichotomy was folded into LeEco's entertainment division, called Le Vision Pictures, which he ran out of Los Angeles. Now he could try to make movies with information based on what people watched online yesterday, rather than what they saw in the theater or bought on DVD last year. And if some of his micro-budget movies didn't turn out well enough to release in theaters, he had an in-house platform that could release them online.

Most important, he had a deep-pocketed backer and was free, for a while at least, from the pressure to hit box-office projections for every film and from the endless hunt for the next Avengers concept — the only things that really mattered to a major studio anymore.

Zhang wanted to make money, of course, but what he wanted most was to run the first Chinese company to prove that his country could make films popular around the globe. An American might run production, but Le Vision would become the Chinese studio that rivaled Paramount and 20th Century Fox.

And in a few years, Zhang might not need the American anymore.

14

Field of Dreams

Studio Defectors and the Future
of Nonfranchise Films

ADAM GOODMAN'S PARTNERSHIP with Le Vision wasn't just an example of the Chinese money flooding the American movie business. It was also a new way for a guy who started working in Hollywood because he wanted to make all types of movies to actually do that, at a time when studios no longer wanted to.

Running production at a studio, as Goodman did at Paramount, used to be the dream job for film lovers because they got to use their taste to decide which movies got made. Think that script is great? Love that director? Studio heads of production can spend millions to turn what they like into an actual movie playing in multiplexes around the world, so long as they stay on budget and don't make so many flops that they get fired. The best-known model for this type of executive is Robert Evans, the colorful head of Paramount in the 1970s who made *Rosemary's Baby, Harold and Maude,* and *The Godfather.* His autobiography *The Kid Stays in the Picture* and its companion documentary are must-sees for anyone fascinated by the halcyon days of Hollywood.

But life atop a studio no longer resembles what it was like for Bob Evans. Now and for the foreseeable future, the heads of production at studios aren't larger-than-life moguls whose relationships and tastes define what we all see. Instead, their job is to identify, cultivate, and grow franchises. Like a senior executive at Procter & Gamble, they have a collection of brands for which they need to maintain consumer interest. But instead of updates to the packaging and ingredients, studio production chiefs come up with sequels, spinoffs, and expansions of their cinematic universes.

Only when that job is done, if they're lucky, might they be able to make a handful of inexpensive comedies, dramas, or thrillers that they personally like and think will succeed — like the kid who gets to watch TV after homework is finished.

Goodman was fired because his bosses blamed him for Paramount's lackluster slate during his last couple of years, and in particular for a shortage of successful franchises. But for him, as for so many other longtime studio executives, the job had become a lot less fun because there was a lot less freedom.

At his new company, Goodman would have the resources and the freedom to make more movies that *he* wanted to make. In his case, that meant micro-budget films, a personal passion because he had long believed that originality in the franchise-dominated environment required experimentation at very low cost, so you could afford to throw a lot of cinematic spaghetti against the wall to see what would stick. "We'll make romantic comedies, we'll make horror, we'll make anything the studios aren't making, really," he said.

But Goodman didn't see Le Vision as a competitor to the major studios; he saw it as a partner. That's because his new Chinese-backed company lacked one key asset that only Paramount and Universal and their four huge competitors possessed: the infrastructure and resources to market and distribute a movie in all media — theaters, DVDs, digital formats, and television — around the world. Building such a system takes years and hundreds of millions of dollars. Le Vision might get there someday, but for now, Goodman would need to sign deals with major studios to release his films. The exact types of movies that studios weren't making would actually be back on their slates — just financed and produced by somebody else.

It was a potentially transformative concept, once you stepped back to think about it. A studio executive could leave the traditional Hollywood system, start his own venture with outside money, and in the process start giving studios exactly the types of movies he couldn't make while on the inside. For movie fans who wanted more than what the franchise-dominated slates of Universal, Fox, Paramount, Warner Bros., Disney, and Sony contained, this was a big deal. Here was a way for studios to start releasing the kinds of movies they weren't making anymore. Not in a limited number of theaters and not on digital streaming platforms, but in thousands of theaters, the way "real" movies had come out for decades.

Of course, one former executive with one Chinese backer wouldn't make a dent at a time when Hollywood was releasing an *Alien* sequel, a *Pirates of the Caribbean* sequel, a *Baywatch* reboot, a *Mummy* reboot, and a *Wonder Woman* superhero adaptation all within a three-week period. But Adam Goodman was in fact not alone. By late 2016, former executives from every major studio were starting their own ventures, with the goal of producing the types of movies that they had been struggling to make on the inside.

Even Steven Spielberg, who spent much of the 1990s and 2000s trying to build his own studio, called DreamWorks, had given up on that dream. His company, now called Amblin Partners, raised more than $800 million to make movies that would be released by other studios.

One of the most interesting of these efforts was set up at Sony Pictures, led by a man who had spent nearly his whole career at the side of Amy Pascal.

COMPANY MAN

After twenty-seven years working his way up the corporate ladder at Sony Pictures, Doug Belgrad made a huge career move — to an office on the other side of a parking lot.

But though his new digs in the Sidney Poitier Building were just a few hundred feet from where he used to work, in the Irving Thalberg Building, Belgrad's job was dramatically different. His office was a lot smaller, his volume of incoming phone calls and e-mails had dropped by about 75 percent, and he no longer had a multi-billion-dollar studio budget to help oversee as president of Sony's motion picture group.

But now, as the head of his own company, dubbed 2.0 Entertainment, Doug Belgrad has the opportunity to do something new, something that would let him make the kinds of movies that he loved but were difficult to focus on in his old job. It could spark a change in Sony Pictures' slate in the years to come.

Belgrad started his career in Columbia Pictures' executive training program in 1989, after a brief stint following media industry stocks on Wall Street. He seemed fated to build a career on the business side of Hollywood, analyzing earnings on spreadsheets, but he decided that was not all he wanted. So in 1992, he became a junior executive in the studio's production division, where he started to work his way up. He built his career by forging relationships in the 1990s with the hot young stars Adam Sandler and Will Smith and by working on some of their early films for the studio, such as *Big Daddy* and *Men in Black*.

In 2003 he ascended to Sony Pictures' top ranks, first as president of production, then president of Columbia, and finally president of the motion picture group. But whatever his title, Belgrad essentially had two primary responsibilities. One was helping to pick and make the studio's movies. He read scripts, talked to talent, visited sets, and oversaw editing — all the key jobs of a production chief.

Belgrad was close to Sandler, and later Kevin James, and played a key role in some of their dumbest but most lucrative comedies, such as *Paul Blart: Mall Cop*. He also helped launch a successful R-rated comedy business for Sony that included *Zombieland* and *This Is the End*. Having grown up with dreams of working in TV news, he took a particular interest in real-life dramas such as *Moneyball*, *The Social Network*, and *Captain Phillips*.

Belgrad's second role was less official but, to many people in the studio, more important. They called him the consigliere, the chief of staff, or the therapist-in-chief. What they meant was that he was Amy Pascal's closest aide and confidant, the person who managed anything he could — agents, budgets, her late-night anxiety attacks — to make her life easier. "I think of myself like the executive officer on a naval ship for her," he said of his relationship with his boss. "I make sure she spends her time and energy on the right things and keep stuff away from her that she shouldn't be bothered with."

Because of his years working in development and production, Belgrad and Pascal spoke the same language. But he was uniquely valuable to her because he was also fluent in finance, budgets, and the bottom line, a lingo Pascal spoke haltingly and reluctantly at best. That combination is why she had pulled him up through Sony's ranks. "I owe my entire career to you," Belgrad told Pascal in 2014.

As Pascal's closest aide and a steady yin to her manic yang, Belgrad was often the recipient of her trademark e-mails freaking out about the latest script problem, conflict with Lynton, or the overall state of the studio's slate. A big part of his job was absorbing the tension and helping his boss refocus.

"I know you want to win more than anyone I've ever come across," he wrote to her one night at 12:25 a.m. "I will leave you tonight with this particular platitude that, believe it or not, has been very helpful for me lately. If trying hard doesn't yield the results, then try easy."

"I will try easy," she wrote back. "You are my bestest pal."

The bestest pals were separated, though, when Pascal was fired in early 2015. Some thought Belgrad had a shot at succeeding her, but when Lynton selected Tom Rothman instead, the speculation shifted as to how long it would be until Belgrad left Sony.

He had, in fact, been contemplating an exit since renewing his contract in 2014. Sony was in the midst of a multi-year rut in its motion picture business at the same time that the industry was shrinking and focusing on big branded films above all else. Though he didn't wear the stress on his sleeve like Pascal, the job was becoming less rewarding for Belgrad too.

He had grown up in an entrepreneurial family, with a father and grandfather who ran a furniture-manufacturing business in suburban Chicago, and had visions of being his own boss. This dream had been long delayed as he ascended the studio ladder. Always the loyal corporate soldier, he helped Rothman make his transition into Pascal's job for more than a year, staying through the critical, and ultimately unsuccessful, release of the Melissa McCarthy–led *Ghostbusters* reboot in the summer of 2016.

A NEW START TO DO THE OLD THING

At the end of that year, sitting in an office in the only corner of the second floor of the Poitier Building not taken up by Will Smith's Overbrook Entertainment, Belgrad talked about his plans to make mid-budget movies when they were decidedly out of fashion in the industry. "The pressures on executives at studios more than ever are to think of movies as brands," he reflected, his salt-and-pepper beard complementing the gapped teeth, glasses, and closely cropped thinning hair, which have long made him easily recognizable in Hollywood. "They're fun things to play with, but the creative opportunities are not what they once were. If you're interested in a broad spectrum of movies, it makes sense to do your own thing."

At the time we spoke, Belgrad was in the process of raising $250 million from investors. His plan was to leverage that money into about twenty movies over the next five years. Most would be co-financed and released by Sony, though his deal allowed him to take projects to other studios if his former employer passed.

Most of Belgrad's movies would cost between $30 million and $60 million, he said, the exact range that studios are largely abandoning in favor of big-budget "events" and ultra-low-budget horror films and comedies. They would be thrillers, comedies, dramas, and family films — genres that he knew well and that most studios, including Sony, had cut back on severely.

Among his first projects was a live-action version of the children's story *Peter Rabbit,* with digitally created animals, which had long been in development at Sony but moved to a greenlight with Belgrad's money. He was also developing a vigilante movie he described as "a female-driven *Taken,*" a real-life story of a man who made three attempts to summit Mount Everest before Sir Edmund Hillary, and a film about a military contractor that he described as "halfway between *Zero Dark*

Thirty and *The Social Network.*" None of these were revolutionary, but they were certainly the type of films that were falling out of style — like CDs or, if he was lucky, vinyl records in the age of Spotify. They were not movies for everybody, like *Spider-Man* and *Star Wars,* but if well made, they would certainly be for somebody.

Belgrad didn't know anything about film economics that Michael Lynton or Bob Iger didn't, and he wasn't arrogant enough to think he could simply make better movies on a more consistent basis than other producers. But as an experienced insider, Doug Belgrad saw the holes in the studio system.

On one side of the equation were Sony and the other studios that would release his films. All of them, except perhaps Disney, he argued, still wanted original mid-budget movies. Their worldwide distribution and marketing systems, in fact, were built to handle around twenty movies per year, but they would be lucky to come up with a half dozen legitimate franchise tentpoles in any given year. The fewer films that movie studios released, the more free time their employees had and the easier it would be for them to release movies on behalf of other companies, for a fee.

In addition, Sony and its competitors all had "output" deals with television and digital networks like HBO or Netflix around the world, which promised to pay several million dollars for the rights to air or stream any movie the studio released. Most of those agreements included up to about twenty-five pictures per year.

But studios weren't using all those slots anymore because they didn't want to devote time and resources to identify and develop mid-budget movies and then take the complete financial risk to make them, particularly because profits from even successful smaller films were so paltry compared to what could be earned by the big brands. It was the exact problem Amy Pascal had faced with *Steve Jobs,* repeated over and over again. The economics of the movie business consistently pushed studios like Sony to make one $200 million reboot rather than four original $50 million films.

For Belgrad, it was an opportunity. He could make mid-budget movies and take advantage of studio executives' free time and the open slots in their television "output" deals. Belgrad's new company would handle all of the up-front work and shoulder half the risk itself. So he would develop his female-vigilante script until it was polished enough to be produced, hire a star and director, and then present Sony with a ready-to-go movie, for which half of the modest budget was already covered.

The profits from a hit would be quite small for Sony, but the risk was low too, particularly because the studio could collect a fee off the top to cover its distribution and marketing expenses. Most important, such a deal would allow Tom Rothman and his team to spend most of their time where it belonged in the year 2016: on the next Spider-Man and Bad Boys and Men in Black and Jumanji movies.

All Belgrad needed, meanwhile, was a few hits. Four or five of them, to be exact, among the twenty-something movies he planned to produce, would make his business a success if the rest ranged from break-even to total flop. The key was keeping his overhead low. Studios were built for an age of abundant profits and annual slates of more than twenty, or even more than thirty films, which is why they had thousands of employees around the globe. As is true for any large corporation, downsizing had been painful and slow, and most studios were still struggling to get to the right size, particularly as the ground kept shifting beneath them with the rise of digital distribution, the ascendancy of television, and changes in consumer behavior.

Belgrad planned to employ no more than a dozen people at his company, including a few creative executives to help him develop and make the movies, along with business and legal staff. "The studio appetite hasn't really changed, but their focus has shifted tremendously," he observed. "There's an opportunity to complement the movies they care about most with the ones they still need that won't move the needle on a major corporation's ledger but could be hugely meaningful to a small supplier."

Whether it's a hit or a flop, Belgrad's vigilante movie is unlikely to merit even a raised eyebrow at the headquarters of the $36 billion Sony Corporation in Tokyo. But it could be a big deal for a company with a dozen employees and total investments of just $250 million. The financial incentives for Belgrad, in other words, are the inverse of those of the major studios. The risk of movies costing more than $100 million to make is too high for him, but the benefits of modest $35 million hits are actually meaningful.

The unanswered question is whether audiences still care about the type of films he wants to make.

Belgrad knows that in an age of high-quality TV, certain types of films are very risky, particularly true-life stories with a political bent, which Belgrad happens to love. One example is a book he optioned while at Sony, by the journalist Glenn Greenwald, about the cyber-surveillance whistleblower Edward Snowden. But he knows those films are absolutely the most challenging at the box office now. *Steve Jobs* was a flop for Universal, and the movie DreamWorks made about WikiLeaks, *The Fifth Estate*, was a total disaster, grossing just $3 million domestically.

"I like those movies but I've got to be careful," Belgrad admitted.

SATELLITES

Nonetheless, his company is premised on the belief that people still want to see mid-budget thrillers and dramas and comedies and family films. Studios may not have much reason to produce them anymore, but "satellite companies" like Belgrad's do, and he wants to pump them through the studio system. His goal is to produce the kind of mid-budget hits that still pop up on the box-office charts, like *Sully* and *Bad Moms* and *Sausage Party*, all of which made solid if not mind-blowing profits in 2016.

But 2016 was also a year in which the top five films vacuumed up a massive 22 percent of total ticket sales in the United States and Canada for the second year in a row. Audiences, particularly overseas, still love their franchises above everything else. And for every *Sully* or *Bad Moms*, there are innumerable mid-budget movies that disappear from multiplexes without a trace, unable to puncture the overloaded pop-culture zeitgeist at a time when almost nobody heads to the theater without already knowing what buzzed-about film they want to see.

After a quarter-century in Hollywood, Belgrad isn't blind to the challenges. He knows that for his or Goodman's or anyone else's studio "satellite" to succeed, it needs ambitions that go beyond the big screen. Belgrad called his company 2.0 Entertainment because he now sees himself as a "content executive" who develops scripts or ideas and then figures out which platform they are suited to. So though his background is in film, and big-screen releases will be a core part of his business, he also expects to be making television shows, such as a legal procedural set in ancient Rome. In fact, if his new company ever got the chance to adapt Greenwald's book, which he bought at Sony, Belgrad would not make it a feature film. He now thinks it would work better as a limited series on cable or a streaming service.

"I think the scarce resource is curation, understanding the marketplace opportunity and filling it for the right price, whether it's on TV or digital or in features," he said near the end of our conversation.

Doug Belgrad was for years widely regarded as one of the smartest studio executives in Hollywood, and with good reason. He knows the financial challenges of the movie business better than almost anyone. But his career peak was in the first decade of the 2000s, which means that what he knows and loves most of all are mid-budget star vehicles, the dramas and comedies that drove Sony's success back then. They were the reason he ran production at a major studio.

If his new company succeeds by making those types of films in the years to come, it could mark a mini-revolution. It would mean that the tastes and talents of Belgrad and so many other former studio executives launching similar ventures are still relevant despite the massive changes in the studio system. And it would mean that audiences really are still hungry for a broader set of movie options than what Disney and Sony and Warner are feeding them.

15

The Last Picture Show?

MICHAEL LYNTON HAD NEVER REALLY managed to fit into Holly-wood, but by 2017, he was the longest-serving CEO of a major studio. Finally, in January of that year, he announced that he was leaving the company he had led since 2004 to focus on his other job: chairman of the board of Snapchat, which that March went public at a valuation of $24 billion.

Few in Hollywood were sad to see Lynton leave. To his friends, he had endured too much corporate chaos for too long, whether it was in-fighting with Steve Mosko, profit pressure from Tokyo, or the devastating fallout of the hack. To his enemies, it was long overdue justice for the man who had backstabbed Amy Pascal after the hack and had spent more than a decade believing he was better than the industry in which he worked, as evidenced by his efforts to escape Hollywood for the more refined world of academia. How did a CEO who didn't even want to be there get to stay an additional four years, they murmured at parties, while the woman who lived and breathed movies got the ax?

Just two weeks after Lynton revealed his plans to leave, it became clear just how bad a state he was leaving Sony Pictures in. Sony Corporation announced it was taking a $1 billion write-down on the studio, due primarily to a drop in profit projections for the movie business as

DVD sales continued to plummet and it had no *Star Wars*–size hits to make up the difference.

In general, 2016 and 2017 were tough years for Hollywood. The pile-up of box-office flops boggled the mind. Some tried to claim that the failure of so many big-budget franchise movies, like *King Arthur,* a reboot of *The Mummy* starring Tom Cruise, the sixth Alien movie, the third Smurfs, the fifth Transformers, the sixth X-Men, the second Alice in Wonderland, the third Divergent, and the fifth Teenage Mutant Ninja Turtles, indicated audiences were losing interest in recycled fare and wanted originality.

But people weren't rushing to mid-budget original films either. The top-grossing films of both years were, as of this writing, all sequels, spinoffs, remakes, and reboots based on well-known brands like Star Wars, Marvel, the X-Men, Warner's DC superheroes, Fast & Furious, and Disney animated classics. The growing number of franchise flops was a symptom of the fact that studios were making more and more of this type of film while chasing the same audience, who weren't actually going to theaters more frequently.

Even though the number of bombs was sure to grow as a result of the heightened competition, studios attempting to act rationally had no choice but to focus primarily on expensive franchise movies, with just a few cheap horror films and comedies to round out their slates. Studios that didn't have massive global franchises already in their pocket, like Sony, were still stuck in a hole that seemed all but impossible to climb out of.

It was no coincidence that around the same time that Sony announced Lynton's departure and the $1 billion write-down, Hollywood's second-longest-serving studio CEO, the head of Paramount, Brad Grey, was fired. Like Sony, Paramount had also suffered from years of underinvestment by its parent company and strategic missteps that left it with bad box-office results, poor employee morale, and few globally popular franchises. Midway through 2017, Sony and Paramount were ranked at the bottom among major studios at the box office for the third year running.

Paramount's parent company, Viacom, had sold almost 49 percent of the studio to China's Wanda Group the prior summer, and as Sony tried to determine a future for its studio post-Lynton, many questioned why it didn't get out of the entertainment business entirely. Promises to find synergies with the rest of the company had never come to fruition after all, and fundamental questions existed as to whether a studio like Sony or Paramount could really come back in the current environment.

Perhaps Amazon would significantly expand its entertainment ambitions, or Apple or Google would launch their own by buying a studio and merging the old-fashioned movie business with a digital giant that represented the future. Perhaps Wanda's Wang Jianlin or another Chinese giant would finally fulfill the ambition of becoming a global entertainment powerhouse by buying one of the studios. Or maybe a more successful Hollywood company, like CBS or Fox, would use its profits to simply acquire a struggling competitor.

One way or another, it was clear by 2017 that Hollywood was unlikely to continue much longer with six major studios pursuing similar business models. There was sure to be consolidation, and Sony Pictures was at the top of most people's list of studios that might not exist in a decade.

TURNAROUND EFFORTS

In the meantime, though, Sony's leaders had no choice but to try to turn things around. Tom Rothman in particular was a ferocious competitor who badly wanted to win. After replacing Amy Pascal in 2015, he attempted to refocus the movie division on international markets and global franchises — the areas in which the studio under Pascal had long been weak. But two years later, there was little to show for the effort.

The Melissa McCarthy–led reboot of *Ghostbusters* in 2016 was a money-losing flop. That December's *Passengers*, a science-fiction thriller starring Jennifer Lawrence and Chris Pratt, which was the biggest bet on an original script by any studio that year, also proved a disappointment. It was decimated at the holiday box office by the Star Wars spinoff *Rogue One,* demonstrating once again that spending big money on anything original in the age of franchise film dominance is usually a suicide mission.

Things were better at the television group, but leadership questions remained in the wake of Mosko's controversial ouster. In June, just a year after Mosko's departure, his former deputies and widely respected heads of TV production, Zack Van Amburg and Jamie Erlicht, were poached by Apple to head up its new original content efforts. It was another blow for Sony and a threat to Hollywood, as America's richest tech company signaled it was going to start making its own TV shows, and possibly movies too.

Tony Vinciquerra, the low-key but well-liked former Fox TV executive who was named to replace Lynton in May, now faced massive challenges: finding new leaders for the TV division that provided most of his profits, coming up with strategies to fend off the threats of new technology, and salvaging his still flailing movie business.

What was the future of Sony's movie business? Nobody knew for sure whether reboots like *Jumanji,* long-awaited sequels within series like Bad Boys and The Girl with the Dragon Tattoo, or a new animated family film about emojis would turn into the next major franchise. But the odds, most people in Hollywood believed, didn't look good.

The only sure thing, it seemed, was the most valuable asset Sony Pictures has had this century. *Spider-Man: Homecoming* was one of the most anticipated movies of summer 2017, in large part because fans knew the web-slinger had finally come home to the Marvel universe, with a reboot produced by Disney-owned Marvel Studios and featuring its superstar, Iron Man. Sony didn't have to worry about making the movie, in other words. It handled the marketing and kept all the profits (while Marvel got the money from toys and other merchandise that a hit movie would spawn).

It would also mark a turning point for Amy Pascal, who was on set for every day of *Homecoming*'s shoot in Atlanta, as its producer. Since leaving the Sony executive suites, Pascal kept her head as far down as humanly possible, staying out of the press and quietly starting life as a producer out of a bungalow on the Sony lot that used to be the schoolhouse for young stars like Judy Garland and Mickey Rooney.

She was the happiest she had been for years, free from the pressures of developing franchises and meeting profits targets for a Japanese electronics company. Though she was making less money and no longer had a grand office and impressive title, she could spend her time making the movies she wanted, including the mid-budget dramas for adults that she struggled so hard to make as a studio chief.

On a Friday in October 2016, an executive at Pascal's production company showed her an original screenplay by an up-and-coming writer about the *Washington Post*'s decision to publish the Pentagon Papers. She fell hard for the script and bought it that night.

Sony, which had first right of refusal on any movie Pascal produced, passed on making the movie. But as the Trump presidency made freedom of the press a more relevant issue than it had been in decades, Pascal's project became a hot one in Hollywood, and she attracted Steven Spielberg to direct and Tom Hanks and Meryl Streep to star. Co-financed by Spielberg's Amblin Entertainment, one of the new breed of companies like Doug Belgrad's that are making more diverse types of films, and Fox, it looked likely to earn Pascal an Oscar nomination less than three years after her ouster.

WHY WE MAKE MOVIES NOW

Films like *The Post* are still an endangered species in Hollywood, but if you're willing to open your mind to something beyond traditional movies made by traditional studios for traditional reasons, things get a lot more interesting.

By 2017, the most successful and revolutionary film companies were the ones making films for nontraditional reasons. Amazon and Netflix were upending the lower tiers of the film business, from low-budget indie productions all the way up to $100 million star vehicles, in order to sell video subscriptions, shoes, and garden hoses. Apple looked like it might soon follow in their footsteps, making movies in order to sell more Apple TVs and iPads.

The biggest, most successful studios had ulterior motives too. Disney may have been generating record-breaking profits from its Marvel, Pixar, and Star Wars films and live-action remakes of animated classics, but ultimately its movie studio existed to launch and maintain franchises that sold toys and T-shirts and drew tourists to theme parks. Universal was the second most successful studio of the 2010s, but its parent company, Comcast, made movies first and foremost to ensure that there would be compelling content on its cable and video-on-demand systems.

Warner Bros., the studio that consistently made the most movies, was poised to join that group in 2017. The wireless giant AT&T had agreed to buy its parent company, Time Warner, for $85 billion, and the business-friendly Trump administration appeared likely to approve the deal. For executives at Warner, it was a reason to cheer. No longer would they, like Sony, live and die by the profits of their movie slate each year. Now their primary purpose would be to create films that kept people paying to gobble up data on their phones and tablets.

Branded franchises would remain important because what better reason could passionate fans have to subscribe to AT&T than getting the best offering of Warner's DC superheroes, Harry Potter wizards, and Lego animation?

But it was good news for people who wanted other types of movies too. Indie films were a terrible business on their own, as Bob Iger correctly observed, but perhaps they made more economic sense if they kept people subscribing to a certain wireless or cable company. It wasn't a coincidence that Universal saved its specialty film division, Focus Features, despite years of red ink and the threat of Amazon and Netflix. Executives at the very top levels of Comcast insisted that the studio keep trying to make it work so art-house films would always be available to rent and stream on cable boxes.

Whether they're making *Fast and Furious 27* or *Moonlight*, however, it became very apparent that companies like Comcast, AT&T, and Disney view film as a means to an end, not as a special part of our culture in which they are privileged to participate. If the 2010s were the peak of the age of franchise films, the 2020s were starting to look like the age in which films would become nothing more, or less, than another type of content.

This was most clear in a long-simmering debate that reached a boil in 2017 over how long movies should play exclusively in theaters before they could be watched at home. Cinema chains like AMC and Regal had long insisted on a minimum of about ninety days during which people would have no choice but to watch a movie on the big screen, and studios had dutifully, if reluctantly, agreed. But as leverage in the movie business started to tilt away from theaters and toward the studios with mega-franchises that accounted for most of the box office, the argument shifted. The ninety-day window was archaic, studio executives argued, because millennials were used to getting what they wanted when they wanted it, on the device of their choosing, and companies like Netflix were offering great movies online the same day they opened in theaters.

Theater owners had obvious motives to oppose such a move, but certain directors who worship the silver screen and believe film is much more than a type of content that plays in theaters on its way to the iPad were horrified too. "The only 'platform,'" said Christopher Nolan at an industry convention, while scornfully throwing up air quotes, "I'm interested in is theatrical exhibition."

The plan for "premium video-on-demand" was to offer movies somewhere between two and six weeks after they debuted in theaters for $20 to $50, a high enough price that wouldn't immediately undercut theatergoing, but a reasonable price for a family or group of friends who wanted to see a new movie but couldn't or wouldn't head out to a multiplex. Studio heads argued that such a move would help preserve, rather than undermine, theaters. While premium VOD was sure to make his soon-to-be bosses at AT&T happy, the Warner Bros. CEO, Kevin Tsujihara, also made a compelling case that premium VOD would help save the "adult dramas we're having problems with right now on the theatrical side" because it would create a much-needed new stream of revenue for them.

By mid-2017, negotiations continued between the theater owners and studios as to how exactly premium VOD would work, but few doubted that it would happen. And everyone knew that once it launched, the prices were sure to fall over time, as would the number of weeks between a movie's launch in theaters and when it could be watched on an Internet-connected TV, a tablet, or a pair of Snapchat Spectacles.

FILMS OR CONTENT?

For those who viewed moviemaking as a unique art form and the Hollywood studios, for all their flaws, as one of the great American achievements of the twentieth century, this was alarming. The easier it was to watch movies at home, the less special they might become. Films at their best are cultural moments, when millions of us gather to laugh, cry, scream, or dream together in a theater with a huge screen and a state-of-the-art sound system. These movies completely immerse us and for a few hours make us forget about our Snaps and our Instagram likes.

Would *Wonder Woman* have sparked a national conversation about the representation of women in our culture, or would *Get Out* have everyone talking about the intersection of horror and the African American experience, if so many of us weren't watching the same movie together at the same time? Perhaps these films would have suffered the same fate as the Brad Pitt political satire *War Machine,* which debuted on Netflix with as much hype as the streaming service could muster but made about as much impact on popular culture as skywriting on a windy day.

It's easy to be a pessimist and conclude that if movies simply take their place on our content queues, in between the latest seasons of *The*

Walking Dead and *Fuller House,* they'll have been devalued beyond repair. The fact is, though, that since VCRs became ubiquitous thirty years ago, cinema has not actually been a cinematic experience for most people. Regardless of how movies are intended to be watched, or "should" be watched, most movies *are* watched on the TV in the living room. And no matter what studios and film lovers do, that living room TV will be replaced by portable digital devices sometime in the next few years. Pragmatically speaking, the golden age of television is in the process of becoming the golden age of digital visual content, and movies will become a part of it.

The traditional economics of film, whereby each production aims to be profitable through a mix of box-office dollars, DVD sales, and television licensing, will become more and more challenged. That's sure to further narrow down the types of movies that old-school studios like Sony make to the big, loud, and financially safe superheroes, sequels, and spinoffs.

But the new economics of film, in which two- to three-hour visual stories are funded by subscriptions to video services, wireless packages, and free product shipping, will flourish. The studio executives working under this model will no longer have to obsess, as Amy Pascal did, about whether every individual movie will be profitable enough on its own to satisfy a corporate parent's expectations. They won't have to gin up laughable revenue projections to justify making the films their gut tells them will work, or that they simply want to make.

If you love movies, you should be thrilled to realize there will be as many and perhaps more of them than ever. If you want to buy a ticket and see them on a big screen, you'll still be able to do so.

Of course, it'll be a lot easier if it's a Marvel movie or one of its many offspring in competing cinematic universes. Original, mid-, or low-budget motion pictures for adults will increasingly play for just a few weeks, in a few dozen theaters, in major cities.

Most of the time, we'll be watching those types of films the same way we watch television, YouTube clips, and virtual reality experiences: at home and on the go.

The terminology we use for visual content is already antiquated, given how often we watch TV shows on devices other than TVs and view films without any cellophane in sight.

But if movies aren't stories we go to movie theaters to see, then what are they? Are they just, as Ted Sarandos argued, visual stories we can watch in a single night, rather than the several nights it takes to watch a television series? Realistically, the answer is yes. Most people already watch more movies at home than in theaters, and the bigger chunk that Netflix and Amazon and perhaps eventually Apple take of the business, the truer that's going to be.

Nonetheless, I think something will be lost if we don't preserve cinemas as a gathering place where hundreds of us can watch the same story in the same room at the same time and then collectively talk about it as a culture. *Get Out* is a great movie, no matter when and where you watch it, but it becomes a culture-shifting event when millions of us find ourselves scared and shocked and provoked in groups together over a period of a few weeks.

But you can't force that to happen. If studios want people to go to movie theaters, they have to make movies worthy of getting off our asses. That might be because the film is an eye-popping spectacle you can't fully enjoy on a TV or because it's a zeitgeist-busting event that everyone wants to see together, right now.

The fact is, however, that there won't be enough releases like that each year to sustain a healthy movie industry and a vibrant movie culture. For those to survive, we have to accept that most films will be streamed to digital devices at viewers' convenience, whether a few weeks after they play in theaters, or at the same time, or having never played on a big screen at all.

Theater attendance, which has fallen by 5 percent this century despite our rising population, is going to keep going down. The number of multiplexes will shrink, and studios will release fewer movies. Those who still go will likely pay higher and higher prices, albeit for a more luxurious experience, with reclining seats, food ordered by app and delivered by hand, and the absolute best visuals and sound systems.

Are they still movies, though, if more than 99 percent of the people who watch them don't do so in a movie theater? Who cares. Take out the commercial breaks and "previously on"s, and *Breaking Bad* is a forty-five-hour movie that's better than anything most movie studios have made this century. And no matter how many billions they earn at the box office, no one can convince me that the third Avengers offering and the fourth Captain America film aren't super-expensive episodes in the most successful television series of our era.

The more digital our entertainment becomes, the more creators are going to discard old ideas about how long a "movie" should be and how many minutes define an "episode" of a television show or how many episodes define a "season." Movies, as most of us watch them most of the time, will just be one part of a spectrum that also includes mini-series, television shows, digital shorts, and forms that haven't yet been invented. The lines that divide these types of content will blur to nonexistence.

As long as we're getting great visual stories, with the option to watch them on screens big and small and enough variety to satisfy fans of Iron Man and Almodóvar, how could we possibly complain?

The changes that are roiling Hollywood and revolutionizing the ways we watch movies will continue to be bad news for struggling studios like Sony Pictures and traditionalists who think cinema is first and foremost a physical location. I don't think studios or theaters will disappear, but if they're an essential part of your definition of film, the future undeniably looks a bit bleak.

But for those of us who simply want to sit down, turn off the lights, and be immersed in the magic of stories told in images on a screen, the future has never looked brighter.

Acknowledgments

After years of covering the entertainment industry, I've seen firsthand that what makes or breaks a film is usually the quality of the collaboration behind it. In the two and a half years I spent on this project, I learned the same is true for a book. If you enjoyed what you just read, much of the credit belongs to the people I have been blessed to work with on it and to know in my life leading up to it.

This book wouldn't exist if not for an e-mail I received out of the blue from my agent, David McCormick. David played a critical role shaping my early thinking as he guided me through multiple versions of my proposal, before landing it with the right publisher.

Eamon Dolan edited this book with a sharp eye, an inquisitive mind, and a consistently supportive attitude. Our conversations always left me invigorated with new ideas that made their way into the manuscript, and his notes led me to change the final product you hold in your hands significantly for the better. He is, to me, the Platonic ideal of an editor, and I feel lucky to have worked with him and his many talented colleagues at Houghton Mifflin Harcourt.

I didn't always feel naturally suited to be a journalist and the fact that I have built a career as one is in large part thanks to the mentors I have had. First is the one and only journalism instructor I had in college, Michael Vitez. He taught me to pay attention to details, to write as if the most seemingly tedious set of facts make a great yarn, and to try and see the world from my subjects' point of view. When Mike found out I was working on this book, he told me to "report the shit out of it and write with felicity." I hope I followed his advice well.

I've had many editors who helped me develop my skills as a reporter and understand the entertainment industry. I'm indebted to Peter Bart, Sallie Hofmeister, John Lippman, Claudia Eller, and Charles Fleming for their guidance. I'm particularly indebted to my editor at the *Wall Street Journal,* Ethan Smith, who supported me in writing this book and has been a champion for me and the talented team of reporters with whom I work. I feel proud to work for one of the world's great newspapers and I thank our many leaders, including Gerard Baker and Matt Murray, for maintaining its standard of journalistic excellence, which I tried to apply to this book.

Hollywood has a deserved reputation as a place where truth is often not welcome, which doesn't make life as a reporter easy. So I'm very grateful to the dozens of sources, from the highest ranks of the industry to the lowest, who candidly shared their experiences and knowledge with me in interviews. Some are named in this book but many are not, often because they put their careers at risk in talking to me. I'm particularly grateful to current and former employees of Sony Pictures who had every reason to be wary of a book that uses internal e-mails and documents from their company, but assisted me nonetheless.

I wouldn't enjoy the life and career I have today if I hadn't always been encouraged to pursue my passions and be myself by my parents, Bruce Fritz and Elise Godfrey. I'm also lucky to have many friends who have made my life richer. I'd particularly like to thank Brendan Nyhan and Warren Zeger for the valuable feedback they provided on drafts of this book.

My most heartfelt thanks are reserved for Alicia Kirk, my partner and dearest friend, who has always believed in me more deeply than anyone I've known. I am a far, far better person because she is part of my life.

Hudson Fritz won't be able to read this for a few years and probably won't be interested for many years after that. But whenever he does, I want him to know that watching him grow has been the best part of my life over the past few years and that our time together has kept me sane and happy amid the stress of this project.

I end these acknowledgments on a tragic but important note. My sister Riley Fritz died in the Oakland Ghost Ship warehouse fire while I was writing this book. Her personal integrity, her gentleness, and her acceptance of other people were examples I will carry with me for the rest of my life. I am grateful to the people who loved and supported Riley, and I'm grateful to those who supported me and her family and friends when she was stolen from us. This book is certainly not a worthy tribute to her too-short life, but it is dedicated to her nonetheless.

Notes

INTRODUCTION: GROUNDHOG DAY — HOW FRANCHISES
KILLED ORIGINALITY IN HOLLYWOOD

page

xiv   *"nobody knows anything":* William Goldman, *Adventures in the Screen Trade*
(Grand Central Publishing, 1983).

xvi   *preparing to shoot a scene:* Details on preparations for Investor Day come from
people involved in the event.

xvii *more than $75 million:* Sony financial details come from internal documents
leaked in the hack and people who currently work or previously worked at the
company.

"it's an investor conference": E-mail from Amy Pascal to Michael De Luca, Nov.
21, 2013. No subject.

"U know its bs": E-mail from Amy Pascal to Doug Belgrad, Nov. 21, 2013. No
subject.

xviii *"and always will":* E-mail from Amy Pascal to Doug Belgrad, July 17, 2014. No
subject.

double the number created in 2010: Stephen Battaglio, "Scripted Shows Continue
to Grow as 'Peak TV' Hasn't Peaked Yet." *Los Angeles Times,* Jan. 12, 2017.

1. THE ODD COUPLE: LYNTON AND PASCAL'S
GLORY DAYS AT SONY

3   *"and so here we are":* E-mail from Michael Lynton to Amy Pascal, Oct. 3, 2014.
Subject: a reflection.

4   *"turn the company around"*: E-mail from Amy Pascal to Tom Rothman, April 3, 2014. No subject.

5   *"the history of the business"*: Nancy Griffin and Kim Masters, *Hit & Run* (New York: Touchstone, 1996), back cover.
     and Blazing Saddles: Dennis McLellan, "John Calley Dies at 81," *Los Angeles Times*, Sept 14, 2011.

6   *middle-class Jewish intellectual*: Jewish Women's Archive, accessed June 23, 2017. http://jwa.org/encyclopedia/article/pascal-amy
     parents, who live in New York: No author, "Amy Pascal," *Hollywood Reporter*, Dec. 19, 1998.
     she would later say: Tim Arango, "Sony's Version of Tracy and Hepburn," *New York Times*, Oct. 25, 2009.

7   *"That's always been the plan"*: Claudia Eller, "Ted's Ready for His Build-Up, Ms. Pascal," *Los Angeles Times*, July 7, 1995.
     annual budget of $100 million: Claudia Eller, "Unhappy Ending at Turner Pictures a Sign of the Times," *Los Angeles Times*, Nov. 19, 1996.
     "they're more like you": Eller, "Ted's Ready for His Build-Up."
     "the greatest studio boss out there": E-mail from Ron Howard to Amy Pascal, Nov. 1, 2014. Subject: Emma — confidential.

8   *"studio that loves film"*: E-mail from George Clooney to Amy Pascal, Jan. 30, 2014. Subject: Re: It's getting worse.
     "I actually love her": Ben Fritz, "Sony Executive Needs More Than 'Spidey Sense,'" *Wall Street Journal*, May 1, 2014.
     "(ebullient)": Jess Cagle, "The Women Who Run Hollywood," *Time*, July 21, 2002.
     "a chance to begin": Eller, "Unhappy Ending at Turner Pictures."

10   *fiscal discipline was needed*: Here and elsewhere, motion picture group profit details come from internal Sony documents.

11   *"to become a CEO"*: Author interview with a former colleague of Michael Lynton's.
     "stranger in a strange land": Claudia Eller, "A Stranger in a Strange Land Is Hollywood Pictures' New Player," *Los Angeles Times*, Aug. 17, 1994.

12   *he said of himself*: Michael Wolff, "Executives at the Gate," *Vanity Fair*, Dec. 1, 2004.
     "henry miller sculpter": E-mail from Amy Pascal to Andrew Blum, Sept. 19, 2014. No subject.

13   *Lynton's brother-in-law*: E-mail from Michael L. Ryan to Michael Lynton and Peter Lattman, Dec. 3, 2014. Subject: Introduction.
     about Lynton's departure: Claudia Eller, "Michael Lynton's Brief Film Career," *Los Angeles Times*, Aug. 19, 1996.

"That is a horror": Robert S. Boynton, "The Hollywood Way," *The New Yorker* (March 30, 1998).

14   *traditional entertainment world*: No author, "The arrogance has gone," *The Guardian*, July 14, 2003.

"weird, arranged India marriage": Arango, "Sony's Version of Tracy and Hepburn."

15   *declared Stringer*: Claudia Eller, "For Sony Pictures, It's Complicated at the Top," *Los Angeles Times*, Dec. 11, 2003.

more than he needed: E-mail from Craig Schwartz to Amy Pascal, Nov. 8, 2014. No subject.

"what it means," she wrote: E-mail from Amy Pascal to Michael Lynton, Nov. 8, 2014. No subject.

"who runs this place": Interviews with former Sony employees.

16   *"he delegated a lot"*: This and other De Luca quotes are from author interview.

"what's good about us": E-mail from Amy Pascal to Michael Lynton, Nov. 8, 2014. No subject.

boasted Stringer: Merissa Marr, "Expanding Sony's Web," *Wall Street Journal*, Dec. 15, 2004.

17   *(her peak pay, in 2011)*: This and details on Amy Pascal's compensation are from e-mail from Amy Pascal to Alan Wertheimer, Oct. 22, 2014. Subject: deals.

$13 million in 2013: E-mail from Michael Lynton to Marc Goldberg, Dec. 4, 2013. Subject: Gifts.

"movie gods": Kate Kelly, "'Stealth' Leaves Sony Grounded at the Summer Box Office," *Wall Street Journal*, Aug. 2, 2005.

a profit of about $15 on each disc: Author interviews with home-entertainment industry experts.

"welfare state": Ben Fritz, "For Movie Producers, a Golden Age Fades," *Wall Street Journal*, Jan. 22, 2014.

18   *its stars, director, and producers*: Claudia Eller, "Higher Profile Role for Ace Pictures Picker," *Los Angeles Times*, Oct. 22, 2003.

peaked at 204 in 2006: MPAA theatrical market statistics reports. http://www.mpaa.org/research-and-reports/

a high of almost $25 billion: From annual home-entertainment spending reports at degonline.org. Accessed June 24, 2017.

19   *"If she doesn't get it"*: Fritz, "Sony Executive Needs More Than 'Spidey Sense.'"

"comfort zone": Ibid.

2. REALITY BITES: HOW EVERYTHING WENT WRONG
FOR THE MOVIE BUSINESS

21   *from nearly $22 billion to $12 billion:* From annual home-entertainment spending
      reports at degonline.org. Accessed June 24, 2017. Excludes subscription stream-
      ing, which is more equivalent to television than DVD.

22   *International box office exploded:* These and other annual box-office statistics
      from the Motion Picture Assn. of America's annual Theatrical Market Statistics
      Reports. Mpaa.org. Accessed June 24, 2017.
      DVD sales declines were smallest: From data in a Sony Pictures internal report.

25   *"businesses for the future":* E-mail from Amy Pascal to Doug Belgrad, July 3, 2014.
      No subject.
      Sony made only $57 million: Profit and loss details on *Skyfall* and other individ-
      ual movies are from Sony internal documents.
      "who else is gonna make": E-mail from Amy Pascal to Barbara Broccoli, Oct. 21,
      2014. No subject.

26   *"it was a shitty year":* E-mail from Amy Pascal to Bryan Lourd, Aug. 19, 2014.
      Subject: Re: steve knight update.

27   *"It was two fucking movies":* E-mail from Amy Pascal to Michael Lynton, Nov.
      24, 2013. No subject.
      "Mark Poppins": E-mail from Amy Pascal to Mark Seed, Mar. 26, 2014. No sub-
      ject.
      more than $250,000 per year: Tatiana Siegel, "New Life for Amy Pascal," *Holly-
      wood Reporter,* Nov. 25, 2013.

28   *"Why is everyone freaking out[?]":* E-mail from Amy Pascal to Michael Lynton,
      Nov. 24, 2013. No subject.
      "It's not so easy": E-mail from Amy Pascal to Scott Rudin, Nov. 24, 2013. No sub-
      ject.
      "and hence confused": E-mail from Tom Rothman to Amy Pascal, Nov. 19, 2014.
      No subject.
      "The un marvel marvel world": E-mail from Doug Belgrad to Amy Pascal, Jan. 22,
      2014. No subject.

29   *"I've been miserable for two years":* E-mail from Amy Pascal to Bryan Lourd, Aug.
      19, 2014. Subject: re: steve knight update.
      wasn't about to be fired: E-mail from Amy Pascal to Doug Belgrad, Nov. 24, 2013.
      No subject.
      "Work is drudgery": E-mail from Michael Lynton to Elizabeth Salt, Sept. 15,
      2014. Subject: re: long time, no etc.
      "harmful to the company": When Lynton's job search was revealed after the
      hack, it didn't do any apparent harm to Sony, but it did fuel resentment among

those in Hollywood who already believed that he had no passion for their business.

more than $500 million: Details on Lynton's involvement in Snapchat are from a person with knowledge of the matter.

30   *"Where's our tentpole?!":* This and other Michael De Luca quotes are from author's interview.

"jump street merging with mib": E-mail from Jonah Hill to Neil Moritz, Nov. 6, 2014. Subject: Re: title.

31   *"getting the big ones done":* E-mail from Michael Lynton to Amy Pascal, Dec. 3, 2013. Subject: concerns.

"so I'm writing you": E-mail from Amy Pascal to Doug Belgrad, Nov. 6, 2014. No subject.

32   *"enablement sessions":* This and other details of the greenlight process at Sony Pictures are from current and former employees.

more than $100 million domestically: Greenlight projections for Sony movies are from internal documents and interviews with current and former employees.

35   *to demand an update:* E-mail from George Rose to Michael Lynton, Oct. 3, 2014. Subject: Re: Amy.

"to agree to": E-mail from Amy Pascal to Alan Wertheimer, Oct. 22, 2014. Subject: deals.

"You know ml will be as rude": E-mail from Amy Pascal to Bryan Lourd, Aug. 19, 2014. Subject: Re: steve knight update.

36   *"3 years I'm done for good":* E-mail from Amy Pascal to Elizabeth Cantillion, Nov. 1, 2014. No subject.

3. INCEPTION: THE SECRET ORIGIN OF
THE SUPERHERO MOVIE

37   *"ive lost my marbles":* E-mail from Sam Raimi to Amy Pascal, Nov. 4, 2014. No subject.

38   *it made less than $20 million:* E-mail from Kathryn Nielsen to Michael Lynton and other recipients, June 13, 2014. Subject: Ultimate Reports.

"and wrong casting": E-mail from Amy Pascal to Doug Belgrad, Mar. 26, 2014. No subject.

"They just kicked our ass": E-mail from Amy Pascal to Doug Belgrad, May 12, 2014. Subject: Re: Pineapple Express.

39   *"eaten by Marvel":* E-mail from Amy Pascal to Jeff Robinov, Nov. 10, 2014. No subject.

40   *one that caught his eye:* Details on the Spider-Man movie rights before Marvel's bankruptcy come from author interviews with knowledgeable people and Ron-

ald Grover, "Unraveling Spider-Man's Tangled Web," *BusinessWeek,* Apr. 14, 2002.

41 *an astounding 62 percent of Marvel's total profits:* Estimate from an internal Sony document.

42 *Marvel in late 1996 filed for bankruptcy:* Details on Marvel's bankruptcy are from Dan Raviv, *Comic Wars* (New York: Broadway Books, 2002).
  Landau put together a $500 million offer: Details on Sony's bid for Marvel are from author's interview with Yair Landau as well as Raviv, *Comic Wars.*

43 *An Israeli veteran of the Six-Day War:* Ike Perlmutter's early biography is from Raviv, *Comic Wars.*
  Perlmutter agreed to buy all its fixtures: This and other details about Ike Perlmutter are from author's interviews with people who have worked with him.

45 *"all the products and the other rights":* Raviv, *Comic Wars.*

46 *"Nobody gives a shit":* This and other details of Sony's purchase of the film rights to Spider-Man are from author's interview with Landau, as well as other people involved in the process.

47 *"delusional":* John Lippman, "Sony Plans New Bond Films, but MGM Claims to Own 007," *Wall Street Journal,* Oct. 14, 1997.
  "The idea is to do it now": Michael A. Hiltzik, "Studio Rights to Spider-Man Are Untangled," *Los Angeles Times,* Mar. 2, 1999.

48 *"I remember seeing a cut":* Author's interview with Landau.

49 *$442 million in profits:* This and other details on Spider-Man movies' financial results, as well as money flowing between Sony and Marvel, are from Sony internal documents and author's interview with current and former employees of both companies.

50 *A* Newsweek *article:* Stephen Levy, "Sony's New Day," *Newsweek,* Jan. 27, 2003.
  "they're getting all the benefit": This and other Avi Arad quotes are from author's interview.
  "What's the meaning of this?": Author's interview with Landau.

51 *$3.2 million condo:* Dawn Chmielewski, "Ike Perlmutter Holds the Reins of Superheroes at Marvel," *Los Angeles Times,* Aug. 16, 2012.

52 *Peter Parker would be a heterosexual male:* Sony internal documents.
  Both sides were regularly auditing each other: Details on Marvel's clashes with Sony are from author interviews with knowledgeable people at or close to both companies.

4. REVENGE OF THE NERDS: THE RISE OF MARVEL STUDIOS

53 *he wanted to spend $80,000:* Author's interview with Avi Arad.
  slash the salary: Raviv, "Comic Wars."

54 *It took an outsider:* Unless otherwise noted, details on the history of Marvel come from author interviews with Amir Malin, Avi Arad, David Maisel, and others who have worked at or with Marvel.

  "Why don't you finance your own pictures?": Author's interview with Amir Malin.

55 *"Ike's scared of the film business":* This and other quotes are from author's interview with Avi Arad.

56 *"This is an opportunity worth billions!":* This and other quotes are from author's interview with David Maisel.

61 *"you would really turn to?":* Geoff Boucher, "Ka-pow, Spidey! Marvel Studios Taps Second-String Superheroes to Grab Box Office," *Los Angeles Times,* July 22, 2006.

62 *"Steel cannot fly":* Author's interview with Arad.

66 *selling Marvel stock worth nearly $60 million:* Steven Zeitchik and Ben Fritz, "Marvel's 'X' Man Makes Cushy Exit," *Daily Variety,* May 31, 2006.

69 *The clashes intensified:* Peter Sciretta, "The Incredible Hulk: The Truth About Edward Norton vs. Marvel," *Slashfilm,* June 14, 2008. http://www.slashfilm .com/the-truth-about-edward-norton-vs-marvel/

70 *as their next target:* Details on Disney's purchase of Marvel are from author's interviews with Bob Iger and David Maisel.

71 *"I like this man":* Author's interview with a knowledgeable person.

  "He's great": Author's interview with a person with knowledge of the conversation.

72 *Chris Hemsworth was paid $150,000:* Jay A. Fernandez and Borys Kit, "How Marvel Went from Near-Bankruptcy to Powerhouse Game-Changer for the Entire Movie Industry," *Hollywood Reporter,* Nov. 2, 2010.

  He earned more than $50 million: Kim Masters, "How Marvel Became the Envy (and Scourge) of Hollywood," *Hollywood Reporter,* July 23, 2014.

5. SPIDER-MAN: HOMECOMING — WHY SONY GAVE UP
ITS MOST VALUABLE ASSET

75 *"I am sure you are getting this":* E-mail from Michael Lynton to Amy Pascal, July 15, 2014. Subject: Re: Give Marvel back the rights to Spider-Man.

76 *were $159 million:* This and other financial details on Spider-Man movies are from Sony internal documents.

77 *"rich universe":* Ben Fritz, "Why Can't Marvel's Movie Superheroes Be Friends?" *Wall Street Journal,* May 1, 2014.

  "No superhero team up here": E-mail from Jeff Robinov to Amy Pascal, Nov. 10, 2014. No subject.

  a deal in 2011: Details on Sony's amendment to its arrangement with Marvel are from Sony internal documents and people with knowledge of the negotiation.

78 *"In a million years I would never advocate"*: E-mail from Alan Fine to Michael Lynton, July 31, 2014. Subject: FW: Spider-Man 5 Fwd: Amazing Spider-Man 2 script.

79 *Under the 1998 deal:* E-mail from Andrew Gumpert to Michael Lynton and others, Oct. 31, 2014. Subject: Spidey univ time frames.
Perlmutter needed to convince Sony: Details on negotiations for Marvel to reclaim the right to produce Spider-Man movies, and final deal, are from people involved in the negotiation.
He targeted Lynton: E-mail from Ike Perlmutter to Michael Lynton, Nov. 4, 2014. Subject: Marvel Announces Phase 3 Slate!
"get the fuck out of here": A person with knowledge of what occurred at the lunch.
He approached Hirai: A person briefed on Iger and Hirai's discussion.

80 *"right babysitter for this moment":* E-mail from Amy Pascal to Michael De Luca, Sept. 12, 2014. No subject.
"Can't go back to marvel": E-mail from Jeff Robinov to Amy Pascal, Nov. 10, 2014. No subject.
"Michael had no ego": Author's interview with Michael De Luca.

81 *Sony had already given up:* E-mail from Doug Belgrad to Amy Pascal, Aug. 2, 2014. Subject: Re: Fury Publicity.
"the Marc Webb experience": E-mail from Amy Pascal to Michael Lynton, Nov. 14, 2014. No subject.
paying him $6 million: E-mail from Amy Pascal to Matthew Tolmach and Doug Belgrad, Mar. 18, 2014. No subject.

6. STAR WARS: THE DECLINE OF THE A-LIST

83 *"Michael seems to have gotten annoyed":* E-mail from Amy Pascal to Doug Belgrad, Aug. 18, 2014. Subject: Re: brief but imp updates
"make us very much money?": Ibid.

86 *Made Sony a $179 million profit:* Financial details on *The Da Vinci Code, Angels & Demons,* and other movies in this chapter are from Sony internal documents.

87 *and Grazer 10%:* Some *Angels & Demons* compensation details are from e-mail from Andrew Gumpert to Amy Pascal and others, June 10, 2014. Subject: inferno caa proposal.
it would make a profit of about $50 million: Some financial details on *Inferno* and the Da Vinci trilogy are from e-mail from Doug Belgrad to Amy Pascal, Oct. 29, 2014. Subject: Fwd: Inferno.

"This is getting pricey": E-mail from Michael Lynton to Amy Pascal, July 30, 2014. No subject.

88 *"the most talent-friendly studio in town:"* Patrick Goldstein, "The Studio Report Card," *Los Angeles Times,* Feb. 8, 2009.

"My goal is to have": Ibid.

"it was our strategy": E-mail from Amy Pascal to Doug Belgrad, July 3, 2014. No subject.

89 *"I want to be the biggest movie star"*: This and other details on Will Smith's early career are from Rebecca Winters Keegan, "The Legend of Will Smith," *Time,* Nov. 19, 2007.

90 *"really means to produce movies"*: Tatiana Siegel, "Smith, Lassiter Bent on World Conquest," *Variety,* Dec. 12, 2008.

"Home is a place": Dana Harris, "Sony, Overbrook Ink," *Daily Variety,* Jan. 30, 2002.

92 *$20 million against 20 percent:* Details on Sandler's and Smith's compensation and perks are from current and former Sony employees and people close to the stars.

94 *lost $42.5 million:* Financial details on Adam Sandler and Will Smith movies come from Sony internal documents.

96 *"I think one of the answers"*: E-mail from Michael De Luca to Amy Pascal, Oct. 30, 2014. No subject.

"very difficult": E-mail from Doug Belgrad to Amy Pascal, Sept. 22, 2014. Subject: Re: Candy Land.

"You said yourself": Ibid.

97 *"back on track"*: E-mail from Amy Pascal to James Lassiter, Feb. 12, 2014. No subject.

$15 million against 15 percent of the gross: Details on Will Smith's negotiation and compensation for *Concussion* and from interviews with knowledgeable people and e-mail from Michael Lynton to Amy Pascal, July 8, 2014. Subject: Re: Concussion.

"I don't know what to do with that": E-mail from Amy Pascal to James Lassiter, June 5, 2014. No subject.

"fired with the last movie": E-mail from Amy Pascal to Michael Lynton, June 5, 2014. Subject: Re: ha ha ha.

98 *Lynton pressured his executives:* E-mail from Michael Lynton to Doug Belgrad, Feb. 22, 2014. Subject: Re: Pixels sensitivities.

"It was brilliantly funny and engaging": E-mail from Amy Pascal to Michael Lynton, May 31, 2014. No subject.

"dimwitted": Justin Chang, "Film Review: 'Pixels.'" *Variety,* July 22, 2015.

7. A STAR IS BORN: NETFLIX,
THE NEW HOME FOR MOVIE STARS

102 *about $30 million per year:* Details on the Sony-Netflix-Starz arrangement from Ben Fritz, Joe Flint, and Dawn Chmielewski, "Starz to End Streaming Deal with Netflix," *Los Angeles Times,* Sept. 2, 2011.

Kevin Spacey movies had long done well: Details on the use of data to greenlight *House of Cards* from David Carr, "Giving Viewers What They Want," *New York Times,* Feb. 24, 2013.

103 *"It's incredible how consistent":* Ted Sarandos quotes are from author's interview.

104 *Netflix had been prepared to pay about $1 billion:* Ben Fritz, Joe Flint, and Dawn Chmielewski, "Netflix Offered $300 Million-Plus, but Starz Wanted Higher Consumer Prices," *Los Angeles Times,* Sept. 1, 2011.

105 *theater attendance had been falling:* Data from National Association of Theatre Owners. http://www.natoonline.org/data/admissions/

Sony lost more than $10 million: Sony internal documents.

106 *Sandler got word that Netflix:* Details on the deal-making for Adam Sandler with Netflix, as well as Brad Pitt's *War Machine* and Will Smith's *Bright,* come from author interviews with people close to those projects.

109 *Netflix wrote a check for more than $90 million:* Some details on the sale of *Bright* to Netflix from Mike Fleming Jr., "Netflix Commits $90M+ for David Ayer–Directed Will Smith–Joel Edgerton Pic 'Bright.'" *Deadline,* Mar. 18, 2016. http://deadline.com/2016/03/netflix-bright-will-smith-90-million-deal-david-ayer-joel-edgerton-max-landis-1201721574/

"I was after the creative freedom": Peter Bart and Mike Fleming Jr., "'Bright' Scribe Max Landis and Director David Ayer Tell Why $90M+ Netflix Deal Wasn't Just About $$$," *Deadline,* Mar. 22, 2016. http://deadline.com/2016/03/max-landis-david-ayer-will-smith-90-million-dollar-netflix-gawker-hulk-hogan-verdict-1201724354/

8. FROZEN: WHY STUDIOS STOPPED MAKING
MID-BUDGET DRAMAS

112 *"I just made the worst decision":* E-mail from Amy Pascal to Matt Tolmach, Nov. 19, 2014. No subject.

"In man gram machine": E-mail from Amy Pascal to Scott Rudin, Nov. 20, 2014. No subject.

a healthy profit of about $45 million: This and other films' financial details in this chapter are from Sony internal documents.

113   *"I would take that bet everyday"*: E-mail from Michael Lynton to Amy Pascal,
        Nov. 7, 2014. No subject.

115   *"There just is no floor anymore"*: E-mail from Amy Pascal to Tom Rothman,
        Nov. 24, 2013. Subject: Re: I really feel for Stacey.

116   *"If ever there was a fact pattern"*: E-mail from Andrew Gumpert to Amy Pascal
        and Doug Belgrad, Nov. 5, 2014. Subject: Fw: Jobs RENT A SYSTEM is the
        way to go.
        "We need Megan": E-mail from Doug Belgrad to Scott Rudin, Nov. 8, 2014. No
        subject.
        Inside Annapurna's offices: Information on Annapurna and Megan Ellison is, un-
        less otherwise noted, from author interviews with people who have worked with
        her; and from Ben Fritz and Steven Zeitchik, "Megan Ellison Is Energizing In-
        die Film World," *Los Angeles Times,* May 8, 2012; Vanessa Grigoriadas, "Caution:
        Heiress at Work," *Vanity Fair,* Mar. 2013; and Michael Cieply and Brooks Barnes,
        "Silicon Valley Scion Tackles Hollywood," *New York Times,* Aug. 28, 2011.

117   *"The kind of movies"*: Fritz and Zeitchik, "Megan Ellison Is Energizing Indie
        Film World."
        estimated to be worth $62 billion: Forbes.com. http://www.forbes.com/profile
        /larry-ellison/. Accessed June 25, 2017.

120   *"I have such admiration for you"*: E-mail from Amy Pascal to Megan Ellison, Oct.
        17, 2014. Subject: Re: Us.

121   *"We left messages for her everywhere"*: E-mail from Scott Rudin to Amy Pascal,
        Nov. 6, 2014. Subject: Re: Megan E.
        "We're in crazy-land here": E-mail from Scott Rudin to Amy Pascal, Nov. 10,
        2014. Subject: Fw: Boyle/Ellison.
        "Very interesting discussion": E-mail from Doug Belgrad to Amy Pascal, Nov. 11,
        2014. Subject: Fwd: Megan.
        "Megan 'sees' it": Ibid.

122   *"It would depend on who it was"*: E-mail from Amy Pascal to Scott Rudin, Nov.
        13, 2014. No subject.
        "When I say that": Ibid.
        "I simply have to do": E-mail from Megan Ellison to Amy Pascal, Nov. 13, 2014.
        No subject.
        "Why did she do this???": E-mail from Amy Pascal to Scott Rudin, Nov. 13, 2014.
        No subject.
        "$50 million on a biopic": Mike Fleming Jr., "Plan B Closes Overall Annapurna
        Deal," *Deadline,* May 4, 2017. http://deadline.com/2017/05/plan-b-annapurna
        -brad-pitt-adam-mckay-dick-cheney-movie-megan-ellison-christian
        -bale-1202079165/

"a fucked situation": E-mail from Amy Pascal to Scott Rudin, Nov. 13, 2014. No subject.

"fair and honorable thing": E-mail from Amy Pascal to Scott Rudin, Nov. 16, 2014. No subject.

"ILL DO IT": E-mail from Amy Pascal to Danny Boyle, Nov. 19, 2014. No subject.

"cried and acted like an idiot": E-mail from Amy Pascal to Elizabeth Cantillion, Nov. 20, 2014. No subject.

"I am devastated": E-mail from Amy Pascal to Bryan Lourd, Nov. 19, 2014. No subject.

"without jobs but much wiser": E-mail from Amy Pascal to Tom Rothman, Nov. 20, 2014. Subject: Re: how are you doing??

124   *"Why have the job"*: E-mail from Scott Rudin to Amy Pascal, Nov. 15, 2014. No subject.

lost about $50 million: Universal's estimated loss on *Steve Jobs* is based on projections from an internal Sony document and a person close to the project.

9. TRADING PLACES: HOW TV STOLE MOVIES' SPOT ATOP HOLLYWOOD

125   *"There is now a narrative being told"*: E-mail from Amy Pascal to Steve Mosko, Feb. 26, 2014. No subject.

"Of all the people in the world": Ibid.

126   *Mosko made little secret of his unhappiness:* Details on Steve Mosko's relationship with Lynton and Pascal are from people who work or have worked at or with Sony Pictures.

128   *total profits of $2 billion and $1 billion:* Sony internal documents.

"new black baby": E-mail from Michael Lynton to Amy Pascal, Steve Mosko, and others, July 9, 2014. Subject: Re: priv and conf — Robinov — work product — for your review.

130   *Netflix paid Lionsgate:* Ben Fritz and Joseph Flint, "Netflix Less About Flicks, More About TV," *Los Angeles Times,* Feb. 4, 2012.

131   *7 percent drop:* Richard Verrier and Ben Fritz, "Movie Industry Hits Ticket Sales Decline on the Note," *Los Angeles Times,* Mar. 30, 2011.

"All of us are looking": Ibid.

132   *a janitor and truck driver:* Early background on Steve Mosko from Joe Schlosser, "Mosko on the Coast," *Broadcasting & Cable,* Mar. 9, 1998.

"our numbers would double": Ibid.

134   *"That is the craziest"*: From the documentary "No Half Measures: Creating the Final Season of 'Breaking Bad.'"

"Hey, guys, it's your career": Ibid.

Sony executives initially projected: Unless otherwise noted, financial details on *Breaking Bad* are from a person close to the show and Sony internal documents.

Averaging fewer than two million viewers: Breaking Bad ratings from https:// en.wikipedia.org/wiki/Breaking_Bad

135   *they sold 100,000 copies:* E-mail from Steve Mosko to Sheraton Kalouria, Dec. 5, 2013. Subject: Fw: Breaking Bad Week 1 Sales.

Breaking Bad's *profit from DVD:* E-mail from Steve Mosko to Chris Elwell and Drew Shearer, Mar. 17, 2014. Subject: Re: Q4 HE Ultimates — TV Product.

136   *"ML told me tonight"*: E-mail from Amy Pascal to Stefan Litt, Feb. 3, 2014. No subject.

Sony produced a pilot based on an idea of Pascal's: Some details on Amy Pascal and *Vatican* from Tatiana Siegel, "New Life for Amy Pascal." *Hollywood Reporter,* Nov. 25, 2013.

137   *"disappointment"*: E-mail from Amy Pascal to amya@scottfree.com, Jan. 9, 2014. No subject.

"Wow, is Pascal having an impact" and *"Jeez zzz"*: E-mail from Steve Mosko to Amy Pascal and others, Feb. 5, 2014. Subject: Fwd: Blacklist L3 record.

"I have never ever gotten in your business": E-mail from Amy Pascal to Steve Mosko, Feb. 26, 2014. No subject.

"With SPE's leadership standing by": Nellie Andreeva, "Sony Hack Deepens Rift Between Film and Television Group," Dec. 17, 2014. http://deadline.com /2014/12/sony-hack-rift-film-television-group-1201325868/

138   *"Steve Mosko is actively campaigning"*: E-mail from Nicole Seligman to Michael Lynton, Aug. 19, 2014. Subject: Re: IP Intake — confidential.

In fiscal 2012: Financial details are from Sony internal documents.

139   *"Growth in tv profitability"*: E-mail from Michael Lynton to David Goldhill, Nov. 23, 2013. No subject.

10. THE TERMINATOR: DISNEY, THE PERFECT STUDIO
FOR THE FRANCHISE AGE

143   *But the men who ran Disney animation:* Unless otherwise noted, details on Disney's movie business are from current and former employees and people who have worked with the studio.

146   *"There's a difference"*: Iger quotes from author's interview.

148   *"You can't eat vanilla"*: Jill Goldsmith and Cathy Dunkley, "Disney Looks to Rejig Slate," *Daily Variety,* Oct. 10, 2004.

149 *"try very hard to get the PG"*: Claudia Eller, "Disney Comes of Age with PG-13 Rating for 'Pirates,'" *Los Angeles Times,* June 20, 2003.

"very, very out there": Ben Fritz, "Pirates' Treasure," *Daily Variety,* July 9, 2006.

158 *Cook ran the studio too much like a silo*: Some details on Dick Cook's firing are from Claudia Eller and Dawn Chmielewski, "Disney's Clash at the Top," *Los Angeles Times,* Sept. 21, 2009.

11. THE PRODUCERS: CREATIVITY MEETS FRANCHISE MANAGEMENT

168 *Dan Lin was on a very traditional Hollywood career path*: Details on Dan Lin and quotes are from author's interview.

174 *And he is on set*: Details on Simon Kinberg and quotes are from author's interview.

182 *On a soundstage on the Paramount Pictures lot*: Details on the Hasbro writers' rooms are from author's interviews with people involved and Ben Fritz, "Film Studios Recast Writers' Rooms," *Wall Street Journal,* Oct. 13, 2016.

183 *"Movies and TV have inverted"*: Akiva Goldsman quotes are from author's interview.

"It allows us to activate our brand": Author's interview with Stephen Davis.

"get out of my room": Author's interview with Michael Chabon.

12. THE SHOP AROUND THE CORNER: AMAZON SAVES THE INDIE FILM BUSINESS

188 *"TV at this point of my career"*: David Ng, "Weinstein Co. Serves Up 'The Founder' amid Smaller Film Slate and Shift to TV," *Los Angeles Times,* Jan. 16, 2017.

189 *Amazon.com's offer for* Manchester by the Sea: Details on Amazon's purchase of *Manchester by the Sea* are from Mike Fleming Jr., "Sundance Sensation 'Manchester by the Sea' Nears $10M Amazon Deal," Jan. 24, 2016. http://deadline.com/2016/01/manchester-by-the-sea-10-million-deal-amazon-casey-affleck-sundance-1201689425/ and Brent Lang "Amazon, Retail Behemoth, Taking Smaller Steps into Hollywood," *Variety,* Mar. 8, 2016.

192 *"requires me to deliver"*: http://trulyfreefilm.hopeforfilm.com/2013/12/i-am-no-longer-going-to-produce-films-for-my-living.html

"I want to make films": Ibid.

193 *"wanted to make the equivalent"*: Ted Hope, *Hope for Film* (New York: Soft Skull Press, 2014), 11.

"complete systems reboot": Ibid.

194 *"Instead of thinking of ourselves"*: Ibid.
195 *"We look for something artful"*: Author's interview with Ted Hope.
196 *"Our customers wanted"*: Author's interview with Bob Berney.
197 *"We're trying to deliver"*: Author's interview with Jason Ropell.
 "They are often very good": Ben Fritz and Laura Stevens, "Oscar Nominations Validate Amazon's Hollywood Ambitions," *Wall Street Journal*, Jan. 24, 2017.
198 *"They're like the kings"*: Author's interview with Nicolas Winding Refn.

13. APT PUPIL: CHINA'S SHIFTING RELATIONSHIP WITH HOLLYWOOD

201 *"We focus much more"*: E-mail from Andrew Gumpert to Michael Lynton, Amy Pascal, and others, Feb. 3, 2014. Subject: Fw: Shanghai Media Group/PIXELS and spiderman response.
202 *wasn't even released in China:* Patrick Brzeski, "'Ghostbusters' Denied Release in China," *Hollywood Reporter*, July 13, 2016.
 Sony signed a deal: Details on Sony-Wanda deal and Sony's record in China from Wayne Ma and Erich Schwartzel, "Sony and Wanda Team Up to Market Films in China," *Wall Street Journal*, Sept. 23, 2016, and Jonathan Kaiman and Jessica Meyers, "Wanda Group Partners with Sony Pictures," *Los Angeles Times*, Sept. 23, 2016.
203 *The head of Wanda had so many meetings:* Some details on Wang's dealings in Hollywood come from people in the film industry who have met with him.
204 *eighteen new screens were being built every day:* Clifford Coonan, "China's Box Office Surges 30 Percent in First Quarter," *Hollywood Reporter*, May 3, 2014.
 grossed $11.7 million: http://www.china.org.cn/english/2006/Jan/155614.htm
 "When studios greenlight": Rich Gelfond quotes and details on IMAX's experience in China are from author's interview.
205 *"no ceiling"*: Brooks Barnes, "Dalian Wanda of China Offers a Carrot to Hollywood," *New York Times*, Oct. 17, 2016.
 "China is now the wallet": Author's interviews with several people in Hollywood, including Adam Goodman.
206 *"a narcotic which the capitalist class"*: Jim Mann, "'Superman' Shanghaied in Peking Screen Test," *Los Angeles Times*, Jan. 25, 1986.
 "the 10 best foreign movies": Rone Tempest, "How Do You Say 'Boffo' in Chinese?" *Los Angeles Times*, Nov. 29, 1994.
211 *The filmmakers used digital technology:* Ben Fritz and John Horn, "Hollywood Tries to Stay on China's Good Side," *Los Angeles Times*, March 16, 2011.
 a remake of The Karate Kid: Details on the movie are from John Horn, "'Karate

Kid' Update Breaks Down Some Chinese Walls," *Los Angeles Times,* May 30, 2010.

Sony trimmed several minutes: Steven Zeitchik, "Will Smith's 'Men In Black 3' Censored in China," *Los Angeles Times,* May 31, 2012.

212   *Marvel worked with a Chinese production partner:* Clarence Tsui, "'Iron Man 3' China-Only Scenes Draw Mixed Response," *Hollywood Reporter,* May 1, 2013.

Sony cut a glimpse: Erich Schwartzel, "Hollywood's New Script: You Can't Make Movies Without China," *Wall Street Journal,* Apr. 18, 2017.

"They want to have a Chinese component": Erich Schwartzel, "Hollywood Under Pressure to Put More Chinese Actors in the Spotlight," *Wall Street Journal,* Sept. 19, 2016.

"We hope those protective measures": Ben Fritz, "'Dark Knight,' 'Spider-Man,' 'Prometheus" to Open Close in China," *Los Angeles Times,* Aug. 13, 2012.

213   *it was critical to the government:* Lilian Lin and Laurie Burkitt, "China's Movie Executives Cry Foul over Propaganda Film's Box-Office Success," *Wall Street Journal,* Sept. 9, 2015.

215   *On a sunny September day:* Details and quotes are from author's interview with Adam Goodman and Zhang Zhou.

217   *"Working with a company like Universal":* Ben Fritz, "Chinese Videogame Maker Investing $250 Million in Universal Movies," *Wall Street Journal,* Feb. 17, 2016. In late 2017, LeEco experienced severe financial problems due to its high debt, stalling Goodman's plans for Le Vision Entertainment at least temporarily. See Patrick Brezski, "China's LeEco Collapse Clouds Future for Exec Adam Goodman," *Hollywood Reporter,* Aug. 2, 2017.

14. FIELD OF DREAMS: STUDIO DEFECTORS AND THE FUTURE OF NONFRANCHISE FILMS

222   *"We'll make romantic comedies":* Author's interview with Adam Goodman.

223   *raised more than $800 million:* Ben Fritz, "Steven Spielberg's DreamWorks Relaunches as Amblin Partners," *Wall Street Journal,* Dec. 16, 2015.

224   *"I think of myself like":* Ben Fritz, "Columbia Pictures President Had a Knack for Numbers," *Los Angeles Times,* Jan. 15, 2012.

225   *"I owe my entire career":* E-mail from Doug Belgrad to Amy Pascal, July 16, 2014. Subject: Nice story.

"I know you want to win": E-mail from Amy Pascal to Doug Belgrad, Nov. 12, 2014. No subject.

226   *"The pressures on executives":* Doug Belgrad quotes and details on his new company are from author's interview.

232   *Brad Grey, was fired:* Several months later, Grey passed away from cancer.

237 *"The only 'platform'"*: Christopher Nolan remarks at Warner Bros.' Cinema-Con Presentation in Las Vegas, Nevada, Mar. 29, 2017.

The plan for "premium video-on-demand": Many details about Hollywood's premium video-on-demand plans are from Ben Fritz, "From Multiplex to Living Room, in 45 Days or Less," *Wall Street Journal*, Mar. 26, 2017.

238 *"adult dramas we're having problems with"*: Kevin Tsujihara comments on Time Warner earnings call, Feb. 8, 2017.

240 *Theater attendance:* National Assn. of Theater Owners. http://www.natoonline.org/data/admissions/. Accessed June 26, 2017.

Index

actors. *See* talent

After Earth, 26–27, 94–96

Ali, 90

Alice in Wonderland, 143, 160

The Amazing Spider-Man, 26, 38, 75–78, 212

The Amazing Spider-Man 2, 38, 75, 77–78, 79, 113, 201–2

The Amazing Spider-Man 3, 75–76, 81

Amazon Studios
  audience, 197
  flops and impact, 198–200
  formation of, 191–92
  independent film financing by, xxiii, 187–90, 198–200
  Netflix versus, 195, 196–97
  originality mission of, 190, 191–92, 194–97, 200

Amblin Partners, 216, 223, 235

AMC, 134–35, 203, 216

America Online (AOL), 14

American Hustle, 117, 120

Anderson, Paul Thomas, 119

Angels & Demons, 86–87

animated movies
  China's release of, 213
  Disney live-action of, 143–44, 160–62
  DreamWorks, 70
  Lego, 166, 171–74
  Pixar, 152–53, 157

Annapurna Pictures, 116–22

AOL. *See* America Online

Apollo 13, 208

Apple iPod, 152, 154

Arad, Avi
  as Marvel competitor, 73
  Marvel film logo by, 53
  Marvel resignation by, 65–66
  Marvel vision of, 44–45
  Marvel World pitch to, 54–55
  Marvel's slate deals and, 62–63

Artisan Entertainment, 54

AT&T, 236

audience
  actor loyalty decline, 83–88, 93–99

audience (*cont.*)
    actor loyalty success, 88–93, 106–7
    Amazon Studios, 197
    binge-watching by, 129–30
    Breaking Bad, 135
    China's, 209–10
    cultural collective of, 238–41
    data analytics on, 102, 218
    franchise desire of, xv, 23, 115, 150,
        209–10, 240
    future trends, 238–41
    international shift in, 22–23
    Netflix analytics of, 102–3, 106–7
    rating advisory, 149–50
    theater attendance trends, 21–23,
        105–6, 115, 131, 232, 238–41
    theater's future and, 239–41
    theatrical release window and,
        195–97, 237–38
Avatar, 208–10
Avengers franchise, xx, 63, 72, 73, 179
Aviv, Oren, 151
Ayer, David, 109

Bailey, Sean, 162, 163–64
bankruptcy, 25, 42–44
Batman franchise
    The Dark Knight trilogy, 169, 170,
        175, 203, 212
    flops, 74
    as inspiration, 42, 48
    reboots, 67
    spinoffs, 74, 172
Battsek, Daniel, 155–56
Bay, Michael, 175
Beasts of No Nation, 105–6
Beauty and the Beast, 161
Belgrad, Doug
    as independent producer, 226–30
    at Sony, 34, 38, 83, 223–26

Berney, Bob, 195, 196, 198
Bewkes, Jeff, 139
Bezos, Jeff, 194, 195, 200
big-budget "event" movies (tentpoles),
    xix, 18, 24, 30–33, 210. *See also*
    franchise era
Bigelow, Kathryn, 119
binge-watching, 129–30
The Birth of a Nation, 189
box-office revenue
    animation remakes, 143–44
    audience's actor loyalty and, 83–88,
        97
    Avengers, 72
    China's, 22, 202, 204, 209–10,
        212–14
    Disney, 144, 150, 151, 160–61
    documentaries, 105, 155
    franchise era proof by, xix–xx, 22–23,
        97–98
    Guardians of the Galaxy, 72
    Hulk, 62, 69
    independent films, 187–90
    international shift of, 22–23, 202
    Iron Man, 68–69, 72
    Marvel, 62, 68–69, 72, 180
    mid-budget profit and, 112–16, 120,
        153–54, 163
    Pirates of the Caribbean, 150
    projection and greenlighting, 31–32
    Spider-Man, 26, 49, 51, 202
    star vehicles, 83–88
    theater attendance and, 21–23,
        105–6, 115, 131
    X-Men, 48, 180
Boyle, Danny, 121
branding
    Disney's, 147–51, 159–64
    importance of, 144, 146, 159–64,
        171, 182–83

Marvel, 53
producer's role in, 167
Breaking Bad, 133–36
Bridges, Jeff, 65
Bright, 109
Brooks, James L., 26
Brooks, Katherine, 118
Brown, Dan, 86
Bruckheimer, Jerry, 147, 149–50, 158
budget. *See also* financial backing; mid-
    budget films
  big-budget "event" movies (tent-
      poles), xix, 18, 24, 30–33, 210
  micro-, 216, 222
  Netflix talent and, 109
Burke, Steve, 11
Burton, Tim, 42, 143–44, 147–48, 160

cable television, 101–2, 127–30
Cage, Nicolas, 151
Calley, John, 5–6, 8, 9, 42, 47, 51
Cameron, James, 41, 47–48, 166, 208–9
Captain America franchise, xx, 72, 80,
    82
Captain Phillips, 112–13
Carolco Pictures, 41
Cassavetes, Nick, 61
Catmull, Ed, 152–53, 163
censorship, 210–12
Chabon, Michael, 182, 183
China
  3D technology in, 208–10
  audience in, 209–10
  censorship by, 210–12
  domestic competition, 212–14
  financial backing from, 23, 201–5,
      211, 214, 216–17
  government control in, 204, 206,
      210–14
  IMAX growth in, 205–10, 214

independent producers in, 215–19
Chi-Raq, 195–96
Cinderella, 161
cinematic universes
  1000 A.E., 94–95
  audience loyalty to, 83–88, 93–99
  DC Comics, 162, 169–70
  defining, xx, 66
  director's role in, 166–67
  end to, 184–86
  endless possibility of, 166, 171–72,
      182–84
  Harry Potter, 172
  Hasbro, 182–84
  Lego, 166, 171–74
  producer's role in, 67, 165–68
  Star Wars, 161
Clooney, George, 7, 158
Columbia Pictures, 5, 40, 132
Concussion, 97
Cook, Dick, 143, 148–49, 158, 216
Cranston, Bryan, 135
creativity. *See also* originality
  business and, xvi–xviii, 43–44, 53–54,
      65, 73, 168–69, 195
  director's role change in, 166–67,
      175–76
  franchise symbiosis with, 165–68,
      173, 184–86
  Marvel executive changes for, 43–46,
      65–67, 175–76
  personal experiences used for, 177,
      179
  producers of Lego, 166, 171–74
  producers of X-Men, 174–76,
      178–81
  writer's role change in, 165–67,
      174–84
Cruise, Tom, 61, 85
cultural collective, 238–41

Da Vinci Code series, 86–87

The Dark Knight trilogy, 169, 170, 175, 203, 212

DC Comics. *See also specific characters of DC Comics*

  cinematic universe of, 162, 169–70

  comeback, 73–74, 169–70

  Marvel versus, 42, 67, 170

De Luca, Mike, 16, 28, 30, 61, 80, 96

Deadpool, 180–81

Depp, Johnny, 148–49, 150, 158

Despicable Me franchise, xx

digital content, future of, 239–41. *See also* Amazon Studios; Netflix

director role change, 166–67, 175–76

Disney

  branding of, 147–51, 159–64

  China and, 206

  executive changes at, 13, 150–53, 158–59, 160

  franchise flops of, 157–59

  franchise success strategy of, xx, 143–46, 157, 160–64

  franchise vision of, 143, 148–59

  Hollywood Pictures of, 11, 13

  live-action remakes, 143–44, 160–62

  Lucasfilm merger with, 161, 164

  Marvel merger with, 70–73, 159

  mid-budget before franchises, 146–52

  mid-budget phasing out, 153–57, 163

  Miramax label of, 148, 153–56

  Pixar and, 71, 152–53, 157

  quality of, 162–64

  Touchstone label of, 147–48, 153–56

distribution disruption, 60, 103–5, 152, 154, 222–23, 227–30

documentaries, 105, 155, 205–6, 207

The Do-Over, 108

Dope, 187, 188

Downey, Robert, Jr., 64–65, 72, 170

DreamWorks, 70, 156, 223

Drive, 198

DVDs, 17, 21, 103, 129, 148, 210

DVR, 129

Earth Girls Are Easy, 7

Eisner, Michael, 151–52

Ellison, Larry, 117, 216

Ellison, Megan, 116–22

Erlicht, Jamie, 134, 234

Evans, Robert, 221

"event" movies (tentpoles), xix, 18, 24, 30–33, 210. *See also* franchise era

executives. *See* studio executives

Fahrenheit 9/11, 155

Fantastic Four, 180

Fast & Furious franchise, 204, 214

Favreau, Jon, 64

Feige, Kevin

  early importance of, 56, 62–63, 66

  as sole producer, 67, 69, 72–73, 78, 79–80, 82

financial backing

  from Amazon Studios, xxiii, 187–90, 198–200

  from China, 23, 201–5, 211, 214, 216–17

  for independent films, xxiii, 187–90, 198–200

  independent producers, 116–20, 215–19

  Marvel mergers for, 44–45, 70–73

  for original mid-budget films, 116–20, 198

  from talent, 122

from Wall Street, xvi–xvii, xx, 3, 27, 58
financial bubble, 58
Fincher, David, 102
Fine, Alan, 78
The Finest Hours, 163
Focus Features, 188, 193, 236
foreign interest, 22–23, 139, 202. *See also* China
Fox. *See* 20th Century Fox
franchise era. *See also* cinematic universes; Disney; Marvel
arrival of, xv, xviii, 21–23, 143–46, 159–64
audience desire for, xv, 23, 115, 150, 209–10, 240
audience's loyalty shift to, 83–88, 93–99
box-office proof of, xix–xx, 22–23, 97–98
branding importance for, 144, 146, 159–64, 171, 182–83
China's box-office in, 22, 202, 204, 209–10, 212–14
China's financial backing in, 23, 201–5, 211, 214, 216–17
Chinese audience in, 209–10
creativity propelled by, 165–68, 173, 184–86
director's role change in, 166–67, 175–76
end to, 184–86, 232
executive organization in, 67, 159–60, 161–62
flops, 49–50, 73–74, 75–78, 157–59, 169–71, 180, 185–86, 232
IMAX and, 205–10, 214
originality versus, xviii–xxi, xxiv–xxv, 23, 122, 146, 155, 187–90

producer's role in, 67, 165–68
profit of mid-budget versus, 112–16, 120, 153–54, 163
Sony's efforts in, xvi–xviii, 30–33, 37–40, 86, 233–35
strategy before, xiii–xiv, xviii, 18, 146–51
strategy success, xx, 30, 39–40, 73–74, 143–46, 159–64, 171–74
study resources, ix–xi, xxi–xxiii
television versus, xviii–xix, xxiv–xxv, 23
theatrical release window in, 195–97, 237–38
theme-park adaptations, 152, 155, 158
video-game adaptations, 157, 204, 214
visions of, 44–45, 53 60, 143, 148–59
writer's role in, 165–67, 174–84
The Fresh Prince of Bel-Air, 89
Fritz, Ben, xxi

Garfield, Andrew, 76, 81
Gelfond, Rich, 205–8, 209, 210, 214
Get Out, 238, 240
Ghostbusters reboot, 31, 32, 233
G.I. Joe, 183–84
Goddard, Drew, 81
Godzilla, 170–71, 184–85, 203
Golan, Menahem, 40, 41
Goldhill, David, 139
Goldsman, Akiva, 177–78, 182–84
Goodman, Adam, 213, 215–16, 218, 221–22
Grazer, Brian, 86–87
The Great Wall, 217–18
greenlighting, 31–32, 166

Greenwald, Glenn, 229, 230
GSN, 139
Guardians of the Galaxy, 46, 72
Guber, Peter, 5
Gumpert, Andrew, 116, 202
Gyllenhaal, Jake, 51, 109

hack of Sony Pictures, ix–xi, xxi–xxiii,
    33–36, 81, 137–38
Hanks, Tom, 84, 86–87, 112, 235
Harry Potter franchise, 24, 172, 204
Hasbro, 42–43, 182–84
The Haunted Mansion, 148
HBO, 128, 129
Her, 119
Hill, Jonah, 8, 30, 32
Hirai, Kaz, 79–80
home entertainment. *See also* Amazon
    Studios; Netflix
  cable television, 101–2, 127–28,
    129–30
  disruptors and revenue, 21–22, 152,
    154
  DVDs, 17, 21, 103, 129, 148,
    210
  future of, 239–40
  profit, 17, 21–22
  rights, 41–42, 45, 104
  theatrical release window and,
    195–97, 237–38
Hope, Ted, 192–97
Horn, Alan, 160, 161–62
House of Cards, 102
How Do You Know?, 26
Howard, Ron, 86–87
Howard, Terrence, 64
Hughes, John, 82, 168, 215
Hulk, 62, 67. *See also The Incredible
    Hulk*
The Hundred Regiments Offensive, 213

Icahn, Carl, 42
Iger, Bob, 70–73, 146, 151–61
IMAX, 205–10, 214
The Incredible Hulk, 69, 76
Independence Day franchise, 89, 212
independent films
  Amazon's backing of, xxiii, 187–90,
    198–200
  Amazon's mission and, 190, 191–92,
    194–97, 200
  closing studio divisions of, 188
  documentary, 105, 155, 205–6, 207
independent producers
  Belgrad as, 226–30
  China's investment in, 215–19
  Ellison's work, 116–22
  executives defecting to, 215–16,
    221–30
  Goodman as, 213, 215–16, 218,
    221–22
  Pascal as, 82, 235
  studio system's future with, 222–23,
    227–30
independent studios, 122, 188
Indiana Jones reboot, 164
Inferno, 86–87
international focus, 22–23, 139, 202. *See
    also* China
The Interview, 33–36
investors. *See* financial backing
Iron Man franchise, 61–69, 72, 212

Jack & Jill, 93
Jacobson, Nina, 149
James Bond franchise, 25, 47
Jobs, Steve, 71, 120–21, 146, 152. *See
    also Steve Jobs*
Jonze, Spike, 119
Joon Ho, Bong, 109–10
Jump Street franchise, 30, 33, 171

The Jungle Book, 161, 162
Jurassic World, 203
Justice League: Mortal, 169–70

The Karate Kid reboot, 211
Katzenberg, Jeffrey, 146, 154
Kennedy, Kathy, 162, 163
Kidman, Nicole, 177
Kinberg, Simon, 174–81
Kundun, 206

Landau, Yair, 42, 45, 46
Lasseter, John, 152–53, 163
Lassiter, James, 89–90, 97
Le Vision Pictures, 218–19,
      221–22
Lee, Roy, 171
Lee, Spike, 195
Lee, Stan, 40, 53
LeEco, 218
Legendary Pictures, 171, 203, 217
Lego, 166, 171–74
Liman, Doug, 178
Lin, Dan, 166, 168–74, 185
Lin Pictures, 165–66, 169–74, 185
Lionsgate, 130, 155, 216
Little Miss Sunshine, 154, 188
Loeb, Dan, 27
Lonergan, Kenneth, 189, 190
Lucasfilm-Disney merger, 161, 164
Lynton, Michael
      background of, 10–15
      Pascal and, xvii–xviii, 14–19, 27–28,
            31, 35–36, 75
      Sony decline and, xvii–xviii, 3–4,
            27–29, 34–35, 231–32
      Sony departure of, 51, 231
      Sony early years of, 10–15
      Sony hack and, 34–35
      Sony successes and, 15–19

Sony television politics and, 134,
      138–40
Spider-Man rights and, 51, 75, 77–78,
      79, 80
talent loyalty decline and, 83–84, 97,
      98

Mad Men, 130, 134
Maguire, Toby, 48, 51
Maisel, David, 55–63, 66–67,
      70–72
Maleficent, 160
Malin, Amir, 54–55
Man of Steel, 74
Man on a Wire, 105
Manchester by the Sea, 187–90, 200
marketing. *See* branding; distribution
Marvel. *See also specific characters of
      Marvel*
      bankruptcy, 42–44
      box-office revenue, 62, 68–69, 72,
            180
      branding, 53
      DC Comics versus, 42, 67, 170
      executive roles at, 43–46, 65–67,
            175–76
      first film production by, 63–69
      first slate deals with, 58–63
      flops, 180
      franchise success formula, xx, 39–40,
            73–74
      franchise vision of, 44–45, 53–60
      Marvel World pitch for, 54–55
      merger with Disney, 70–73, 159
      merger with Toy Biz, 44–45
      Netflix success of, 102–3
      offices, 56, 73
      rights, 40–47, 50–52, 62–63, 75–82
            Spider-Man rights, 42–47, 50-52,
                  75-82

Marvel (*cont.*)
　Sony and, 39–40, 42–47, 50–52,
　　75–82, 234
　stock value, 50, 66, 69, 70
　talent earnings, 51, 64–65, 72
The Master, 119
Me and Earl and the Dying Girl, 187, 188
Men in Black franchise, 26, 30, 94, 211
merchandising
　branding importance and, 182–83
　Breaking Bad, 135
　classic versus film, 44, 47, 50–51
　conglomerates, 236
　Iron Man, 63, 68–69
　lawsuit, 50–52
　Marvel-Toy Biz merger, 44–45
　Spider-Man, 42, 47, 50–51, 77
　theme-park, 152, 155, 158
mergers
　Disney-Lucasfilm, 161, 164
　Disney-Marvel, 70–73, 159
　Disney-Miramax, 148
　Marvel-Toy Biz, 44–45
Metro-Goldwyn-Mayer (MGM), xiii,
　　25, 41, 47
micro-budget films, 216, 222
mid-budget films
　comeback of, xxiv, 106–10, 122,
　　187–90, 200, 221–30
　decline of, xvi–xviii, 3–4, 21–29,
　　83–88, 112–16, 153–57
　Disney history with, 146–52
　Disney phasing out, 153–57, 163
　distribution outsource for, 103–5,
　　222–23, 227–30
　financing originals and, 116–20, 198
　golden age of, xiv, xix, 18
　Netflix talent strategy and, 106–10
　profit of franchise versus, xix–xx,
　　112–16, 120, 153–54, 163

as "star vehicles," 84–85, 88
studio executive defectors for,
　　215–16, 221–30
studio system's future role in, 222–23,
　　227–30
Minghella, Hannah, 28, 30
Miramax, 148, 153–56
Moore, Michael, 155
Mosko, Steve, 125–27, 131–33, 136–40
Mozart in the Jungle, 192
Mr. and Mrs. Smith, 177–78

National Treasure, 151, 155
Neighbors, 38
The Neon Demon, 198–99
Netflix
　Amazon Studios versus, 195, 196–97
　audience analytics, 102–3, 106–7
　binge-watching, 129–30
　DVDs, 21, 103
　independent films saved by, 189–90
　original programming strategy,
　　102–6, 109
　streaming rights, 130
　studio system disruption by, 103–5,
　　107–10
　success overview, 101–3
　talent strategy with, 106–10
New Line Cinema, 61–62
The Nightmare Before Christmas,
　　147–48
Nolan, Christopher, 166, 169, 175, 237
Norton, Ed, 69

Okja, 109–10
1000 A.E., 94–95
originality. *See also* mid-budget films
　Amazon's mission for, 190, 191–92,
　　194–97, 200
　Annapurna's contribution to, 116–20,
　　122

corporate support of, 187–90, 200
executives defecting for, 221–30
franchise versus, xviii–xxi, xxiv–xxv,
    23, 122, 146, 155, 187–90
Netflix strategy for, 102–6, 109
studio system's future role in, 222–23,
    227–30
television's lead on, xviii–xix, 23,
    102–3, 191–92
Overbrook Entertainment, 89–90, 92,
    95–96

Paramount Pictures
    China's investment in, 203,
        213–14
    downturn of, 221–22, 232
    Marvel's first slate and, 60
    writers' room attempt by, 182–84
Paranormal Activity, 216
Pascal, Amy
    background of, 6–10
    Belgrad and, 34, 38, 83, 224–25
    Ellison and, 117, 120
    as independent producer, 82, 235
    investor pressure for, xvi–xviii, 3–4
    Lynton and, xvii–xviii, 14–19, 27–28,
        31, 35–36, 75
    Marvel collaboration with, 82, 236
    mid-budget profit and, 112–16
    Mosko and, 125–26, 131–32,
        136–40
    Sony decline and, xvi–xviii, 3–4, 9,
        24–29, 33–35, 75–76,
        79–82
    Sony departure of, 35–36, 82
    Sony early years of, 6–10
    Sony franchise efforts of, xvi–xviii,
        30–33, 37–40, 86, 234
    Sony hack of, 33–36
    Sony successes and, 15–19, 48,
        87–88, 112–13

Sony television branch and, 125–26
Spider-Man making by, 48, 51, 82,
    234
Spider-Man reboot by, 26, 32, 37–38,
    75–82, 234
Spider-Man rights and, 42–47,
    50–52, 79–82
Steve Jobs and, 111–13, 115–16,
    120–24
talent importance to, 6–8, 87–88,
    90, 91
talent loyalty decline and, 97, 98
television age viewed by, 130, 131
television efforts by, 136–38
Passengers, 212, 233
Paul Blart: Mall Cop, 93, 224
Perelman, Ron, 42, 44
Perlmutter, Ike
    business acumen, 43–44, 53–55, 65,
        73
    Disney-Marvel merger and, 70–73
    on Iron Man, 68–69
    Marvel backing by, 43–46
    Marvel production pitch to,
        55–60
    personal frustrations with, 65–66,
        72–73
    Spider-Man rights and, 43–46,
        50–52, 79–80, 82
Peters, Jon, 5
Pirates of the Caribbean franchise,
    148–50, 155, 157, 211
Pitt, Brad, 108–9, 122, 179–80
Pixar, 71, 152–53, 157
Pixels, 98
Plan B Entertainment, 122
The Post, 235
Pratt, Chris, 96, 212
Price, Roy, 191–92, 193–95,
    197
price discrimination, 104

producers. *See also* financial backing;
　　independent producers
　　Lego creativity of, 166, 171–74
　　rise of, 67, 165–68
　　writers as, 167, 178–81
　　X-Men creativity of, 174–76,
　　　178–81
profit
　　bankruptcy and, 25, 42–44
　　China's box office and, 204
　　Disney's formula for, 143–46,
　　　161–64
　　greenlight projections of, 31–32
　　home entertainment, 17, 21–22
　　mid-budget versus franchise, xix–xx,
　　　112–16, 120, 153–54, 163
　　Netflix model of, 107
　　Spider-Man, 76, 77, 82, 113
　　studio model of, 103–4, 112–16
　　television versus film, 127–28,
　　　134–36

Queen of Katwe, 116, 163

Raimi, Sam, 37, 40, 48, 76
Rain Man, xix
rating advisory, 149–50
reboots
　　Batman, 67
　　defined, 76
　　Fantastic Four, 180
　　Ghostbusters, 31, 32, 233
　　Godzilla, 170–71
　　Indiana Jones, 164
　　The Karate Kid, 211
　　Spider-Man, 26, 32, 37–40, 75–82,
　　　234
　　Superman, 74
Red Dawn, 210–11
Redbox, 21

Refn, Nicolas Winding, 198–99
revenue. *See also* box-office revenue
　　home entertainment, 21–22, 152,
　　　154
　　studio model of, 103–4, 112–16
　　talent earnings and, 17–18, 86, 92
　　television versus film, 127–28,
　　　134–36
Rideback Ranch, 185
The Ridiculous 6, 106, 108
rights
　　character portrayal, 171–72
　　Disney animation, 143–44
　　home entertainment, 41–42, 45, 104
　　Hulk, 62
　　Iron Man, 61–62
　　James Bond, 25, 47
　　Marvel, 40–47, 50–52, 62–63,
　　　75–82
　　merchandising, 44, 47, 50–51
　　royalties and, 50–52
　　Spider-Man, 40–47, 50–52,
　　　75–82
　　television streaming, 130
　　Thor, 62–63
　　X-Men, 42–43, 175
Rogue One, 161, 234
Ropell, Jason, 195
Rosenblum, Bruce, 139
Ross, Rich, 158–59, 160
Roth, Joe, 10, 13
Rothman, Tom, 28, 36, 105, 115, 225,
　　233
Rudin, Scott, 7, 120–22, 123–24
Ruffalo, Mark, 69

Sandler, Adam, 88, 90–94, 96–98,
　　106–8
Sarandos, Ted
　　background of, 101

Netflix originality strategy of, 102, 103–6

Netflix talent strategy of, 106–10

Schlessel, Peter, 40, 41

Scott, Ridley, 136

Seed, Mark, 27

sexism, 8

Shanghai Film Studios, 207

Shanghai Media Group (SMG), 201–2

Shaye, Bob, 62

Sherlock Holmes, 170

Showtime, 129, 136

Shyamalan, M. Night, 95, 96

Singer, Bryan, 175

The Sinister Six, 81

Six Degrees of Separation, 89

Skyfall, 25

SMG. *See* Shanghai Media Group

Smith, Will, 88–90, 91–92, 94–97, 109

Snapchat, 29, 231

Sony Pictures

    Annapurna backing of, 117, 120–22

    Belgrad's role at, 34, 38, 83, 223–26

    Breaking Bad, 133–36

    China's investment in, 201–4

    Da Vinci Code series of, 86–87

    decline of, xvi–xviii, 3–4, 9, 24–29, 33–35, 75–82, 231–32

    executive changes at, 5–6, 28, 36, 139–40, 225, 231

    franchise efforts by, xvi–xviii, 30–33, 37–40, 86, 233–35

    hack, ix–xi, xxi–xxiii, 33–36, 81, 137–38

    independent film division of, 188, 189

    Lynton's departure from, 51, 231

    Lynton's early years with, 10–15

    Marvel and, 39–40, 42–47, 50–52, 75–82, 234

    Mosko's role at, 125–27, 132–33, 136–40

    Pascal's departure from, 35–36, 82

    Pascal's early years with, 6–10

    revenue and talent earnings, 17–18, 86, 92

    Spider-Man making by, 48–49, 51, 234

    Spider-Man reboot by, 26, 32, 37–40, 75–78, 234

    Spider-Man rights of, 42–47, 50–52, 75–82

    Starz channel of, 101–2

    Steve Jobs, 111–13, 115–16, 120–24

    studio lot, xiii–xiv

    success in film, 10, 15–19, 25, 47–52, 87–93, 112–13

    success in television, 133–36, 139–40

    talent decline with, 93–99

    talent focus of, 6–8, 88–93

    television failure, 136–37

    television network, 133

    television politics, 125–27, 131–33, 136–40

    television revenue, 128

Spacey, Kevin, 102

Spider-Man, 39, 76

Spider-Man 2, 39, 76

Spider-Man 3, 39, 75–76

Spider-Man franchise

    The Amazing Spider-Man, 26, 38, 75–78, 212

    The Amazing Spider-Man 2, 38, 75, 77–78, 79, 113, 201–2

    The Amazing Spider-Man 3, 75–76, 81

    box-office revenue of, 26, 49, 51, 202

Spider-Man franchise (*cont.*)
  China's interest in, 201–2
  fan petition for, 75
  history, 40–47
  Marvel rights to, 42-47, 50-52, 75–82
  merchandising, 42, 47, 50–51, 77
  profits, 76, 77, 82, 113
  Sony's making of, 48–49, 51, 82, 234
  Sony's reboot of, 26, 32, 37–40,
      75–78, 234
  Sony's rights to, 42–47, 50–52, 75–82
  spinoffs, 77, 81
  talent, 48, 51, 76, 81
Spider-Man: Homecoming, 82, 234
Spiegel, Evan, 29
Spielberg, Steven, 156, 166, 216, 223,
    235
spinoffs. *See* cinematic universes
"star vehicles," 84–85, 88
Star Wars franchise, 161, 234
stars. *See* talent
Starz, 101–2
Steve Jobs, 111–13, 115–16,
    120–24
streaming, future of, 239–41. *See also*
    Amazon Studios; Netflix
Streep, Meryl, 235
Stringer, Howard, 9, 14, 15, 133
studio executives
  Amazon's mission and, 194–97
  backseat film editing by, 62, 65
  binge-watching by, 130
  defecting to independent producers,
      215–16, 221–30
  director's role and, 166–67
  Disney turnover, 13, 150–53, 158–59,
      160
  earnings of, 17, 35
  franchise era organization of, 67,
      159–60, 161–62

Marvel's creativity and, 43–46,
    65–67, 175–76
  producer's role and, 67, 165–68,
      221–22
  Sony turnover, 5–6, 28, 36, 139–40,
      225
  television versus film, 125–27,
      131–33, 136–38
studio system
  broadcast networks in, 133
  conglomerate ownership of, xx, 236
  end of, xv, 87, 231–33, 239
  future mid-budget role of, 222–23,
      227–30
  Netflix disruption of, 103–5, 107–10
  revenue and profit model, 103–4,
      112–16
Suicide Squad, 74
Sundance Film Festival, 187–90
Superbad, 32
superhero movies. *See* DC Comics;
    Marvel
Superman franchise, 74, 169, 175, 205

talent
  A-list decline, 83–88, 93–99
  A-list golden days, 87, 88–93
  audience loyalty decline, 83–88,
      93–99
  audience loyalty success, 88–93,
      106–7
  B-list/newcomer over A-list, 48, 76,
      169–70
  casting challenges, 61, 64–65, 76,
      115, 117–18, 131, 170
  China's stars, 212
  difficult, 51, 69, 89, 93–94
  earnings, 17–18, 51, 64–65, 72,
      85–87, 92, 108–9
  financial backing from, 122

gifts and perks, 69, 92–93
Netflix strategy with, 106–10
Sony's focus on, 6–8, 88–93
television move by, 131
technology
3D, 208–10
audience analysis, 102, 218
distribution, 152, 154
golden age of television and, 128–31
television. *See also* Netflix
broadcast networks, 133
cable, 101–2, 127–30
director's role in, 167
executive politics in, 125–27, 131–33, 136–40
film adaptations for, 137
future of, 239–41
golden age lead-up, 129, 131, 133–36
golden age of, xviii–xix, xxiv–xxv, 23, 127–31, 239
international, 139
originality led by, xviii–xix, 23, 102–3, 191–92
profit and revenue versus film, 127–28, 134–36
talent's move to, 131
technology and, 123–31
tentpoles, xix, 18, 24, 30–33, 210. *See also* franchise era
Terminator franchise, 170, 213
That's My Boy, 93
theater attendance
change in, 21–23, 105–6, 115, 131, 232, 238–41
as cultural collective, 238–41
future of, 239–41
IMAX, 205–10, 214
release window, 195–97, 237–38
theme-park adaptations, 152, 155, 158
Thor, 62–63, 72

3D technology, 208–10
Time Warner, 8, 14, 127–28, 139, 236
TiVo, 129
Touchstone Pictures, 13, 147–48, 153–56
Toy Biz, 44–45
toy-based franchises
Hasbro, 182–84
Lego, 166, 171–74
toys. *See* merchandising
Trank, Josh, 180
Transformers franchise, 171, 183, 213–14
Transparent, 191–92
TriStar Pictures, 105, 115, 132
Tsujihara, Kevin, 139, 172, 237
Turner Pictures, 7, 8
20th Century Fox, 42, 49, 154, 161, 175, 188, 189
2.0 Entertainment, 224, 230

Universal Pictures
DreamWorks move to, 156
independent label of, 188, 193, 236
Marvel and, 67
Overbrook Entertainment and, 89–90
Steve Jobs picked up by, 123–24

Van Amburg, Zack, 134, 234
The Vatican, 136
VCRs, 239
Viacom, 41, 232–33
video-game adaptations, 157, 204, 214
video-on-demand, 21, 237–38. *See also* Amazon Studios; Netflix
Vinciquerra, Tony, 234

Waking Madison, 118
The Walk, 105

Wanda Group, 202–3, 205, 216
Wang Jianlin, 202–3, 205
War Machine, 108–9, 238
Warcraft, 204, 214
Warner Bros.
    AT&T and, 236
    Fox squabble with, 175
    franchise flops of, 73–74, 169–71
    franchise success of, 24, 74,
        172–74
    internship at, 168
    talent gifts and perks, 93
    Time Warner and, 8, 127
The Wedding Singer, 91
Weinstein, Harvey and Bob, 148, 155,
    188
White House Down, 26–27
Wonder Woman, 74, 238
writers
    rise of, 165–67, 174–81

strike, 170
team process for, 181–84

X-Men
    box-office revenue, 48, 180
    competition, 50
    creativity behind, 174–76, 178–81
    rights to, 42–43, 175
    talent, 48, 212
X-Men: Apocalypse, 180
X-Men: Dark Phoenix, 178, 181
X-Men: Days of Future Past, 179–80,
    212
X-Men: The Last Stand, 178

Yun-fat, Chow, 212

Zero Dark Thirty, 117, 119, 120, 128
Zhang Zhou, 218, 219
Zhou Yuan, 201